Planning Support Systems
for Cities and Regions

Planning Support Systems for Cities and Regions

Edited by **Richard K. Brail**

LINCOLN INSTITUTE
OF LAND POLICY
CAMBRIDGE, MASSACHUSETTS

Library of Congress Cataloging-in-Publication Data

Planning support systems for cities and regions / [edited by] Richard K.
Brail.
    p. cm.
  Includes index.
  ISBN 978-1-55844-182-8
  1. City planning--Data processing. 2. Regional planning--Data processing.
  3. Land use--Planning--Data processing. 4. Information storage and
  retrieval systems--Land use. I. Brail, Richard K.
  HT166.P542 2008
  307.1'2160285--dc22
                                2008032821

Designed by Peter M. Blaiwas, Vern Associates, Inc., Newburyport, Massachusetts

Art Development by Maggie Powell Designs, Inc., Asheville, North Carolina

Composed in Goudy and ITC Franklin Gothic

Printed by Puritan Press Incorporated, Hollis, New Hampshire

MANUFACTURED IN THE UNITED STATES OF AMERICA

Contents

Figures

Tables

Boxes

Acknowledgments

In September 2007, the Lincoln Institute of Land Policy sponsored a conference in Cambridge, Massachusetts, at which the papers in this volume were first presented. The authors, discussants, and attendees were drawn from the United States and abroad, and were connected through research and practice to the use of information technology in urban and regional planning and policy formulation. Four discussants were invited to the conference to review and comment on the papers: Richard S. Bolan, University of Minnesota; Joseph Ferreira, Massachusetts Institute of Technology; Lewis D. Hopkins, University of Illinois; and Lyna Wiggins, Rutgers University. Their insights fed into spirited discussion among conference participants and were well received. John Landis, University of Pennsylvania, was also a welcome addition to the program. A particular note of appreciation is due to Richard Klosterman for assistance in developing the theme and structure of the fall conference.

Lincoln Institute was an excellent host. We deeply appreciate the support of Gregory K. Ingram, its president, and the Institute's board of directors. Armando Carbonell, senior fellow and chair of the Department of Planning and Urban Form, provided strong guidance throughout the conference planning period. Lisa Cloutier was a tremendous help with organization and arrangements. Brooke Digges of ResourcePlus did an excellent job handling conference logistics. Book production was similarly well supported. Ann LeRoyer, senior editor and director of publications, has provided superb guidance as well as access to Brian Hotchkiss and Peter Blaiwas of Vern Associates, an excellent editor and book designer, respectively.

A final thank you is due to all who supported and participated in this effort. I hope this book will highlight the potential of planning support systems in assisting the growth and development of cities and regions.

— Richard K. Brail

Foreword

Planning Support Systems for Cities and Regions invites the reader to join in a virtual dialogue with its authors—educators, theorists, model builders, and planners—about technology and the social context in which technology is employed. It is also the trace of a face-to-face dialogue that took place at Lincoln House in Cambridge in September 2007, when we convened the authors and several invited planning experts to discuss earlier drafts of these chapters on the state of the art in planning support systems. (This term dates only to 1989 and is attributed to Britton Harris, if not first coined by him.)

This dialogue, or perhaps dialectic, revolves around the almost unlimited potential of computer-based tools to enhance the effectiveness of planning and the serious challenges in applying these tools within real-world planning environments. The Lincoln Institute of Land Policy has focused on tools for planners in a number of its recent books, including Kwartler and Longo's *Visioning and Visualization: People, Pixels, and Plans* (2008), Campoli and MacLean's *Visualizing Density* (2007), and Hopkins and Zapata's *Engaging the Future: Forecasts, Scenarios, Plans, and Projects* (2007).

All three of these books and the current volume have in common, albeit to varying degrees, an interest in the spatial and visual side of planning. However, it is useful to differentiate the two visualization/design books from this volume and *Engaging the Future*, which are less about "showing" the tools and more about promoting a critical understanding of their strengths and limitations. The intended audience, therefore, is both the user—and potential user—of these tools, and those who seek to continue to improve them.

Richard Brail, the editor of this comprehensive and ambitious volume, has been notably successful in bringing together the wisest of the field's thinkers, the most inventive of the toolmakers, the most experienced of those working at the interface with real clients, and the most battle-seasoned practicing planners (and many of these individuals occupy more than one of these niches). Together they present a broad view of the field, in-depth developmental histories of the most important models and tools as told by their creators, and a provocative, in-the-trenches critique of the state of the art. In part, it is a book about "matching the user to the instrument"; and, if not yet the *Consumer Reports* some have called for, it is a helpful guide for those new to the field.

But I think this book is also much more than that. It is an invitation to think about how planning support systems can help in shaping the uncertain future that planners must visualize and communicate to an increasingly participative public. These tools have emerged during an age where the expectations of communities to be able to "take control" of their futures have increased, where fragmentation of interests is more the rule than is confluence, and where complexity is seen to trump rationality.

Planning support systems aspire to enable the expert and the citizen to meet on an equal footing in a new communicative planning process. The structure of the book moves from the broadest conceptual level, through regional and local applications including project planning and regulatory review, to the perspective of the practitioner. I sense, in following this transect from the heights of the academy to the front lines of practice, a gradient of increasing pessimism and lowered expectations, ending with a call for ease of use and simplicity in the face of a task that is irreducibly complex and unpredictable.

Planning will never be easy; it needs and deserves the best support systems that modelers and system developers can deliver. This volume not only reports that they are "working on it," but also gives us a glimpse at future tools suited to a planning process that has become, as Brail says, "more visual, more public, more accessible, and more collaborative."

— Armando Carbonell
  Chairman
  Department of Planning and Urban Form

Introduction

Richard K. Brail

PLANNING SUPPORT SYSTEMS (PSS) THAT INTEGRATE SPATIAL MAPPING, analysis, and visualization have evolved substantially over the past decade. Significant resources have been devoted to making these computer-based systems operational and meaningful in public decision making. In September 2007 the Lincoln Institute of Land Policy held a conference focusing on planning support systems that highlighted the current state of the art and pointed to future developments. Leading scholars at the intellectual and operational centers of current work in the area contributed the eleven chapters included in this volume.

The term *planning support systems* has been defined both broadly, to encompass a range of technology-based solutions useful to planners, and more narrowly as GIS-based models that project urban futures and/or estimate impacts. In the broadest sense, PSS encompasses analysis, design, participatory planning, communication, and visualization.

The Lincoln Institute conference focused on mature planning support systems that have been implemented in a number of applications, and have received broad recognition. Yet, they vary in their theoretical frameworks, data inputs, and types of output. The one common theme to the PSS models in this book is that they are all operational and have been implemented in real-world applications. The systems were selected for this reason as well as for representing different design approaches. These models are not speculative and unproven, but rather show that a powerful concept such as PSS can be translated into operational frameworks useful in planning and public policy.

The book is divided into four sections. In the first section, "A Broader Perspective," Michael Batty's and Harry Timmermans's essays provide an overview of planning and decision support systems. Batty introduces the concept of a planning support system and highlights the movement of urban planning over the past decades from a top-down, "professionals know best" attitude to a participatory approach involving a broad spectrum of citizens, interest groups, and public officials. Today planners and public officials interact with multiple communities and increasingly do so with digital technology. Batty develops the concept of a planner's toolbox of digital tools and applications that focus on the visualization of models and processes.

Batty states, "communication through visualization is rapidly becoming one of the main foci in PSS as the computer revolution moves ever more swiftly to graphic and related media in contrast to its origins in numerical data processing" (Batty, chapter 1, page 5). He demonstrates the power of visualization with a set of interesting examples, including a land use model, a "virtual" London, and Google-based implementations. These remarkable examples illustrate the power of graphics-based tools and their place in a planning support system.

Harry Timmermans looks broadly at spatial decision support with particular focus on land use and transportation models (LUTMs) and offers an excellent review of their evolution. While these models comprise only one class of planning support system, there are lessons to be learned from their implementation because their broad dissemination has had a mixed history. Some have been used widely, while others are little more than academic exercises. Based on the experiences of LUTMs, Timmermans suggests that developing a model does not mean that it necessarily will be used. Even more, emerging planning support systems often are "toy" enterprises, developed as stand-alone projects presented at academic conferences. In "on the street" legitimacy, there is a substantial gap between operational PSS used in live situations and research designs that show promise but have never been tested in the real world. For Timmermans, cities and regions are complex and require substantial resource commitments and complex modeling solutions.

The second section of the book, "The Regional Scale," contains three chapters about operational PSS that work at broader geographic scales. These three systems are generally focused on groups of cities, counties, or other regional-scale entities such as river basins or watersheds. These models reflect different methodological approaches to projecting into the future. The first chapter, by Keith Clarke, describes SLEUTH, a cellular automaton model that uses the grid cell as the unit of analysis. SLEUTH is widely used, having been applied to more than 100 cities and regions. Key to its development is the availability of the model code on the Internet and the host of researchers and students who have worked with and improved the model design. Clarke outlines the history of SLEUTH, discusses unresolved issues, and shows how this complex and computationally intensive model is evolving into a PSS with visualization, scenario construction, and alternatives analysis.

The second chapter in this section, by Brian Deal and Varkki Pallathucheril, presents the Land-use Evolution and impact Assessment Model (LEAM), which integrates a grid-based cellular automata (CA) approach with regional socioeconomic models—a "hybrid CA" framework. LEAM balances the results of model runs against stakeholder and professional review and comment. Developed at the University of Illinois at Urbana-Champaign, the model has been used in Chicago and St. Louis. The St. Louis case, where LEAM is loosely coupled to a regional transportation model, is described in detail. This connection permits the simulation of the classic interaction between development and the transportation infrastructure impacts. The authors emphasize the connectivity between models and citizens, where scenarios are put in the public arena for discussion and consensus building.

In the final chapter of this section, Richard Klosterman offers a view of planning that underlies the development of the What if?™ planning support system. Klosterman reviews the evolution of planning theory and practice from top-down design and analysis to collective reasoning. Successful PSS should consider a set of design principles that recognize the difficulty of prediction, the inadequacy of available data, and the need to keep model implementations understandable.

Klosterman reinforces Deal and Pallathucheril's comments about involving the community in developing the model and exploring the policy alternatives. What if? responds to these design principles since the model "is an explicitly policy-oriented model that suggests *what* might happen in the future *if* clearly specified public policies are adopted" (Klosterman, chapter 5, page 90). This model employs vector-based developable land units (DLUs) and builds future scenarios based on user-defined policies and rankings. What if? has been used broadly, with installations in the United States, Australia, China, Italy, Korea, Malaysia, Spain, and the United Kingdom.

The third section, "Moving from Region to City," contains four chapters that examine how planning support systems transition from the regional scale down to neighborhoods and into the planning office. The chapter on UrbanSim, authored by Paul Waddell, Xuan Liu, and Liming Wang, describes a complex and powerful model used in a variety of city sizes and locales, including Brussels, Honolulu, Rome, Salt Lake City, San Francisco, Seattle, Tel Aviv, and Zurich. UrbanSim simulates interactions through agents representing persons and jobs, and contains an urban land market at the parcel, zone, and grid-cell levels. Unlike many other simulation efforts, UrbanSim models real estate interactions and prices, and integrates directly with urban transportation models. The development of UrbanSim has been fostered by broad and extensive funding support and recognition of the strength of the conceptual framework and the need for such a model system. This PSS is also widely known for open source licensing.

Eliot Allen authored the next chapter, focusing on the INDEX PSS, which was designed as a straightforward scenario generator and scoring tool. INDEX contains a set of indicators that can be used to evaluate alternative land use designs in terms of their environmental and sustainable impacts. These indicators are embedded in the PSS and described in detail in a dictionary. The focus of INDEX is on the assessment of current projects and plans, rather than long-range activities. Its intent is to improve the numerous planning decisions made daily by the thousands of agencies in the United States that deal with land use and transportation issues. The INDEX consulting group has also used "smart boards" as an interactive design device for citizen planning. This innovative tool, Paint the Region, permits broad citizen participation in planning issues. INDEX has been used widely—in 690 locations across 36 states as well as internationally.

The section's third chapter is by George Janes and Michael Kwartler of the Environmental Simulation Center (ESC). The center directed the research effort that developed CommunityViz®, a highly ambitious effort supported by the Orton Family Foundation. The original CommunityViz was a bold attempt to integrate cutting-edge technology and theoretical concepts into a unified framework. The initial design included a scenario builder connected to both a two-dimensional GIS and a three-dimensional visualization environment. Users could work across 2D maps and 3D scenes, seeing the results of planning and development decisions in both media, and actually flying through a computer-generated landscape.

Coupled to this integrated 2D and 3D framework was an agent-based urban microsimulation model, the Policy Simulator™, which is no longer supported as part of the original CommunityViz. The Policy Simulator represented an innovative attempt at simulating a city at the level of the individual activities of households and firms. Today CommuntyViz consists of Scenario 360™, the 2D PSS that offers indicator-based evaluation, and SiteBuilder 3D™, the three-dimensional interactive viewing module. Scenario 360 provides an excellent tool for building indicators with the Formula Wizard, and has been used in a variety of localities.

The last chapter in this section focuses on the use of the PSS as an administrative tool in the planning office. Anthony Yeh details how PSS is being used in Hong Kong and China for development control, in particular for processing project applications. The primary objective of these PSS implementations is to rationalize the planning and administrative decisions made about applications for new development projects. The chapter provides a detailed window into the use of two interesting conceptual and methodological approaches, Computer-Supported Collaborative Work Flow (CSCWF) and case-based reasoning (CBR). This PSS implementation uses GIS, database management, and visualization tools as well as knowledge-based frameworks, complementing the other systems presented in the book.

The final section, "Planning Support Systems in Practice," focuses on using PSS in planning and public policy applications from two different perspectives. Stan Geertman, a professor in the Netherlands, has researched and written about planning support systems, while Terry Moore is a practicing planner in the United States. Both offer critical assessments of the application potential of PSS in practice and recommendations of how to move PSS further into the mainstream.

Geertman sees PSS as an information technology tool that requires user acceptance to be successful, requiring a solid understanding of planning decisions and decision makers. Context is important; the nature of the problem, the predilections of the staff, and the level of available resources all matter. He calls for a research agenda that supports the continuing development of PSS, noting that we have a long way to go. Critical in this future work is the matching of the user to the PSS instrument used.

Moore reinforces the need for user acceptance and argues that planning support systems should be more flexible, easier to use, and focused on producing needed and useful outputs for planners and the community. He also presents the dilemma of complexity versus simplicity. As Moore states: "A dilemma for planners is that the decision makers make irreconcilable demands of PSS. On the one hand, they know metropolitan areas are complex, and that everything affects everything else. They want a model that deals with that complexity and especially with the myriad policy choices that they want investigated" (Moore, chapter 11, page 252).

But planners and policy makers also "want transparency. They claim not to want a black box, implying that they want to understand all the relationships and be able to adjust on the fly" (Moore, chapter 11, page 253). Moore offers insights on how to deal with this issue by focusing on the PSS design process.

What can we learn from these authors? Planning support systems already exist to help professionals and citizens better understand the consequences of their decisions and better "see" the future. This book presents a range of operational systems that do a variety of tasks, and these modeling frameworks have been used widely. SLEUTH has been run in more than 100 regions; UrbanSim is used both in the United States and internationally; and INDEX has been applied in about 700 places in the United States, as well as internationally. PSS can do projections to the future, can estimate impacts of development options, visualize urban environments, and help manage the office. Yet, there are still many gaps between what PSS offers and what is needed by cities and regions. There is the continuing frustration that PSS has not entered the planning and policy arena more broadly.

There is the gap between the ideal PSS, an analytic tool useful in communicative planning, and the reality that many planning organizations do not use these systems. This lack of use is attributed to a wide range of causes including tool and user mismatch, lack of resources, and inadequate knowledge. We face the obvious question: How do we find the resources and commitment to develop PSS so that these decision support tools can be better connected to planning and public policy?

In the United States the urban transportation planning community benefited from a large influx of federal dollars that assisted in developing a coherent and robust analytic framework, which has survived and evolved over half a century. Sufficient resources would be welcome, but even without the significant influx of new finances, PSS tools can evolve. As the reader will see in these chapters, there are success stories as well as recommendations about how to move PSS forward.

PSS are a small piece of the larger movements occurring in planning and policy development. The planning process today is more visual, more public, more accessible, and more collaborative than in previous decades. Technology—in the form of models, visual simulations, and the Internet—is feeding the broadened access of citizens to their environment and to the decisions that affect the community. Google Earth and Microsoft's® Virtual Earth™ are two examples of widely available mapping tools as three-dimensional "flying" is becoming commonplace.

Cities and regions are on the digital map. At the same time, the world faces the issues of climate and environmental change and energy depletion. Within this dynamically changing landscape sits urban and regional planning. Planning support systems will evolve; they will have to in order to remain relevant. This book provides ample evidence that this evolution is taking place.

A Broader Perspective

SECTION 1

Planning Support Systems

Progress, Predictions, and Speculations on the Shape of Things to Come

Michael Batty

Defining Planning Support

PLANNING SUPPORT SYSTEMS EMERGED IN THE LATE 1980S AS THE GENERIC term for that loose assemblage of computer-based tools that urban and regional planners had garnered around them. Computers have been applied to human affairs ever since their inception in the mid-twentieth century, and by 1960 planners were experimenting with large-scale systems for data and simulation. These led immediately to municipal information systems and land use transportation models that formed the core of the planner's toolbox until the advent of geographic information systems (GIS). By the 1990s, a sufficiently varied set of tools informed most of the stages of the technical planning process. It thus made sense to consider these collectively as planning support systems (PSS) that could be developed in more integrated fashion and adapted to many different contexts in which planning required such support.

Until the idea of PSS emerged, the conventional wisdom held that scientific or rational planning could and should be underpinned by comprehensive computer models that linked how the system in question actually functioned to how it might function under certain design requirements. In this sense, the planning process itself was articulated as a system both within and without the wider urban and regional system, which was the object of design. This bold and perhaps naïve conception emanating from the systems approach (West Churchman 1968) gradually weakened its grip on planning methodologies. It became ever clearer that such tight structures could not be mapped onto planning problems that were always too diverse, ill-defined, and ambiguous to admit of highly structured decision making supported by well-defined computer technologies.

This conception may have met the requirements for "putting a man on the moon," but it fell far short of solving problems such as "getting us to the airport," in Mel Webber's hallowed words (1979). Once computers became universally available through the PC, then such tight structures were blown apart as many diverse computer-based tools reflecting a variety of applications became available. Geographic information systems were in the vanguard and by 1990 this proliferation could no longer be imagined as integrative. *Planning support systems* came to be used as the collective term for this variety.

Britton Harris (1989a) actually coined the term.[1] Harris, in fact, had been the doyen of the land use transportation modeling field since it began in the late 1950s, being the leading commentator and advocate for how such science might be applied and developed. In a landmark paper in 1989 entitled "Beyond Geographic Information Systems: Computers and the Planning Professional," he argued that just as management required routine support, planning required strategic support, hence his use of the term *planning support systems* in contrast to decision support systems. In the early days, up until networked computer systems really took off, most PSS were focused on nonroutine, strategic planning although the line between the strategic and the routine was inevitably blurred (Batty 1995).

What has changed this context radically is, first, the proliferation of individual software devoted to countless tasks that are relevant to any kind of problem solving and, second, the dissemination of this software and data across the Internet from dumb Web pages that simply provide information to esoteric software collaboratories. This blurring of the field is one of the key themes of this chapter. It traces how the idea of planning support is changing as both the problems to which PSS are applied and the technologies enabling us to generate such support change, both simultaneously and in parallel.

This broadening context is based on three related transitions. First, urban planning has become highly pluralistic based on increasing uncertainty and ambiguity in society at large about well-defined courses of social action. In short, planning problems are no longer regarded as soluble in the classical scientific sense. In Rittel and Webber's (1973) graphic terminology, they are "wicked." The notion that there are optimal products in the form of ideal cities to be designed has given way to the possibility that there might only be optimal processes to be used in negotiating futures that are in some general sense acceptable. In fact, this perspective was widely accepted when planning support systems were first articulated, but since then it has deepened as our collective view of the future has fragmented.

Second, in the last 50 years the process of planning has moved quickly from rigid professionalism to collective negotiation while its methods have been used increasingly to communicate and disseminate a multitude of ideas to many constituencies with a central interest in the future. In this sense, planning support systems are increasingly used to inform. The focus is thus on adapting more esoteric tools and their products to audiences and interest groups that do not ordinarily have the professional expertise to interpret them.

Third, new technologies for disseminating information, now largely digital in one form or another, have rapidly developed in the last 20 years through the

Internet and related systems, and this has led to the common media of communication becoming predominantly visual. Not all these transitions are necessarily ideal, but they form the starting point for this review and the speculations we will develop.

We first outline the development of new computer technologies and their importance for PSS, largely since the advent of the Internet and its visual media in the form of the browser. We pay particular attention to ways in which computers have merged with communications and the way desktop tools are migrating to the Internet. This sets the scene for a rudimentary classification of PSS tools, notwithstanding the great diversity of such tools and the fact that planners and professionals stand at the threshold of developing their own tools for specific situations. This is largely due to the massive growth of generic systems such as GIS and the very high-level processes that are now available for bypassing expert programming. This classification results in what we call the planner's toolbox, which, in this view, contains a series of generic and specialist tools that can be merged with one another and adapted to a wide variety of contexts.

To illustrate these ideas, we chose three exemplars: (1) a land use transportation model that is being developed as part of an integrated assessment of climate-change scenarios in Greater London over the next 100 years; (2) an example of how digital geometric modeling of Greater London, in the form of a virtual city model that has been created, can be used to display and communicate routine measurements of air pollution to interested parties; and (3) the way geodemographic spatial data are being focused on routine applications through linking them to online tools such as Google Maps and online environments or virtual worlds such as Second Life®.

The first example is nonroutine, strategic, and makes use of traditional mathematical models in the first instance as desktop applications. The second and third are much more routine, based on communicating essential content in a user-friendly form across the Web and making use of digital iconic, rather than symbolic, modeling, although both styles are beginning to merge in some applications (Batty 2007). These applications are intrinsically visual and impress the main message of this chapter that communication through visualization is rapidly becoming one of the main foci in PSS as the computer revolution moves ever more swiftly to graphic and related media in contrast to its origins in numerical data processing. This echoes the implicit sentiments of Brail in his earlier emphasis on planning support systems as techniques that "couple analytic tools and computer simulation models with visual displays" (Brail and Klosterman 2001, ix).

New Technologies

Several fundamental themes characterize the evolution of digital computation, but one of the most deep-seated is the development of hardware that is able to process ever-increasing amounts of data. In a sense this might seem an almost trivial characteristic since the entire digital world appears to stem from this. But communication systems, too, have evolved to transmit ever-greater amounts of data ever more quickly on all earthbound scales, and the convergence of computers and communications is now driving the development of computation in all-pervasive ways, of which PSS is just one of many. Miniaturization of computer circuitry through increasingly powerful microprocessors is the key to all of this and there seems to be no end in sight.

For forty years or more Moore's Law, which holds that computer processing power—speed and memory—doubles every two to three years, has held sway, while Gilder's Law suggests that this increase is even faster for bandwidth, with capacity growing at least three times faster than computer power (Gilder 1989). Putting together this growth in the number of computers and increasing bandwidth, Metcalfe's Law suggests that the growth in digital connectivity between identifiable units of social action—people, firms, governments, and so on—grows at least as the square of the number of users, which is even faster still.[2]

By 1990, when PSS were first articulated, part of this technological revolution had taken place in that comparatively massive memories on distributed machines—PCs on the desktop and workstations for more specialized use—were being utilized for computer models of cities and urban information systems. Some of Lee's (1973) critique of the earlier 1960s experience with computer models, where the ability to actually complete such simulation and information retrieval at a scale where such tools were useful, was thus cast in doubt. Moreover, the move to graphics, which was occasioned by such increased memory, was well under way with the development of GIS, although the move to graphical user interfaces following the lead set by Apple and the workstation leaders such as Sun was only just beginning. Visualization was thus significant, but the use of computers for sharing information, for enabling the use of common tools through communication across the Internet, and for disseminating the graphical and numerical outputs from PSS were in their infancy. These later technologies are now forcing the field and this review will be developed from this perspective.

At present, it is the ability to communicate using these new technologies that represents the cutting edge in PSS, rather than any large-scale formal developments in the tools themselves. Urban modeling has moved away from aggregate, cross-sectional models to more disaggregate, agent-based structures that depend on representing more individual-based data (Waddell, Liu, and Wang, chapter 6) and on physical representations of the systems of interest using fine meshes of cells (Clarke, chapter 3), but these developments are largely driven by the existence of fine-scale data and by computation itself rather than by any theoretical advances in our understanding of cities.

In fact, we are living through a time when theories have fragmented and there is much less consensus than there was 50 years ago about what represents the key ways in which cities evolve and grow. Technique rather than theory has come to dominate, and thus developments in computational technologies are tending to drive the field. Developments in large-scale models have not yet availed themselves of the move to communication and visualization other than their embedding within or coupling to GIS for purposes of display. Nor have they moved upstream to avail themselves of super and parallel computer technologies. The ability to distribute such computation across networks has not yet made its mark. Rather, the focus is currently on visualization for much more pragmatic purposes such as the move from two to three dimensions in the construction of virtual city models, and the dissemination of displays for more generic purposes of communication and participation (Batty et al. 2001). The development of PP-GIS (public participation geographic information systems), particularly in North America, is one manifestation of this move.

A nice contrast with our current technologies in terms of visualization is contained in figures 1.1(a) and 1.1(b). Figure 1.1(a) shows the kind of desktop interface available in the early 1990s on a Macintosh computer, where a variety of well-known tools have been brought together for population forecasting. The modules shown on this desktop, which is entitled "The Emergent Desktop Environment for a PSS," can be plugged together in various ways to generate visual outputs, and it is suggested there that "it is only a matter of time before most software moves to this mode" (Batty 1995). In fact, this has not really happened, for the field has become much more fragmented and in so far as such plug-and-play modules have been designed, they have not been generalized in linked software systems. Now, however, there is less consensus that this is the main way forward for PSS. Figure 1.1(b) shows one of the earliest interactive Web pages from March 1995—traffic-flow data being piped from Web cameras in San Diego, California—used as a diagnostic tool for traffic control (Batty 1997b). The Web was then barely known to planning professionals, but this kind of visualization is now writ large and is so routine that it is barely commented upon.[3] Little of this was anticipated a generation ago when PSS was first defined by Harris.

Various hardware environments for visualization are of some significance for PSS, and these revolve around the creation of theaters in which various participants in PSS can interact. In short, this is part of a wider development in which visualization is used to communicate with participants by creating environments in which the participants can interact through computer tools and among themselves. In their extreme form, these are single-user virtual realities in which the software pipes the imagery and interactivity directly into the user's sensory receptors, fully immersive VR through headsets and various interactive hand devices being the original (and now somewhat dated) examples of such environments. VR theatres are good examples of how these technologies have reached out to embrace computer-computer, user-user, and computer-user interactions in a self-contained, purpose-built form. Yet these are still fairly specialized and not yet in general use, notwithstanding reductions in real costs (Batty 2008). Interactivity and communication are still mainly accomplished by users clustering around a desktop or workstation, or interacting across the Web, with this latter technology now forming the cutting edge of interactivity, participation, and communication among diverse remote users.

FIGURE
1.1

Early Graphics (ca. 1995) for PSS:
A. PSS Loosely Coupled on an Apple Mac Desktop
B. Real Time Traffic Display Through Web Technology,
   San Diego, CA

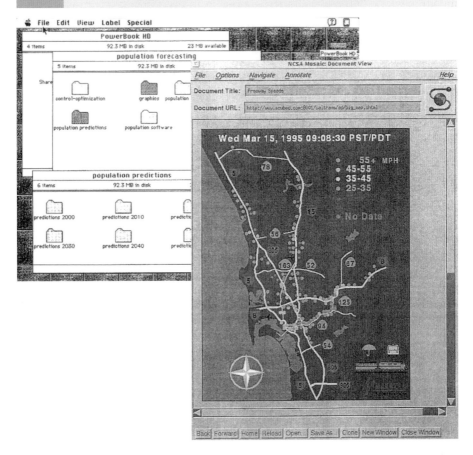

The visualization and communication technologies that are now beginning to influence the development of PSS all revolve around interactivity, mainly using the Web but with grid computing rapidly gaining ground, at least conceptually.[4] The Web is now organized into at least four styles of Web-based services, the collective term for this variety: *vanilla-style Web pages*, which simply present information to users with no interactivity other than simple hyperlinking to other pages; Web pages that enable users to download data and software to their desktops; Web pages that enable users to run software within their own Web page, usually through the form of simple Java-based programs; and Web pages that enable users to import their own data and run software remotely, often in the style of grid computing.

More elaborate systems such as collaboratories—online systems remotely linked through Web pages that enable users to communicate with one another and to run software jointly—are in their infancy. In a sense, these collaboratories are virtual laboratories—virtual worlds, even—that let users communicate in closed environments a little like VR theaters, but remotely with much looser limits on the number of users who can interact. Early systems were pioneered as part of PP-GIS (see, for example, Kingston, Evans, and Carver 2003) although as yet, there are few workable PPS collaboratories, despite some interesting individual attempts. A comparison of the articles in the two edited collections—Brail and Klosterman's (2001) *Planning Support Systems*, which is composed of reviews of tools largely conceived before the early 1990s, and Geertman and Stillwell's (2003b) *Planning Support Systems in Practice*, which contains techniques and models developed up to a decade later—impress this change. Online systems strongly feature in the later collection, although none of them quite reaches the level of collaboratories in the sense implied here. Nevertheless, the rudiments of such systems are now in place and substantial developments in this area are to be expected in the next decade.

As we have suggested, many of the traditional tools that historically dominated computer-aided planning, such as urban or land use transportation models, no longer form the core of PSS, although as Timmermans (chapter 2) suggests, these are still a substantial part of the field. This lesser emphasis is largely due to the extremely specific nature of the problem contexts to which such models need to be applied and the highly variable data that are required. Models such as UrbanSim, MEPLAN, TRANUS, CUF, and the newer generation of cellular automata models of land development (see Maguire, Batty, and Goodchild 2005) are no more widely applied than the Lowry model was in the 1960s and 1970s.

This situation is unlikely to change in the short or medium term for GIS software, which has developed in modular, generic fashion and is still a long way from coupling, incorporating, or embedding such models, despite there now being a visual model–building capability within software such as ArcGIS. Only when software emerges that enables such models to be constructed on the fly will these kinds of tools become more widely used. Even then, it might be that the skill base required to build such models will impose intrinsic limits on what is possible. In fact, even the addition of visualization capabilities to such models has been weak, with attempts limited to loose couplings with GIS, and/or Web-page outputs, such as in the generalization of the MEPLAN, TRANUS, and IRPUD models in the PROPOLIS project (Lautso 2003).

GIS software is more generic, highly descriptive, and much less controversial in terms of its implicit tools of spatial analysis than large-scale urban modeling. The focus in its development has been to generalize such software to be capable of any kind of spatial analysis and representation, and this has tended to keep the tools descriptive rather than predictive. Insofar as they can be used prescriptively, this depends entirely on the way they are used to support the design process. In a sense, GIS is "theoryless," although it depends on the way the user fashions software to the data and whether or not the tools of analysis (such as buffering, simple accessibility measures, overlay analysis, and so on) are relevant. In fact, more specific applications invariably require additional tuning of the software. An example is Klosterman's What if?™ system (2007; chapter 5), which utilizes elements of GIS but is essentially a stand-alone application of overlay analysis tailored to U.S.-style zoning and land use planning.

Within planning support, GIS applications tend to be both routine and strategic as well as applicable across a variety of scales. Visualization can be much larger scale, although more routine, than urban modeling. For example, CAD and 3D iconic models are being generated using GIS as well as other software such as AutoCAD®, and although substantial in terms of size, their application is becoming more routine. This is the fastest growth area of PSS on the Web, where visualization of 2D and 3D map forms are being dramatically accelerated in terms of usage with the availability of nonproprietary software systems such as Google Earth, Google Maps, and Microsoft®'s Virtual Earth™, among others.

It is worth noting that in contrast to early developments of PSS, the dominant applications are much more routine. They are fashioned from the availability of simple desktop tools and vanilla-style Web pages based on creative uses of spreadsheets and related databases and graphics systems ranging from paint packages to simple 2D and 3D CAD and GIS, among a plethora of newer applications that involve merging simple tools. Many of these tools are facilitated by the ability to publish such applications on the Web, thus making them available to a wider group of users. However, these developments are so fragmented and diverse that it is difficult to classify them into coherent themes.

Substantial developments in PSS could arise in the next decade. Embedding one style of model into another is already a major force in the field, and it is likely that we might see symbolic modeling being embedded in iconic—that is, mathematical urban models being coupled to or embedded in 2D and 3D GIS within virtual reality–style environments (Batty 2007). Although there are already examples of this, their routine application remains a long way off. It is more likely that new layers of software will be built up to the point where nonexpert but professional users can fashion many new tools from component parts. This is the way computing has evolved over the last 50 years since its inception and there is no end in sight. However, this model of building successive layers of software comes at a cost: Each additional layer constrains what is possible within that layer. The fact that good urban models cannot be easily built using the tools of GIS, for example, is a limit that is not likely to be resolved due to the theory-laden content of such urban models and its conflict with modular, generic software.

Before we attempt to classify PSS, it is worth noting this last feature of computer technology, the relentless march to develop layer upon layer of functionality in the effort to bring computation to the widest possible constituency. The model of technological development suggests that as computers increase in memory and speed and drop in cost—due to the laws proposed by Moore, Metcalfe, and Gilder—the way users interact with them becomes ever more friendly. The easiest way to achieve this is to add new layers of more generalized software on top of the less generalized. A classic example is the Windows operating system, which was built on top of DOS. In the long term, however, this transition occurs almost continuously. It is seen currently in programming in the object-oriented paradigm and in the introduction of ever more general scripting languages. The same is true of networking with more user-friendly applications of Web services and related communications applications. It is not hard now to foresee a time when users will literally pull windows and their applications around a screen with their fingers, which not so long ago was the stuff of science fiction.

What all this means for the development of our field is that we should not expect it to stand still. In 1989, when Harris developed his vision of PSS, the field was still dominated by large-scale applications such as land use transportation models and GIS, with only spreadsheet applications providing any form of generic media for different kinds of applications. Since then, almost all aspects of planning in its various types, from urban design to regional policy, have been subject to IT support and with the fragmentation of the field, various layers of software have been exploited and built to reflect this diversity. This makes the problem of classification somewhat confusing, or rather much less focused than the rather clear structures we assumed for PSS a generation ago. The tools presented below illustrate all these issues as well as ways in which such problems are being resolved in the wider context of visualization and communication.

A Classification of Planning Support Systems: The Planner's Toolbox

The traditional classification of PSS is based on the various tasks that define the technical planning process (Batty 1995). Insofar as planning can be seen as a technical process, it begins with problem identification, moves to analysis, then to the generation of alternative plans with their subsequent evaluation, and finally to the choice of the best plan to implement. This can be a cyclical or iterative process, as was the model that emerged from the concern for rational decision in the 1960s (Boyce, Day, and McDonald 1970), but in essence it is based on the long-standing tradition of "survey before plan" associated with the pioneering work of Patrick Geddes at the turn of the last century. This process is driven by survey, motivated by goal setting, tested against objectives, with the "best plan" managed through implementation. Once a plan is produced, then the process begins again through implementation but at a lower or different level with various processes of this kind nested within and without one another. One statement of this rational decision or problem-solving process on which PSS is based is given in Batty (1995).

This technical process has always been an ideal type that when applied in practice is massively modified. Moreover, there is much less consensus about its role currently than ever before as the perceived consensus about planning in general, from the top down, has fragmented. Nevertheless the series of tasks defining the sequence of stages in the process is as good a vehicle as any on which to think about planning support using IT. We assume the process can be arranged in the following sequence:

Define Problem → *Set Goals* → *Analyze Data* → *Generate Plan* →

Evaluate Plan → *Choose Plan* → *Implement Plan*

Here distinct theories, models, and techniques can be applied at each of these stages. Specialist tools have been developed for each of these stages. Problem-structuring techniques and goal formulation based on brainstorming technologies are quite well developed and are now widely supported by IT although not much applied in urban planning. Analysis techniques largely revolve around GIS in the spatial analysis domain and many packages of increasing sophistication are being used. In fact, this set of tools is increasingly generic in that they are not only used for analysis and of course for database application (survey) but also for management at all stages of the process. Plan generation is still largely governed by land use transportation models, the predictive capacity and what-if capabilities of which have been widely developed during the last 30 to 40 years. Evaluation methods tend to rely on these models as well as more qualitative assessments of risk and benefit-cost and are informed by the whole range of multicriteria and optimization models. Implementation involves a series of management techniques developed under the more routine rubric of decision support.

In the 1960s, very early in the development of land use transportation models, it was assumed that the entire planning process might be encapsulated into a general systems model with command and control capabilities akin to managing a complex machine. Models that could describe, predict, and prescribe (design) were seen as tools to be aspired to, although this phase was short lived and the complexity and ambiguity of city systems and their planning were quickly realized. In fact, it was probably the inadequacy of the tools that was most clearly sensed, as reflected in Lee's (1973) trenchant critique, rather than any insight into the nature of cities that had not been part of our consciousness already.

Nevertheless, just as the process of planning has broadened and fragmented, so has our vision of what might constitute the planner's toolbox. GIS was added to land use and transportation in the 1980s. Since then the development of much more generic tools such as spreadsheets at a lower level and of wider applicability has begun to inform all stages of the process. The rather narrow technocratic process above can be extended into a much wider domain of public engagement, however. Running alongside or perhaps woven into this fabric is public participation of all kinds, which has provided ways in which the process has reached out to its wider context. Such participation has been fashioned particularly around PP-GIS (Craig, Harris, and Weiner 2002), but increasingly a whole variety of visualization tools making use of more bottom-up technologies as well as 3D virtual city models have come into play. Much of this was anticipated by the mid-1990s as reflected in Brail and Klosterman (2001).

The next set of ideas by which to classify PSS is considerably more generic in the sense of tasks, and these revolve around issues of how the city system is represented and manipulated. In short we can identify the key activities in problem solving and use these to organize PSS. Survey is based on observation and measurement while analysis is based on the representation and organization of these data. Modeling and simulation are key activities in description and prediction while optimization is the activity of generating and evaluating some best plan. Management is reflected in implementation while negotiation occurs at all stages and scales of the process.

The activities of observing, measuring, analyzing, modeling, simulating, predicting, prescribing or designing, optimizing, evaluating, managing, and negotiating, among others, can all be supported by software, and software has and is being developed around them. To show the variety of such classification at this point, however, it is worth noting that distinct packages have been developed that reflect different combinations of these activities to different degrees. These packages can be roughly classified as GIS; land use transportation models (LUTM); multicriteria analysis (MCA); plan-generation techniques such as What if?™, CAD, and 3D GIS; and public participation/multimedia community-visioning methods (Shiffer 2001). This is by no means an exhaustive list, and lower-level, generic software can also be identified that can be adapted to all such tasks in the form of spreadsheets, animation, and visualization packages. At the higher level, several of the standard packages can be added, integrated, or coupled together. For example, CommunityViz® is one such application that has reached the point of wider application, building on agent-based models, GIS, and 3D visualization.[5]

These packages can all be scored against the activities noted above. For example, GIS is focused on measuring and analyzing but can be adapted to prediction to an extent. Various routines are available for simulating and modeling and for optimizing, but in general the focus is more on representation, data, and some limited 2D visualization. Already we see that such tools have a more generic quality than might be assumed at first sight, and an exhaustive list of software products and the tasks they involve could be compiled. Most software has an ambiguous role in PSS in that it can be applied at various stages of the planning process and for various planning tasks. The same is true of planning problems at different scales. This is largely because when software is devised, it is usually in relation to a narrower problem; when it is refined, if it stands the test of time, it is extended in its applicability. Other software, as developed or adapted to some specific stage of the planning process, is often extended into other parts of the process and the entire sequence of tasks is related to this in some way. For example, it is not unusual to find LUTM and GIS being combined to form the heart of the plan-generation and evaluation process with its dissemination often now realized through some Web-based interface. PROPOLIS is such an example (Lautso 2003).

Some software is designed for extremely generic tasks, but even this varies across scales. For example, consider the idea of spreadsheets as PSS tools. Klosterman, Brail, and Bossard's *Spreadsheet Models for Urban and Regional Analysis* (1993) shows a wide variety of analytical and predictive applications (e.g., models implemented in spreadsheets that were initially devices solely used for storing, visualizing, and searching data). Currently, at the other end of the spectrum, several packages are emerging for new classes of the cellular automata model that can be applied to urban development, and for agent-based models, which specify the system in terms of fine-scale disaggregates. These are really toolboxes in their own right that enable users to develop any such model with the generic properties of the particular application. For example, in the case of an agent-based model, the package is often adaptable to represent a very wide range of problems of which spatial ones might only be a subset.

Several other ways exist to classify tools for PSS. The scale of the problem is significant. It is likely that urban design problems, for example, especially those that involve movement in small spaces, require very different types of software from those used to support regional planning. The best-developed agent-based models are in the area of crowd dynamics, making them useful for assessing movement and patronage in small spaces like shopping centers. This type of model, even its more aggregate-agent equivalents, would not find much use at higher spatial scales. Another feature is context. Often a planning task is ongoing, and as it evolves so does software in the outside world; this changes the basis of support. Sometimes the task is not composed of a series of stages as envisaged, but is based on entry at, say, the implementation stage, where some plan has already been cast and requires modification during its implementation. Sometimes the entire plan may be generated by stakeholder involvement through various forms of participatory design. Again, the possibilities are endless and in one sense this makes the quest to classify PSS an unending and controversial one.

Before illustrating what we consider to be the future based on current developments, we will list the main kinds of software packages and applications that characterize the state of the art. It would be useful to provide an unequivocal classification of PSS into which every piece of software and every application would slot but this is not possible because software tools can be fashioned quite differently by different professionals in different contexts. In a sense, this is what the tools that we have alluded to so far are designed to do. We can, however, produce a rudimentary classification into tools and their software focuses on spatial problems (or not) and can be seen as being specialist for a particular spatial focus (or not). This sets up a two-way classification which we can array as Specialist/Generic against Spatial/Nonspatial. We can consider Nonspatial to be Aspatial because many tools are not specifically designed to deal with spatial problems per se, but can be fashioned to do so. This simple classification is shown in table 1.1 with typical examples of the genus contained in each box.

LUTM is highly specialist software that has hardly reached the stage where it can be purchased and adapted to specific situations by users or professionals who are not involved in its development. The traditional applications such as TRANUS, DRAM/EMPAL, etc., have begun to move in this direction but fall far short of being generic in any way. More recent applications of land use transportation models such as TRANSIMS and UrbanSim do offer software as

TABLE 1.1	**A Classification of PSS**	
	Spatial	*Aspatial*
Specialist	e.g., LUTM	e.g., Expert Systems, AI Software, Agent-based models (ABM)
Generic	e.g., GIS, Google Maps, Google Earth, etc.	e.g., Spreadsheets, Math-stat software, Databases

free or shareware but the learning curve is still extremely steep (Waddell, Liu, and Wang, chapter 6). It is not our purpose to review these models here but to get some sense of the field and how it has persisted; it is worth noting Wegener's (2005) review. It is important to note that such applications are so intense and large scale that entire planning processes are often built around them. Attempts to link them to GIS through loose coupling are weak, and visualization technologies are only just beginning to be exploited. Transport models, as distinct from LUTMs, have more or less followed this trend, too.

As part of this tradition, new styles of model such as cellular automata tend to be less applicable to policy and more speculative than LUTM. The software is better developed largely because such automata models that simulate urban development are more visual and simpler in structure, but also less operational (Clarke, chapter 3). For example, they contain hardly any transport activity, and where they have been widely developed as in the RIKS (Research Institute for Knowledge Systems) applications in the Netherlands (see Timmermans, chapter 2), they are invariably coupled with other models. Agent-based models (ABM) are too new to classify although TRANSIMS and UrbanSim are highly operational. Most others tend to be slightly more generic and are often pedagogic applications rather than fully fledged models that support policy making (see Maguire, Batty, and Goodchild 2005). In these kinds of Specialist/Spatial models, various attempts have been made to open them up to supporting tools in the other boxes of table 1.1. Nothing can truly stand alone, but progress is slow.

In contrast, if we examine GIS, which is clearly a much more generic set of tools than LUTM, various stages of the planning process can be supported using individual tools from the GIS toolbox. GIS is primarily about spatial information—storing and then displaying it—but many rudimentary and some more advanced functions have been added to the toolbox over the years. In particular, treating maps as layers and then combining them is a central operation in generating physical plans through overlay analysis, and it has been very well developed within GIS. It is one of the functions that has been present from the beginning. New functions such as spatial statistics of various kinds as well as routing procedures for transport analysis and now the extension of maps in 2D to 3D are all features of the current software. But GIS largely falls short of being applicable at the plan-generating and evaluating stages of the process in that models within GIS are at best descriptive rather than predictive. Linking to other models (LUTM, ABM, and so on) tends to be the way in which this software is extended.

The GIS toolbox has opened up dramatically in the last five years with the appearance of free mapping and visualization software on the Web. Web-based GIS has slowly developed with map-server technology, but it is Google that has led the way through its Google Maps and now in the third dimension, Google Earth, which are being very widely applied for visualization at many stages of the planning process. The third exemplar below builds on these technologies. In fact, Google Earth is beginning to supplant the use of CAD and 3D GIS software for visualizing urban development in 3D as virtual cities. CAD and 3D GIS are usually tailored to specific applications, despite the software being generic. Each application is quite different, which has meant that each author tends to adapt the generic software to the application. Again, the learning curve is steep, as in LUTM, in contrast to GIS, which is becoming ever more user friendly.

Integrated systems that combine the first column of table 1.1—specialist and generic spatial software—are increasingly used to underpin PSS. For example, CommunityViz and INDEX (Allen, chapter 7) fall into this category, and now the list of such applications is quite large. These systems are being fast extended to all stages of the planning process, particularly through visualization, which enables dissemination of results from modeling, prediction, and design. PP-GIS, for example, is built around standard GIS with Web-based applications beginning to predominate, while the whole area of community visioning through the use of multimedia in desktop and Web-based environments is burgeoning. Attempts are now being made to develop software-based conceptualizations of the entire planning process (Hopkins, Kaza, and Pallathucheril 2005a).

The second column of table 1.1, where software exists both in specialist and generic forms but is focused on problems that are not explicitly spatial, makes it clear that many forms of planning support use these. For example, expert systems informing plan-making activities and participation at different stages of the process have been quite widely developed while spreadsheets, mathematical and statistical, as well as database packages are now used routinely to support various parts of the process. This is where our classification begins to fall away as being less useful. What is very clear, however, is that every bit of software in the domains covered by this table can be adapted and coupled, often embedded within every other bit and that this wide array of possible tools makes every application distinct. This was not the case when PSS was first articulated but it is now a dominant feature of the field.

Exemplars

We now develop three exemplars that illustrate many, but by no means all, of the features and characteristics of PSS identified above.

LONG-TERM FORECASTING AT THE STRATEGIC LEVEL: VISUALIZING LAND USE AND TRANSPORTATION   We are designing a land use transportation model for

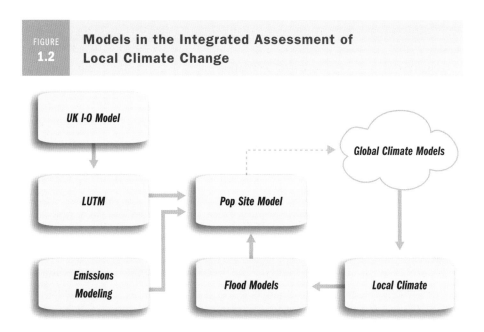

FIGURE 1.2   **Models in the Integrated Assessment of Local Climate Change**

Greater London as part of an integrated assessment of the impact of climate change on the location of population. This process couples a series of models that move down scale from predictions taken from global climate models to their impact on small-scale environments where pollution and flooding are the main concerns. The LUTM we are building is coupled to a global environmental input-output model at the regional scale and, at the site scale, to a detailed population-allocation mechanism that, in turn, is informed by various flooding and emissions models. The sequence of models is being developed by a consortium charged with looking at long-term scenarios to 2050 and 2100 for cities of which Greater London and the Thames Gateway comprise the current application. The models are strung together in the fashion illustrated in figure 1.2, and currently there are no feedback loops to enable adaptation to the various model predictions from the local to the global scale. Although this limits the usefulness of these models, the whole process is embedded in a more discursive structure in which various stakeholders and experts use the information from these models to make informed guesses and judgments about the future.

The LUTM sits between the input-output model, which has already been developed by Cambridge Econometrics, and the population site model, which essentially distributes the population outputs at census tract scale from the LUTM to a finer 100 meter by 100 meter grid used to assess the impact of flooding (see Dawson et al. 2007). What is of concern is the kind of support that this suite of models and the LUTM in particular provide for other professionals and stakeholders involved in the process of informed guessing about the future. Many of the other model builders in this process know little or nothing about LUTM and thus it is essential as a first step to communicate this as easily as possible. Moreover the model is quite large—currently 633 zones—and, thus, to absorb the outputs, we require good visualization so that users can appreciate at a glance what the model is generating. Moreover, setting up scenarios, which are extremely elaborate, needs to be accomplished easily and effectively. Last but not least, the data requirements of the model are large and it is essential to have good and fast ways of checking data.

All this suggests rapid visualization, which most LUTM currently do not have. Moreover, many of the models are almost legacy systems, being based on long out of date code and built in a time when communication was one of the least important problems. But with modern software, it is now possible to develop clear visualization and also to run these kinds of models interactively. This is what we have been developing and we currently have a prototype residential location that the user can calibrate on the fly, applied to 633 zones and four modes of transport—bus, subway, heavy rail, and road—for which trip distributions between all origins and destinations are predicted. This is a classic spatial interaction model and, in time, we propose to add new submodels of the same structure to deal with other relationships in the urban system. Currently we are dealing only with the journey to work, or rather trips between work (employment) and home (population in residential areas).

FIGURE 1.3 Loading the LUTM Toolbar Control, Reading in, and Checking the Data

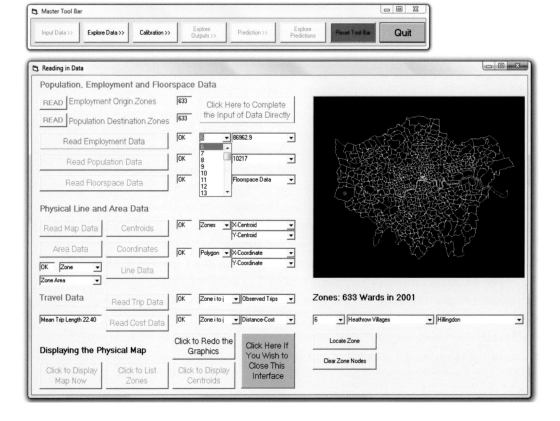

In figure 1.3, we show the data entry (from external files), but also the screen through which the user can first interrogate the data on the fly. The main toolbar moves from data input, to data exploration, to calibration, then exploration of the calibration results, through to the interactive setting of scenarios, and finally to predictions and their exploration. All of this can be done extremely rapidly. The program does not use any external graphics routines in GIS and is entirely self-contained in that users can simply load the executable file from which various options can be chosen at calibration and prediction. Figure 1.4 shows how the model can be interrogated spatially, with six screens showing the employment and population distributions as well as a single trip pattern from one origin to all residential destinations. These can be kept on screen at all times in different windows. More or less the same structure of spatial data exploration can be done after the model is calibrated and also after predictions have been developed. Figure 1.5 depicts a typical scenario being constructed where we have doubled the size of the employment at Heathrow Airport, a major hub in the London region, and also added in a cross rail link from the airport to central London (the CBD). We see some typical predictions in figure 1.6, which shows the impact of this change in population in residential areas across London, which is greater in the west around the airport as we might expect.

FIGURE 1.4   Exploring the Employment, Population, and Trip Data Spatially

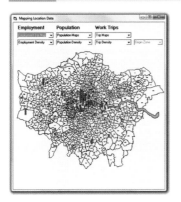 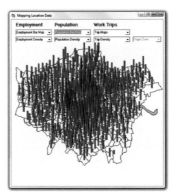 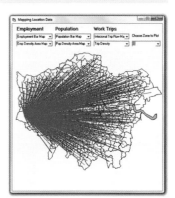

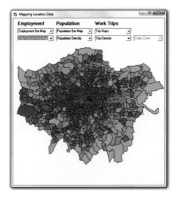 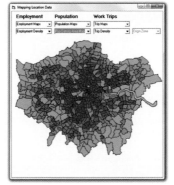 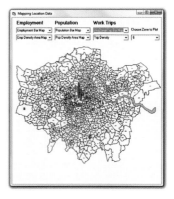

FIGURE
1.5

Creating a Scenario Interactively Using Sliders

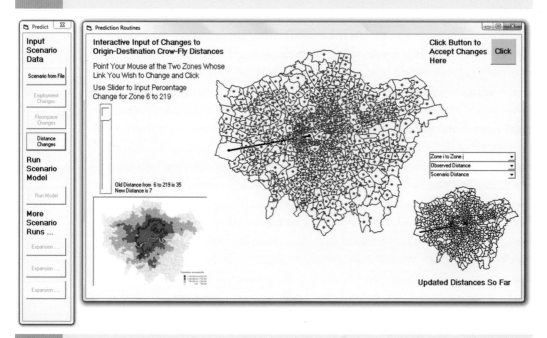

Predicting the Effects of the Scenario Using the Same Techniques for Exploring the Data

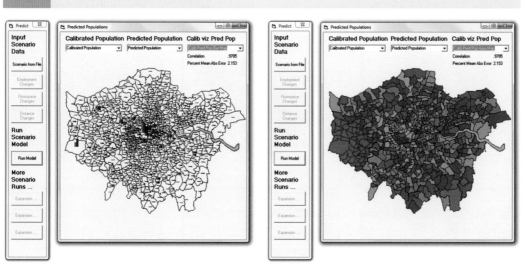

This gives an idea of what is now possible with LUTM. If those involved embraced current technologies, this kind of visualization should become routine, with the models being more widely used, appreciated, and better adapted to real situations. We have not speculated here on how we might embed this model and its running within the Web, giving access to a much wider range of users, but it is easy enough to set up the model for distribution to others in this mode.

IMMEDIATE FORECASTING AT THE LOCAL LEVEL: VISUALIZING THE IMPACT OF AIR POLLUTION USING A VIRTUAL CITY MODEL   Our second case study involves an application using the 3D iconic model—Virtual London—that we have built for the metropolis. This model is quite different in structure from the LUTM. It is not mathematical in the symbolic sense; it is iconic, but nevertheless digital, and constructed from building blocks, land parcels, and street data supplemented in the third dimension by light detection and ranging (LiDAR) data. The model was constructed for general visualization and public participation in Greater London and was funded by a metropolitan agency, the Greater London Authority (GLA), primarily for visualizing the impact of high buildings, which is the traditional use of such models. As it stands, the model now covers Greater London, in which there are 3.6 million building blocks. It was originally built for central London with some buildings rendered in detail but then extended to the metro area, which is largely configured in terms of building blocks. It was built in ArcGIS, improved in 3ds® Max, and now is available for local municipalities/boroughs in Google Earth. For data copyright reasons, it is not available as a public Web site, which is a source of great frustration in terms of its use for public participation.

Visualizations of the 3D form are shown in figure 1.7 for the original model in ArcGIS and also for the new model in Google Earth. The model requires some very powerful hardware to run in ArcGIS but it runs well in Google Earth with detail in the background always suppressed and only loaded as the user flies in. A great deal of multimedia has been ported to the model in order to link it to online panoramas. The products from the model tend to be movies that can be placed online rather than interactive products within which users can navigate. This also minimizes data copyright issues. We have developed several uses in terms of public participation, but a particularly innovative one links with the model to visualize air pollution. The network of air pollution sensors across London provides hourly feeds of data that are mapped and visualized using the surface routines in ArcGIS. We can then overlay these onto the model as shown in figure 1.8. This illustrates the nitrogen dioxide surface for central London where it is clear that this pollutant is strongly correlated with the road system and with key traffic intersections. We can do this for a vast array of pollutants, but to illustrate its potential, we have tagged the data to the static 3D images from the model, coloring the buildings in this manner. This is presented in a Flash-based interface that is available at the London Air Quality Network,[6] a Web site where air pollution data are visualized in somewhat cruder terms, but on a daily basis.

In figure 1.9 the coloring shows the intensity of air pollutants in an area of central London into which the user can zoom. The slider allows the user to see predictions of air quality over the next 10 years, for pollution will drop dramatically here due to new controls, congestion charging, and so on. At various points in the scene, the user can display the pollutants in 3D, where these scenes are taken from the Virtual London model. In fact, the air pollution surfaces are

FIGURE 1.7 Iconic Modeling: Virtual London in ArcGIS (top) and in Google Earth (bottom)

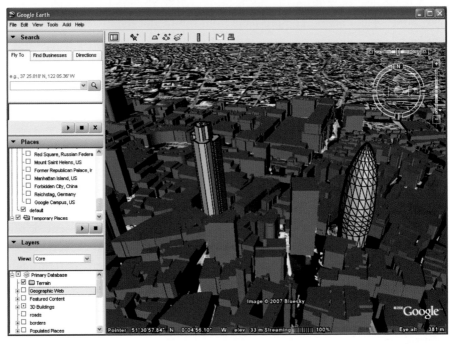

FIGURE 1.8 Nitrogen Dioxide Surface Mapped onto Virtual London as a Surface (top) and as a Flat Map (bottom)

FIGURE 1.9

Predictions from Air Pollution Models Fitted to Current Data Visualized in 2D and 3D Virtual City Environments as a Web-based Service

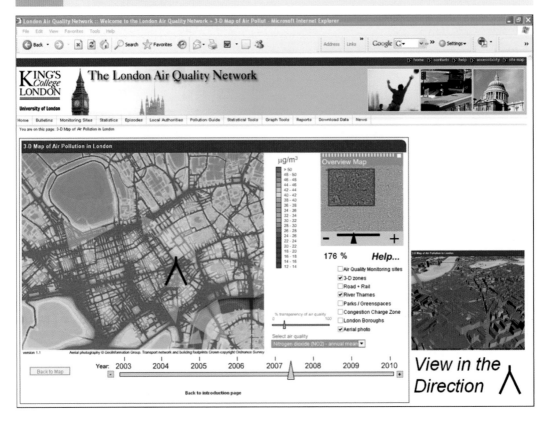

taken from a symbolic model of the hydrodynamics of traffic and pollution, all visualized in a Web-based interface where users can get to grips with the significance of these flows and their location. It is not beyond our wit to consider an online updating of this entire media linked to the sensor network just as we presented for San Diego 12 years ago, as shown in figure 1.1(b). This makes the point quite forcibly that such systems have enormous importance in serving and supporting the planning function in real time. This, too, we expect will be a major development in the next decade.

DESCRIBING AND EXPLORING SPATIAL DATA: TOOLS TO ENHANCE THE UNDER-STANDING OF URBAN PROBLEMS   Our third exemplar is quite different. In 1990 this would not have been thought of as a planning support activity at all because the notion of understanding urban structure and urban problems was largely in the personal domain with no online tools available to add value to data by seeking diverse interpretations through participation. In fact, our current, fast-expanding ability to share data on the Web is leading to new kinds of exploratory analysis that many actors and stakeholders involved in solving planning problems can engage in together. The "wisdom of crowds" is one of the emerging drivers in terms of developing good science and thus any activity that involves sharing data and then adding value by bringing data together from unusual and hitherto unknown and inaccessible sources supports the process of understanding in ways that have not been available until recently. Many of these possibilities are essential in beginning to use software such as Google Maps and Google Earth as these need to be tuned to represent data in ways that inform technical processes.

We are actively engaged in building a Web-based service and resources that enable a user with some spatial data in a standard format to use the free software that is available from Google to display the data. A user with a file in some standard GIS format can easily convert this to ESRI's proprietary but widely used shapefile format and then use our software GMap Creator to generate a Google map from the data file in a one-stop operation. This software is freely downloadable from our Web site,[7] and once the user uses it to convert a file to the Google format it creates a Google map (which is always in a Web page) that can be published on the user's own site. The facility we have developed enables the user to overlay different layers of data and to manipulate them, and it is easy to add more functionality to the interface that is created. Once the map has been created, however, we ask the user to share the URL for the map. If he or she does, we add this to our archive of URLs, which are available for any user on the Web service we are building. This is called MapTube. Essentially MapTube is just a collection of pointers to remote URLs that, when accessed, lets the user grab any map at any of these locations, overlay them, and manipulate them in other ways involving their presentation. In so doing, they add value to the resultant data (as long as the application is meaningful). We show the interface to MapTube in figure 1.10.

In the context of planning support, experts and stakeholders could share their data this way and could take data from remote sources and all have access to it through the Web service. Essentially, storing pointers (URLs) rather than the map data avoids copyright issues, however unwitting. The server will not fall over either as maps are added, for those maps remain on the site where they are currently published. In fact, the data that GMap Creator produces are map tiles from vector data. These can be quite large, which is purely due to the API (application program interface) that Google uses for its maps, and thus we have various stand-alone extensions of this that are Web services in their own right. London Profiler is a server that assembles geodemographic data for London and makes it available to users, enabling them to perform their own overlays. The focus is on spatial variations in health, ethnicity, deprivation, and so on, and this tool enables visual correlations of spatial data to be rapidly assessed in much the same way that any mapping technology lets the user grasp the map pattern quickly and easily, which we show in figure 1.11. We are currently extending the GMap Creator to be able to create 3D pictures that can be displayed in Google Earth; in time the 2D MapTube server will also be extended to 3D.

FIGURE
1.10

FIGURE 1.10

The MapTube Resource for Retrieving, Displaying, and Overlaying Maps

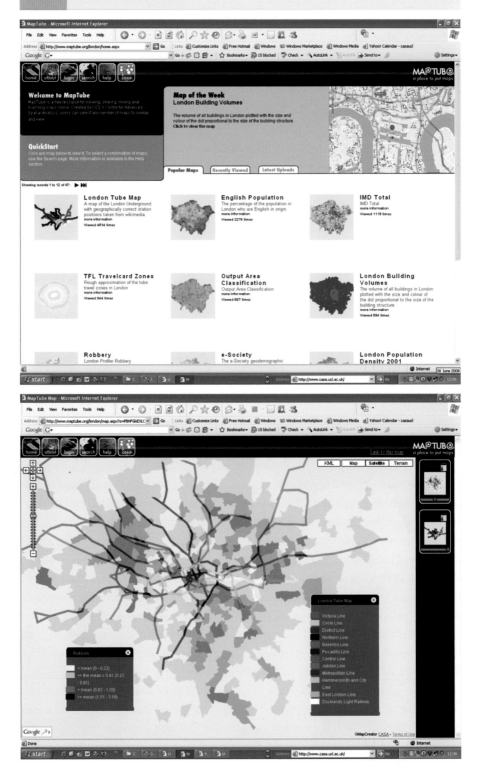

FIGURE
1.11

The London Profiler: A Web Browser Enabling Users to Examine Different Patterns of Spatial Inequality

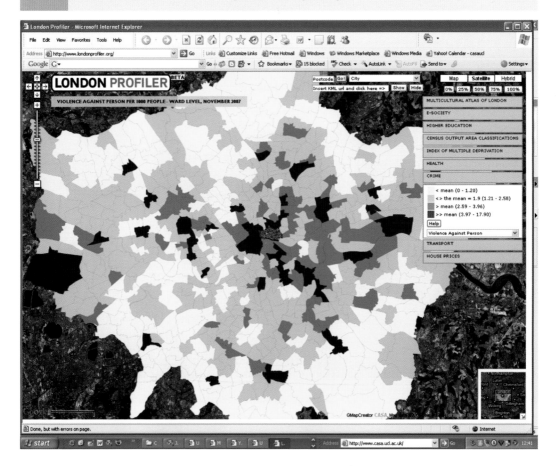

We are also exploring different kinds of environments for the display of spatial data. We noted the Virtual London project above, but increasingly we are interested in remote environments—virtual worlds that enable us to display and manipulate content across the Web where users interact with such media as avatars. Several years ago we placed our Virtual London model into such a world (using Adobe Atmosphere), but currently we are exploring ways in which we can port the kinds of geodemographic data contained in MapTube to such worlds. In fact, when the user allows his or her data to be accessed from Map-Tube, we automatically load that data into the Second Life virtual world so that we can manipulate the media in many different ways, which is akin to placing the data in a virtual exhibition space through which users can interact.

Figure 1.12 shows a picture of Virtual London in such a virtual space, ca. 2001, by the side of the imagery that we now have available in Second Life. Our space in Second Life is part of *Nature* magazine's Second Nature island, which they use to display scientific outputs. The emergence of such domains, which can also be sustained using real-time feeds, provides new ways of generating informed

FIGURE
1.12
Spatial Data in Virtual World: 2D Merges with 3D

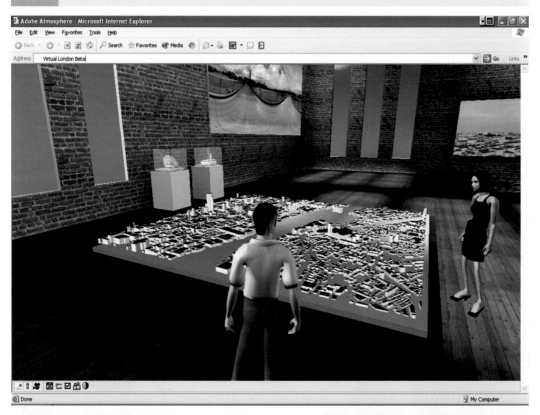

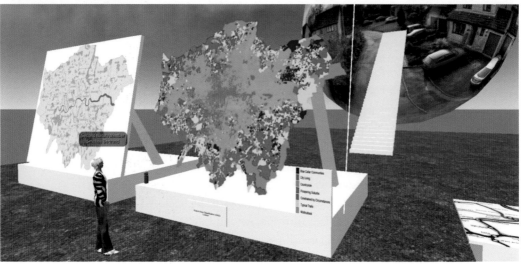

support for planning processes. Finally, it is entirely possible that these kinds of digital environments might also sustain more conventional software with models running within them while users as avatars sit, watch, and manipulate such tools in real time (Batty 2007).

The Future

What portents might the key findings of this review have for the future? The first is that, as software proliferates and is generated at higher and higher levels, it is increasingly possible to support the same kinds of tasks in planning with very different combinations of software. Moreover, there now appear to be examples where every kind of software has been linked to every other as witnessed in the way LUTM and GIS are coupled; how these are linked to 3D and other forms of visualization; how they are supported by routine database, statistical, and mathematical software; and how these support systems are widely disseminated and made accessible on the Web.

Second, visualization is all important. This is particularly the case as the complexity of the models and their data increases and as more and more stakeholders come to be involved in the planning process. Visualization as well as much traditional software is drifting into Web-based contexts and the notion of data, software, and expertise being available at different places and PSS being systems that enable such remote access is likely to become the dominant paradigm. The notion of a user literally picking software off the Web using visual interfaces, as is shown in movies of the near future such as *Minority Report*, is well on the way to becoming a reality as evidenced in the current generation of operating systems.

Third, as planning has fragmented, so have the tools and software necessary to support it. The domain is now quite eclectic and it is hard to predict whether the apparent uniqueness in applications and the relative turbulence in possibilities will subside. Only then will a more uniform paradigm for PSS emerge. The difficulty of finding a coherent framework within which to place PSS dominates the current scene. Much will depend on how physical and land use planning itself matures and evolves and whether or not we move back to a less decentralized, more top-down, perhaps more structured style of planning than the current fragmented and diverse pattern.

Acknowledgments

Richard Milton developed all the software for GMap Creator and MapTube. Maurizio Gibin put together the London Profiler. Dr. Andy Hudson-Smith leads the team in CASA concerned with Virtual London, virtual worlds, and the Google Map server software effort. Steve Evans developed the Air Pollution Visualization. All these colleagues deserve my thanks for their efforts. The ESRC e-Social Science NCeSS program (http://www.ncess.ac.uk/) supported the Web-based work, and the British Oxygen Foundation funded the air pollution work.

Endnotes

1. Harris apparently said that the term was first used by a member of the audience at the 1987 URISA conference in discussion of one of his papers, although he once recalled that someone from the Delaware Valley Regional Planning Commission used the term at the 1988 URISA conference. Its precise origin now lies in the mists of time unless the person from Harris's audience can still be identified, or can still come forward.

2. The rules of thumb were coined by Gordon Moore at Intel in 1965; Robert Metcalfe, coinventor of Ethernet, at Xerox Parc in 1973; and George Gilder in his book *Microcosm* in 1989.

3. The paper referred to by Batty (1997b) was presented first in 1995 at CUPUM '95 in Melbourne, Australia, as an example of how planning could be supported by Web-based technologies. All the hotlinks in that paper are now dead although the paper is still on the Web (e.g., at http://www .acturban.org/biennial/doc_planners/computable_city.htm). An example of what was then possible is archived at The WayBack Machine, with some links intact. To view this go to http://web .archive.org/web/19980124005925/www.geog.buffalo.edu/Geo666/batty/melbourne.html.

4. The "grid" is a euphemism for a new wave of computation that is available in the same sense as the electricity grid delivers electricity, simply by plugging into the Internet and generating whatever software and data resources are required. In essence, the grid is conceptually a system for delivering computational resources—data, software, expertise, etc.—from diverse and remote locations to a user who simply has a device, usually a PC, that controls the way the Internet delivers these resources to the desktop. Usually the grid takes data and software from two or more remote locations and delivers the results of the computation, which possibly takes place somewhere else in the ether, to another remote location, usually the desktop, but possibly to a handheld device connected wirelessly to the Internet.

5. See Janes and Kwartler (chapter 8), and http://www.communityviz.com/. The agent-based model, Policy Simulator, is no longer supported in current versions of CommunityViz, but is detailed in Kwartler and Bernard (2001).

6. See http://www.londonair.org.uk/.

7. See http://www.casa.ucl.ac.uk/software/googlemapcreator.asp.

Disseminating Spatial Decision Support Systems in Urban Planning

Harry Timmermans

THE LITERATURE ON GEOGRAPHICAL INFORMATION AND DECISION SUPPORT systems includes papers that seem to evidence frustration that planning practice has not widely adopted advanced geographical information systems and decision support systems (e.g., Geertman and Stillwell 2003b). A solution advocated to remedy this situation is to develop simplified systems that better capture the needs of planners (e.g., Vonk, Geertman, and Schot 2005; 2006). In this chapter, I argue that this discussion only tells part of the story. The situation in planning does not differ that much from experiences in other disciplines and domains that have also shown evidence of the "technology paradox." In fact, the situation is not much different from marketing any other product—one cannot simply assume that new products more or less automatically find their way to the market.

The dissemination process involves many potential carriers and channels, and a multitude of necessary but not sufficient conditions should be fulfilled for successful dissemination and application of decision support systems. Arguments are supported by discussing successful examples of applications of (spatial) decision support systems in urban planning. Several lines of research, development, and application evidence the relevance of models embedded in spatial decision support systems. From the outset, it should be articulated that other fields of developments such as planners' toolboxes (e.g., Mikkonen et al. 2003; Arentze, Borgers, and Timmermans 2006; Ma et al. 2006; Shen, Kawakami, and Chen 2006) and systems supporting public participation (e.g., Pettit, Nelson, and Cartwright 2004) seem to be less successful.[1]

Retail Planning

When the work on spatial-interaction models was rapidly developing in the 1970s and 1980s, there was a natural need to look for relevant areas of application. Retail planning turned out to be one of the application domains in which there are ample applications. Spatial-interaction models were used to predict retail turnover in shopping centers and shifting market shares of existing centers. Consequently, these models were used to assess the feasibility of new shopping developments and to assess the negative impact new development may have on the performance of existing centers. In addition, the models came with a series of performance indicators, measuring impacts for retailers, consumers, and society at large.[2] In the beginning, these were stand-alone models, but later the models were embedded in decision support systems.

To understand why these models found ample application, it is important to realize that in countries such as the Netherlands, conducting retail research was required by law. In fact, guidelines and standards governing what kind of model to apply, what data to use, etc., were issued. Consequently, the models, which were initially developed by academics, gradually moved from academia to practice, and specialized consultancy firms emerged that do this type of research. In countries such as the United States and Canada, the situation differed in that retail planning was much more liberal. Several cases of litigation arose, however, and modeling results and expert knowledge were brought to court to discuss a case.

In the late 1980s, with changing political powers in Europe together with an economic downturn, the nature of urban planning shifted as well (Guy 2007). In general, trends of liberalization, decentralization of government, and the consequent increased power of the private sector meant that the influence of planners and planning was reduced. The use of shopping models and spatial decision support systems in retail planning seems to have gradually disappeared to some extent. Indeed, planning studies at first almost completely vanished. However, at the same time there is evidence that larger retail organizations, such as TESCO and AHOLD, started their own research and development units, which elaborated and further developed these models and computer systems. Although these firms were less interested in shifting redistributional effects of new development, they were certainly interested in feasibility and cannibalization issues. Several models and systems were presented at conferences such as the Applied Geography Conference and the ICSC (International Council of Shopping Centers) conference, both attended by academics and practitioners alike. The latter conference is large, and I recall many presentations by practitioners on the models, tools, and systems they had developed.

Now that the easy-to-develop locations have been taken and the risk increases, it seems that the interest in applying shopping models—from government, but also real estate agents—is slowly increasing again. It is realized that better informed decisions may reduce the risks of investment and hence may be worth the financial investment.

Transportation Models

Travel demand models have played an important role in transportation planning. Traditionally they have been used to assess investments in new highway development, but more recently they are also utilized in the context of transportation demand management. Unlike retail planning, transportation planning has remained dominantly a matter dealt with by government authorities, and the costs, risks, and externalities are relatively high. It is no surprise that transportation has been and continues to be high on the political agenda.

Since the middle of the last century, the four-step model of transport demand has dominated the field. This model first predicts the number of trips generated for a series of traffic zones as a function of zonal characteristics and travel times/distances. This demand is then allocated to different transport modes and destination zones, resulting in origin-destination (O-D) tables. Finally, the O-D matrices are used as input to a route-choice model, which ultimately simulates traffic intensities at different parts of the network.

Virtually every transportation planning authority has a model at its disposal. In addition, large engineering firms and specialized transportation consultants typically have developed their own models and computer systems, which they routinely apply in their consulting practices. In fact, such firms often serve an intermediate role between academic progress and everyday practice. For example, leading consultancy firms have gradually improved the four-step models by developing (nested) logit models that replace trips with tours and a different model structure. In modern Western countries, such models are routinely applied. For example, in the Netherlands, the LMS (Landelijk Model Systeem) is based on this approach and used by the Dutch Ministry of Transportation. In addition, for the Dutch provinces they have developed versions that are used to assess transportation plans at the regional level. The municipalities typically use the models developed by the engineering firms and local consultants. For example, the latest round of discussions to decide on transportation investments in the Netherlands was, in part, based on applications of the regional models used to identify problems and assess the potential impact of new investments. Each province conducted its own study and the results served as input to the new national plans for the succeeding years.

In the mid-1990s, a discussion emerged, first in the United States and later across the world, that these trip- and tour-based models did not provide sufficient detail and lacked adequate integration to better assess environmental externalities of traffic and simulate sociodemographic changes. An example of an environmental externality of traffic is that the number of cold and hot starts of an automobile is a key variable to predict carbon dioxide emissions better; this information was missing in the traditional models. Moreover, these models tended to focus on peak-hour traffic and thus were too general to be of much use for transport demand management, which focuses on specific, almost real-time situations. A sociodemographic change could be the increasing participation of women in the workforce, which puts pressure on their time use and activities and can be better understood if the focus of attention shifts from transport to activities and from zones to individuals and households.

The policy concerns and the need for more detailed models and systems led to the development and application of various comprehensive so-called activity-based models of travel demand, which predict which activities will be conducted, where, when, for how long, and the travel company and mode choice involved. One of the first models in this tradition is the one developed by Adler and Ben-Akiva (1979). They assumed that individuals evaluate a number of complete, one-day activity-travel patterns and choose the pattern that maximizes their utility. A multinomial logit model was used to predict the choice of activity pattern. The probability of choosing a particular activity-travel pattern was assumed to be influenced by characteristics of the pattern, such as the number of sojourns and tours made for various purposes, the total travel distance traveled by particular modes, the destinations visited, time expenditures to various activity classes, and sociodemographics. The model was later elaborated in the context of dissemination and application projects, jointly with consultants (Bowman et al. 1998; Bowman and Ben-Akiva 1999). Inspired by this seminal work, several other similar nested logit models of activity-travel patterns were developed. Examples include an enhanced version of Wen and Koppelman (1999) and Wen (1998) now being applied in different cities in the United States, and PETRA (Fosgerau 1998) developed for the Danish Ministry of Transport.

Another model is the Prism-Constrained Activity Travel Simulator (PCATS), initially developed by Kitamura and Fujii (1998).[3] It is a system that simulates activity-travel behavior while considering three types of constraints: prism constraints, availability of travel modes, and recognition of potential activity locations. In addition to a stand-alone model, it is used to generate alternative activity-travel patterns to form estimation choice sets that are used by PCATS-RUM (random utility model).

This model assumes that individuals maximize the utility associated within the open periods, subject to the above constraints. Open periods are those during which an individual is free to travel and engage in activities of their own choosing. They contrast with blocked periods, which are characterized by commitments to conduct particular activities at particular locations. The utility associated with a particular activity-travel pattern is assumed to be the sum of the utility associated with activities and the utility associated with trips. It is assumed that the utilities are affected by the attributes of the activities and trips, and other exogenous variables. The model is now part of the FAMOS (Florida Activity Mobility Simulator) model (Pendyala, Kitamura, and Kikuchi 2004), developed and applied by the State of Florida.

The third fully operational activity-based model is CEMDAP (Comprehensive Econometric Microsimulator for Daily Activity-travel Patterns), developed by Bhat and his coworkers. This framework originally considers workers only (Bhat and Singh 2000). Their activity-travel pattern is divided into several periods: before morning commute pattern, morning commute, midday patterns, evening commute, and post-home-arrival pattern. These patterns are described by a series of characteristics, including number of tours, number of stops, mode choice, etc. Bhat, however, also suggested a series of models to predict components of his conceptual framework. Although these have been published largely as isolated modeling efforts, when used in combination a more comprehensive modeling approach is obtained. The State of Texas and some of its major metropolitan areas are now using the system.

The final fully operational activity-based model is Albatross (Arentze and Timmermans 2003), developed for the Dutch Ministry of Transportation. It is an agent-based system that uses decision heuristics to simulate activity-travel patterns. The model assumes a predefined order of decisions, which is derived from an assumed priority ranking of choice facets of activities and a priority ranking of activities by type. Decisions are made from high to low priority for each choice facet and within each facet from high- to low-priority activity. The model first decides on the transport mode for the work activity. Mode choice for work is considered the highest-level decision because this decision determines which person can use the car for a substantial part of the day in cases where there is only one car and more than one driver's license available in the household. In step 2, the model determines which activities and the number of episodes per activity are to be added to the skeleton. Time constraints for each candidate activity episode are initialized based on given static household and institutional constraints, if any. Duration is not exactly specified. Rather, the system chooses between typical duration classes for the activity. A duration class defines a normal duration and a range of possible durations within that class. Step 3 determines the time of day for each flexible activity in the current schedule. Step 4 determines the organization of trips into tours by choosing for each flexible activity whether it is conducted on a Before stop (directly before another out-of-home activity in the schedule), an After stop (directly after another out-of-home activity), an In-between stop, or on a single-stop trip.

The process of model development for Albatross is interesting. In 1995, the Ministry of Transportation, reflecting the international discussion, organized a workshop among policy makers, planners, consultants, end users, and academics to identify major trends in society that would have a significant impact on travel demand, discuss the information needs that emerge from dealing with the identified trends, and assess whether the available models can provide such information in a rigorous manner, or would it be better to develop an activity-based model. The discussion led to the conclusion that certain trends would be difficult to assess with the current models and that the development of a different, more complex model system should be explored.

This conclusion was debated at length with the ministry and after two years it was decided to develop Albatross. In fact, this system was developed in different stages: First, a prototype was posited based on a limited data set and a limited specification; later it was extended in scope using new data; and in phase three it was rigorously tested, compared with other models, and applied in a series of pilots. Simultaneously the model was reviewed in the academic community and introduced in newsletters and other ministry publications; dedicated postgraduate courses were also delivered. The model then received the ministry's stamp of approval and is currently applied in scenario studies.

Although these are examples of applications, it is also fair to say that activity-based models do not yet constitute the state of practice. Workshops and discussions exchange experiences with these models and their advantages and disadvantages. The examples show, however, that the innovation and diffusion processes are slow and require focused efforts from academics and practitioners and their peer networks. Especially if models are used for annual forecasts or monitoring, there is a significant resistance to change and the use of new data-collection methods or new models. Such changes are likely to imply inconsistent results. In that sense, it is often better to introduce new models or new systems in parallel to existing ones to deal with different types of policy issues.

Cellular Automata

Other spatial decision support systems that have gained much attention in academia are the cellular automata models. CA models are simple: In a grid space (array of cells) a series of transition rules is enforced to govern the state of a randomly placed cell depending on a configuration of its neighbors (adjacent cells). If the process is allowed to run iteratively, the resulting spatial patterns show how cities are likely to evolve over time. CA models have two characteristics that make them inherently attractive for applications in urban planning. First, they are in themselves spatial; and second, working with them does not take a great amount of expertise. I have seen many models developed in Microsoft Excel in a few days or weeks by inexperienced students. A few simple rules allow one to generate very complex forms. These "toy problems" were more or less legitimized because early adopters of this approach (e.g., Tobler 1979; Couclelis 1985; 1988; 1989b) were not primarily interested in realistic or predictive representations of urban processes, but used the models and systems primarily as aids in theoretical experiments to provide important insights into the nature of geographical processes.

Serious academic research has significantly elaborated the basic cellular automata model. Based on Couclelis's basic research it was concluded that the regularity assumption of the model makes it almost impossible to apply the cell-space idea to real-world areas containing zones with irregular boundaries and varying numbers of neighbors. In addition, these studies mention the limitation of space- and time-invariant transition rules and the closure of the system to external events. Local laws (for a specific cell) are problematic as they preclude any consideration of global (city-scale) factors such as site accessibility, attractiveness relative to other sites across the city, market conditions of supply and demand, and so on. Space no longer needs to be homogeneous in the properties or in its structure. Neighborhoods need not be uniform across space. One may argue that by allowing for such variation, strictly speaking we are no longer talking about cellular automata models. Yet this flexibility in assumptions has been accepted by the research community primarily because the grid structure and the set of transition rules constitute a simple simulation platform. Consequently, many operational cellular automata models have been developed.[4]

The limited but representative literature review clearly shows the development of CA models over the last three decades. Originally inspired by complexity theory, the models were developed to demonstrate that simple rules can induce complex dynamics and generate emerging patterns. Such "games" serve educational purposes and theoretical explorations very well. Over the years, however, cellular automata models have also been developed as decision-support systems that help planners gain more insight into the likely consequences of their decisions or even provide models that predict urban evolution.

In addition to theoretical and illustrative work on cellular automata, CA models have thus also been developed for planning agencies. Progress here shows increasing sophistication, elaboration, and extension over the years. Early work by White and Engelen (1993a; 1993b) especially has been applied using different acronyms in several countries. In early work, the neighborhood of the cell consists of 113 cells (including the possibility of giving the zero value to the most distant cells). A hierarchy of land use states is used such that a cell may only be transformed from a lower to a higher state. That is, the city will only grow when nonoccupied cells can be converted to vacant ones. In later studies this restriction was relaxed (White and Engelen 1997; White, Engelen, and Uljee 1997). At each iteration the transition potential is calculated for all allowed transitions and sufficient cells are converted to each land use. The cells that are converted to each state are those with the highest potential.

White, Engelen, and Uljee (1997) describe an application of their model to the city of Cincinnati, Ohio. The LOV (Leefomgevings Verkenner) model developed for one of the Dutch National Planning Agencies is another application of the basic framework and has been used by this agency as a desktop planning tool to better understand the impact of certain scenarios. The model has also been used in more detailed applications. The CA model is linked to a transportation model and to various models of environmental emissions and dispersion.

This brief discussion of cellular automata models also illustrates that these models have been used by planning authorities for scenario studies and impact assessments. The number of fully operational and applied CA models may be rather limited, but when judging the literature, I think one should realize that many models have never been developed for serious applications, while others have been primarily developed for educational purposes.

Integrated Land Use Transportation Models

Transportation researchers and urban planners have developed integrated land use transport models since the 1960s. Compared to the other model types discussed in this chapter, the interest in these models has followed a different trajectory. Most early work stems from urban planning, but in that discipline the interest has virtually disappeared completely, although lately there is some evidence of renewed interest. On the other hand, many ministries and departments of transportation and the environment are still using such models.[5]

Early work was based on the Lowry model developed for the Pittsburgh urban region (Lowry 1964). I vividly recall that, when I started my academic career in 1976, in the Netherlands alone at least five such models were developed for different metropolitan areas. Lowry distinguished among population, service employment, and basic (manufacturing and primary) employment, and these activities correspond to residential, service, and industrial land uses. Activities are translated into appropriate land uses by means of land use activity ratios. The division of employment into service and basic sectors reflects the use of the economic base method to generate service employment and population from basic employment.

The model allocates these activities to zones according to their potentials. Population is allocated in proportion to the population potential of each zone and service employment in proportion to the employment potential of each zone. Both are subject to capacity constraints on the amount of land use accommodated in each zone. The model ensures that population located in any zone does not violate a maximum-density constraint that is fixed on every zone. In the service sector, a minimum-size constraint is placed on each category of service employment, and the model does not allow locations of service employment below these thresholds to build up.

Having located the various activities, the model ensures that the population and employment distributions used to calculate the potentials are consistent with the predicted distribution of population. Consistency is secured by feeding back into the model predicted population and employment and reiterating the whole allocation procedure until the distributions input to the model are coincident with the outputs.

In an important paper, Garin (1966) suggested replacing the potential models with production-constrained gravity models and substituted another economic base mechanism for the analytic form. Consequently, the coupling between allocation and generation was much improved. In line with the quantitative revolution in urban planning, the model was elaborated in several directions and gave rise to many similar models based on the concept of spatial interaction. Examples include TOMM (Time Oriented Metropolitan Model), developed by the CONSAD Research Corporation as part of the Pittsburgh Community Renewal Program (Crecine 1964); and the Projective Land Use Model (PLUM) designed by Goldner (1971) for the Bay Area Transportation Study Commission. These more realistic efforts were more like black box and data-fitting exercises. The set of models, developed by Putman and his coworkers, was heavily used across the world because the software was easily made available (e.g., Putman 1983; 1991; Putman and Chan 2001). Other examples are the Leeds Integrated Land-Use Transport model, combining a Lowry-type location model with a four-stage aggregate-transport model (Mackett 1983; 1990; 1991); and IRPUD, developed for the German city of Dortmund (Wegener 1982a; 1982b; 1983; Wegener, Mackett, and Simmonds 1991).

As occurred for shopping models and transportation demand models, spatial-interaction models were gradually replaced in transportation research and, to a lesser extent, in urban planning and geography by random-utility theoretic discrete-choice models in the 1980s and 1990s. It was just a matter of time before logit models were also used in integrated land use transportation models. An early example is the MEPLAN model, developed by Marcial Echenique and Partners through a series of studies in different countries in the world. It started with a model of stock and activities (Echenique, Crowther, and Lindsay 1969), followed by the incorporation of a transport model developed for Santiago, Chile (de la Barra et al. 1975), the incorporation of an economic evaluation system for São Paulo, Brazil (Flowerdew 1977), and the representation of market mechanisms in the land use model for Teheran, Iran (Hirton and Echenique 1979). The model was further enhanced with the incorporation of an input-output component for São Paulo (Williams and Echenique 1978), with a more comprehensive model developed for Bilbao, Spain (Geraldes, Echenique, and Williams 1978). At the heart of the system is an input-output model to predict the change in demand for space (Echenique 1994). Hunt (1994) describes the application of the model in Naples, Italy. Echenique et al. (1995) used the model to simulate the effects of urban policies.

Another example is the TRANUS integrated land use and transport modeling system, which was developed to simulate the probable effects of applying particular land use and transport policies and projects and to evaluate their social, economic, financial, and environmental impacts. A detailed explanation can be found in de la Barra (1989; 2001). The Oregon2 model is currently under development by Hunt, Abraham, and their coworkers for Oregon (Hunt et al. 2001). It has much in common with the above models, although it also contains some new elements. For example, it has a microsimulation household-allocation model and a detailed land development model (Hunt, Abraham, and Weidner 2004a; 2004b).

Yet another example is BASS/CUF. As indicated by Landis (1994; 1995; 2001), the California Urban Futures model (CUF), earlier known as the Bay Area Simulation System (BASS), was developed to simulate how growth and development policies might alter location, pattern, and intensity of urban development. The model differs from the typical integrated transport–land use model in a number of ways. First, regional forecasts are not allocated, but a bottom-up approach is followed. Second, development is not only a function of spatial accessibility but of a wider set of variables.

Central to the model is the notion of the profit potential of each developable land unit as a function of sales price, raw land price, hard construction costs, site improvement costs, service extension costs, development, impact, service hookup and planning fees, delay and holding costs and extraordinary infrastructure capacity costs, extractions, and impact mitigation costs. CUF-2 consists of two multinomial logit models of land use change (Landis and Zhang

1998a; 1998b). The first submodel explores the determinants of land use change among undeveloped sites, while the second model examines the determinants of land use change among previously developed sites. The probability of land use change is a function of initial site use, site characteristics, site accessibility, community characteristics, policy factors, and relationships with neighboring sites. Similar models have also been developed in Europe, including DELTA, developed by David Simmonds Consultancy, MVA Consultancy, and the Institute of Transport Studies, Leeds; and TIGRIS-X developed for the Dutch Ministry of Transportation, Public Works, and Water Management.

Most recent work in the field of application tries to replace traditional transportation models gradually with activity-based models of transport demand. Consequently, aggregate zonal data are being replaced by individual and household data. The best known of these models is UrbanSim, initially designed for Oahu. The model was enhanced in 1996 when the Oregon Department of Transportation launched the Transportation and Land Use Model Integration Project (TLUMIP) to develop analytical tools supporting land use and transportation planning. The model was calibrated for a case study in Eugene-Springfield. Later, the dynamic aspects of the model were calibrated, and the model was applied in Houston, Salt Lake City, San Francisco, and Seattle (Alberti and Waddell 2000; Waddell 2002; Waddell, Liu, and Wang, chapter 6). Several tests are also running in Europe including Paris.

A similar, but at this stage more academic, project is the Integrated Land Use, Transportation, Environment (ILUTE) modeling system under development by a consortium of researchers in Canada from the universities of Toronto, Calgary, Laval, and McMaster (Miller and Salvini 1998; Miller et al. 2004). It represents an experiment in the development of a full microsimulation modeling framework for the comprehensive, integrated modeling of urban transportation and land use interactions and a range of impacts including environmental.

ILUTE differs from earlier work in a number of important ways. First, it differentiates between persons and households. Second, the urban system evolves over time from an assumed known base year with no particular assumptions concerning system equilibrium required. Third, it differentiates between firms, which are modeled as agents. Fourth, in addition to zones, buildings are recognized. Finally, as indicated, activity-based models of transport demand replace the simpler trip- or tour-based models. The goal here is to develop a model that schedules individuals' activity-travel patterns within a household context. This research requires some original work since most current activity-based models are fundamentally person-oriented. Another goal is to develop multiday models as opposed to the single-day models that dominate the field.

Ramblas is a less sophisticated system developed to estimate the intended and unintended consequences of planning decisions related to land use, building programs, and road construction for households and firms (Veldhuisen, Timmermans, and Kapoen 2000a; 2000b). The model allows planners to assess the likely effects of their land use and transport plans on activity patterns and traffic flows.

It simulates the whole Dutch population of 16 million people, for example. The input of the simulation model consists of the distribution of various types of households across the different kinds of dwellings per zone and the distribution of land uses and dwellings per zone. These variables are external to the simulation. Changes in these variables are externally monitored. Households are classified according to their size, and for each class the age and gender of household members is calculated. The spatial attributes of the area (i.e., land use, dwelling stock, and road system) are treated as variables that can be manipulated by planning.

The planning of the road system is also dependent on decisions made by the various planning authorities. The spatial distributions of activities and trips are treated as dependent variables. Thus, the model enables us to predict the likely consequences of possible policy decisions on activity patterns and thus estimate the effectiveness of such policy decisions. In particular, these decisions concern changes in land use, dwelling stock, and road construction. The model has been applied to scenarios focusing on planning issues in the Netherlands.

A final example is ILUMASS (integrated land use modeling and transportation system simulation). This project aims at a microscopic dynamic simulation of urban traffic flows into a comprehensive model system, which incorporates both changes in land use and the resulting changes in transport demand (Moeckel, Schurmann, and Wegener 2002). Microsimulation is used to trace demographic development, household formation, firm lifecycles, construction of houses and buildings, and labor and household mobility. These modules are linked to models of daily activity patterns, travel, and goods movement.

Discussion

The application of decision support systems in planning practice has been the subject of much debate. There seems to be substantial frustration about an assumed lack of dissemination of models and systems to practice. In this chapter, I have identified a series of models for which this does not seem true. What are some of the underlying reasons?

My main point is that one cannot simply expect that a decision support system will be more or less automatically applied after it has been developed. First, it should be acknowledged that many decision support systems and embedded models are developed for toy problems. The serious development of models and systems requires considerable resources: a team of researchers, programmers, large data sets, testing and validation, etc. Moreover, because models become increasingly more complex, practitioners and students must be increasingly more knowledgeable. This implies that one needs research groups of some size with accumulating knowledge to make a substantial difference. Stand-alone projects, which typically dominate many academic conferences, are nice but often aim at illustrating a particular approach as opposed to developing something that is of interest to practitioners and can be used in practice. The fact that progress is slow is also not very helpful with the increasing pressure of publications.

Dissemination is a process that needs to be managed in itself. One cannot expect that practitioners read the journals in which academics publish; the number of conferences attended by academics and practitioners alike is also very small. Consequently, the chance that a practitioner is exposed to a new planning support system is rather slim. Hence, the process needs to be organized, which takes much time in itself and requires champions both on the academic and the practitioner sides. Very few academics seem to make the effort to bring their products to practice. This is understandable in that the benefits are not proportional to the amount of effort it takes. And, even if one would be successful, the use of a system implies a substantial increase in questions and requests for assistance. Very few groups are equipped to handle such activities.

There is also the issue of added value. Planning authorities have their working habits, routine procedures, budget allocations, etc. As in other organizations, there will be resistance to change, especially when considerable risk is involved. There needs to be a sense of urgency and added value, but as the business model in public organizations is typically vague, and the results of any bad decisions often do not bear on the planning organization itself, the circumstances to define added value and act on it are far from perfect. Several times I have encountered a situation where a firm was pleased with a decision support tool that identified their market with 3 to 5 percent more accuracy because this immediately translated into several millions more in profit. This percentage of improved accuracy, however, will generally be irrelevant for planning authorities to support their decision making.   *Why?*

Improved predictions or arguments about this rarely convince planning authorities to use a later generation of models or decision support systems. My experience suggests that innovations were often triggered by the fact that their existing models or work protocols were not sufficiently sensitive to provide answers to new policy questions. The emergence of activity-based models of transport demand is a clear example. Interest in these models was not triggered by the fact that activity-based models are likely to produce more accurate travel forecasts. Interest primarily emerged because activity-based models were a building block for addressing issues of transport externalities and the impact of institutional changes. The existence of clearly formulated policy information needs, as shown by the retail planning example, certainly helps. Otherwise, the dissemination process requires, in addition to the champions and strong teams at both ends, convincing people, showing the potential added value, training, and education.

Often, this process is much like the well-known S shape. Only after some time, when many colleagues or competitive organizations have adopted a new technology, will many others follow. However, it often does take a generation. These are the new students who have gained knowledge about a new approach during their studies and have developed their own perspective on what works, which is often different from what was appropriate to the previous generation.

Endnotes

1. See also Timmermans (1997); Brail and Klosterman (2001); Geertman and Stilwell (2003b); and Van Leeuwen and Timmermans (2004; 2006a; 2006b) for the wide variety of planning support systems.

2. Examples of academic publications in this field of research include Gibson and Pullen (1972); Gautschi (1981); Timmermans (1982); Fotheringham and Knudsen (1984); Guy (1987); Borgers and Timmermans (1987), to name a few.

3. See also Fujii, Kitamura, and Monma (1997; 1998).

4. For example, see White and Engelen (1993a; 1993b); Itami (1994); Batty and Xie (1994); Cecchini (1996); Batty, Couclelis, and M. Eichen (1997); Semboloni (1997); Yeh and Li (2001); Vancher et al. (2005); Jankovic, Hopwood, and Alwan (2005).

5. A more detailed discussion and critical assessment of these models can be found in Timmermans (2006).

The Regional Scale

A Decade of Cellular Urban Modeling with SLEUTH

Unresolved Issues and Problems

Keith C. Clarke

SLEUTH IS A MODEL FOR THE COMPUTATIONAL SIMULATION OF URBAN GROWTH and the land use changes that are caused by urbanization. As a direct result of prior work on modeling the spread of wildfire with cellular automata (CA) (Clarke, Olsen, and Brass 1993; Clarke, Riggan, and Brass 1995), SLEUTH also uses the CA approach. The model grew from discussions on land use change with U.S. Geological Survey (USGS) Geographer Len Gaydos at NASA's Ames Research Center in 1991, and the development of the first operational version of SLEUTH (then called the Urban Growth Model, or UGM) was a component of the Urban Dynamics research program at USGS (Kirtland et al. 1994). Further USGS support allowed the model to be extended to simulate land use change in addition to urbanization (Clarke 1997). The reformulated model was released on the Worldwide Web under project Gigalopolis (Clarke, Hoppen, and Gaydos 1997), first at New York's Hunter College and then at the University of California, Santa Barbara (UCSB).

After 1996, the project Web site was extended to include documentation and a discussion forum, and the model was extended to version 2, with dynamic memory allocation. With further funding from USGS and the Environmental Protection Agency (EPA), the team rewrote the model code and included calls to the message-passing interface, making SLEUTH suitable for EPA's Cray supercomputers. Key programming work was by Tommy Cathey and Mark Feller, resulting in the release of version 3 of the computer code (Clarke et al. 2007), nominally still a beta release since maintenance is only occasional. With federal support, the model has been open source since its outset, and a complete set of source code and test data can be downloaded from the Web site.[1] Recent notable contributions have allowed the model to run under Linux and Cygwin, a Windows-based UNIX emulator.

The initial application of SLEUTH was to the San Francisco Bay area (Clarke and Gaydos 1998), and the animations created by the model had some immediate public acceptance. The San Francisco application completed the simulations for a broad area from San Jose to Sacramento in 1996, but at a coarse resolution of 600 meters and with urban extent data up to 1990. Later work in Washington, DC, and Maryland repeated this experience. SLEUTH is calibrated with historical data, and while the incompatibility of paper maps and remotely sensed imagery was a challenge, eventually many varied sources were employed, including historical road maps (for highways) and the CORONA declassified spy satellite imagery. The USGS still uses SLEUTH in its Urban Dynamics program, and has experience in modeling at least eight urban regions.

Release of the code and documentation to the Worldwide Web was key to the model's success. Through the Web site, a UCSB-based discussion forum open to all users[2] was created and remains active; since then it has been supplemented by another public forum.[3] SLEUTH has been included in two major inventories of land use change models that compare and classify the model and its functionality (Agarwal et al. 2002; Gaunt and Jackson 2003). At last count, there are over one hundred applications of the model to cities and regions. By any measure, this makes SLEUTH a highly successful urban and land use change model.

Nevertheless, in spite of extensive attention to the model's calibration process and exhaustive sensitivity testing, as yet there has been no assessment of the unsolved issues and problems that have arisen in the many applications and computational experiments. In this chapter, the model will be examined from first principles as regards its unexplored assumptions and inherent limitations. This is followed by a practical examination of application and calibration problems and of the inherent assumptions that constrain the models' forecasts. As with all models, SLEUTH makes the world abstract, with urban behavior simplified. Better understanding of these inherent limitations of models in general, and SLEUTH in particular, can enhance the use and application of this and many other models of land use change. Lastly, the 1996 San Francisco application was recovered, and the forecast to 2007 compared with actual urban extents using the Google Earth viewer, with the intent of conducting a forensic examination of a past forecast as a way of evaluating SLEUTH.

How SLEUTH Works

A cellular automaton (CA) is a theoretical framework that permits computational experiments in spatial arrangements over time. Components of a CA model are: (1) a reference set of cells, usually a raster grid of pixels covering an urban area; (2) a set of states associated with the cells, which can be in the set {urban, not urban} or more detailed land uses such as {urban, forest, agricultural, wildland, wetlands, water}, and such that all cells have a state at any given time; (3) a set of rules that govern state changes over time; (4) an update mechanism, in which rules are applied to the state at one time period to yield the states of the same cells in the next time period; and (5) an initial condition of the framework.

In SLEUTH, a gridded raster of the study area is digitized or created from imagery, and the framework has a given and fixed spatial resolution or ground size of the cells and also a fixed spatial extent, usually a bounding rectangle for the study area. Successive application of the rules to the states yields states beyond the initial conditions, and one rule application with synchronous update of all cells is considered a "year" in time.

SLEUTH's rules are fixed, but vary from complete to zero influence at each time step based on behavioral parameters. Five parameters control SLEUTH's behavior entirely, each with a possible integer value between 0 and 100. It is assumed that one set of five parameters best mimics the behavior of an actual urban growth sequence. To select the best parameter set, model sequences are empirically compared against a series of control dates, that is, images for the urban or land use sequence as it actually occurred. For example, a CA may have initial conditions reflecting actual land uses in 1950, with a modeling goal of forecasting the urban pattern on 2050. However, the performance of a parameter set creating feasible system behavior may be controlled by having actual data on urban areas for 1965, 1980, 1990, and 2006. A discussion of the uncertainty that this backcasting method introduces is included in Goldstein, Candau, and Clarke (2004). Successive search using brute force methods, which try all possible combinations of inputs (Silva and Clarke 2002) or genetic algorithms (Goldstein 2004a), reveals the "best" parameter set. These values are used to run the model, with the present day as the starting data set, to any desired distance into the future.

The five parameters are obviously critical to SLEUTH's application. The calibration process is automated, so SLEUTH "learns" the best set for any given application from the data. The parameters were chosen after extensive testing by trial and error. They include parameters that control the random likelihood of any pixel turning urban (dispersion), the likelihood of cells starting their own independent growth trajectory (breed), the regular outward expansion of existing urban areas and infill (spread), the degree of resistance of urbanization to growing up steep slopes (slope), and the attraction of new development toward roads (road gravity). Furthermore, these parameters are interrelated. So, for example, when development is attracted to a road by the road gravity factor, it can relocate via a random walk along the road network a distance in proportion to the dispersion factor. Lastly, the system as a whole allows self-modification. That is, as the entire system grows faster or slower, control parameter values are changed as a consequence. The net effect is to amplify rapid growth and retard stagnation in what are termed "boom" and "bust" stages.

Calibration of SLEUTH begins by first creating historical data for the backcasting. Data sets should be carefully registered with each other, and should include raster maps for topographic slope, land use, excluded areas, urban extent, and transportation and hill shading for the visualizations. Two land use layers are used, so that transition probabilities can be computed from the change matrix. Any set of land use or cover classes is suitable, but only one urban class is permitted. Exclusions include a layer with nondevelopable land (e.g., lakes and parks), and can include probabilities for other land classes, perhaps based on value or zoning. Urban extent is a binary map showing urban and nonurban, and at least four of these are necessary for calibration. Normally, the transportation layer is roads, and multilevel systems (e.g., interstate, state road, local road, and unsurfaced road) are supported.

The user then decides how the five parameters are to be explored. One "run" is a single set of five parameters from the earliest (start) date, to the latest (present) date. The code matches model behavior with the actual data when it reaches the data years, and computes a total of 13 measures of the goodness of fit between a model run and reality. A composite of these measures, averaged over several Monte Carlo iterations, then "scores" the parameter set. Three phases are used in calibration, with user choices between them. At first, large increments of the parameters are used to cover the whole space. When the outcomes are scored and ranked, the highest scoring parameter sets are used to "bracket" the next round of values, and smaller increments are used. Again, runs are scored and ranked, and a last round with unit increments is used to select the "best" parameter set. This set is then used to start the model, and the finishing parameter set saved to start a forecast run into the future. Explanations for the procedure to follow are included in the documentation and have been improved upon in the reported literature.

The land use change component of SLEUTH, called the deltatron model, is a second CA that operates in change space. Two land use layers are differenced to yield a matrix of change probabilities that are first normalized to a one-year time step. Land use change is controlled by the amount of urban growth in the UGM at each year, and pixels are selected for change based on random, topographic slope, feasible class transitions, and the prior changes reflected in the deltatron space. Changes are spread to simulate expansion, and after a short cycle, deltatrons are killed off so that subsequent change can take place at the same location (Candau, Rasmussen, and Clarke 2000).

SLEUTH Applications

SLEUTH's applications were evaluated by contacting all discussion forum users and by conducting a literature search, which identified 32 major studies with published results (Clarke et al. 2007). The result was an addition to the Web site of an inventory of applications and, for about 20 of them, results of the city calibrations and data. Many more applications have been conducted since, including most recently, for multiple California counties (Tietz, Dietzel, and Fulton 2005; Onsted 2007); Honolulu, Hawaii (James 2004); Gdansk, Poland (Rozwadowski 2006); Chiang Mai, Thailand, and Taipei, Taiwan (Sangawongse, Sun, and Tsai 2005); Tijuana, Mexico (Le Page 2000); Alexandria, Egypt (Azaz 2004); Yaounde, Cameroon (Sietchiping 2004); and Sydney, Australia (Liu and Phinn 2004).

The first application of SLEUTH's precursor, the UGM, was to the San Francisco Bay area at a coarse resolution of 600 meters (Clarke, Hoppen, and Gaydos 1997). The urban extent was digitized from maps and remotely sensed images from 1850 to 1990. Forecasts and animations of the spatial growth patterns were created, statistics describing the spatial growth were calculated, and UGM was used to predict future urbanization to the year 2100. The 1997 paper provided the details of the mechanics of the UGM, describing the necessary data layers, the five coefficients, the four types of urban growth behavior, and self-modification. A second application, this time to Washington-Baltimore, and a comparison of the two applications followed (Clarke and Gaydos 1998). This paper examined the role that geographic information systems (GIS) played in modeling and advocated using GIS to loosely couple models and their results using systems of models.

The first applications of the UGM focused solely on the modeling of urban growth, but there was a need to include other landscape changes in the model. In spite of the advocacy for loose coupling, the solution was a code-level tight coupling of a second CA to simulate land use change. The deltatron model (Candau and Clarke 2000) was first used for modeling land use change in the EPA's Mid-Atlantic Integrated Assessment Region. In modeling the eight-state region, land use data were classified using the Anderson Level I categories for 1975 and 1992. This produced a map of predicted land use in the year 2050, and introduced the land use uncertainty map, which SLEUTH calculates and plots.

The principal drawback to using SLEUTH is its time-consuming calibration process. Though discussed in Clarke, Hoppen, and Gaydos (1997) and in Clarke and Gaydos (1998), the definitive description is that documenting the application of the model to Lisbon and Porto, Portugal (Silva and Clarke 2002). This paper presents four key findings: (1) that SLEUTH is applicable to both North American and European cities; (2) that increasing the spatial resolution and detail of the input datasets makes the model more sensitive to local conditions; (3) that using a multistage calibration method can better refine the model parameters to find those that best replicate the historical growth patterns of an urban system; and (4) that the model parameters can be compared across different systems. Following from the last finding, Silva (2004) developed the concept of urban DNA, further explored in a theoretical context by Silva and Clarke (2005) and Gazulis and Clarke (2006). Further large-scale applications of SLEUTH added knowledge of how best to work with the calibration process to yield the best forecasts (Jantz, Goetz, and Shelley 2003; Yang and Lo 2003; Dietzel and Clarke 2004).

Some applications have involved the coupling of SLEUTH outputs with social modeling efforts, while others have linked with physical models. Claggett et al. (2004) coupled SLEUTH with the Western Futures model (Theobald 2001), demonstrating the ability of SLEUTH to categorize the growth into different classes of "development pressure" based on forecasts of population growth. Leão, Bishop, and Evans (2001; 2004) coupled SLEUTH outputs into a multicriteria evaluation of landfill suitability (Siddiqui, Everett, and Vieux 1996) to determine where around Porto Alegre City, Brazil, land was unlikely to be urbanized, and so was suitable for landfills. Arthur (2001) coupled SLEUTH to an urban run-off model in Chester County, Pennsylvania. Syphard, Clarke, and Franklin (2007) examined the consequences of urban development on wildfire regime and vegetation succession in southern California's Santa Monica Mountains and coupled the

LANDIS land use model to SLEUTH, testing the coupling strategy. Cogan, Davis, and Clarke (2001) compared using SLEUTH and the California Urban Futures (CUF) model (Landis 1994) to assess stresses on biodiversity. Solecki and Oliveri (2004) used SLEUTH in simulating climate-change scenarios in New York.

Through the Urban Change–Integrated Modeling Environment project, the value of using scenarios as a presentation of SLEUTH results became evident. SLEUTH's application to Santa Barbara reported by Herold, Goldstein, and Clarke (2002) was part of a study that sought to increase local residents' awareness of smart growth principles through modeling. Both SLEUTH and SCOPE (the South Coast Outlook and Participation Experience model) were used to create a set of scenarios that could be used to experiment with alternative futures. SCOPE is a systems dynamics model in the Forrester tradition, coded in the STELLA modeling language and including various social, economic, and demographic variables (Onsted 2002). SLEUTH allows policy and plans to be incorporated through new transportation layers and through variations in the excluded layer.

Choosing scenarios and using models, including SLEUTH, led to work on the nature of scenario planning (Xiang and Clarke 2003) and on simplicity in modeling (Clarke 2005). An aspect in the modeling for scenarios that was addressed was that of visualization, which was important because of the long series of public meetings that were part of the Regional Impacts of Growth Study (RIGS) by the Santa Barbara Economic Community Project (figure 3.1). Two important visuals were perspective views in which satellite views were simulated by repeating an urban "pattern" across areas forecast to be urbanized under the scenarios (figures 3.2 and 3.3), and items called "Postcards from the Future," which were vehicles to encourage thinking about the future scenarios and their implications (figure 3.4). More recently, the link between parameters, model behavior, and scenario generation has been the subject of further investigation (Dietzel and Clarke, 2007). Onsted (2007) has conducted extensive amounts of SLEUTH modeling for California counties, using information at the parcel level about land-conservation status to prove that a carefully constructed exclusion layer can vastly improve forecasts.

Acevedo and Masuoka (1997) presented the general methodologies used to create 2D and 3D animations of the Baltimore-Washington, DC, region by using SLEUTH to create video frames for animations. Candau (2000) explored ways of visualizing the spatial uncertainty of urban growth in a simulated landscape. Aerts, Clarke, and Keuper (2003) continued this idea by experimenting with human test subjects, using different display methods to question them about their understanding of the uncertainty in urban growth forecasts for a section of Santa Barbara.

SLEUTH has been used as a tool in theoretical investigations of urban processes. Bierwagen's (2003) dissertation focused on simulating generic urban forms and their connectedness in the landscape to assess the viability of different urban growth forms on butterfly habitat. Goldstein, Candau, and Clarke (2004) compared using SLEUTH for the backcasting of urban extent with spatiotemporal

FIGURE
3.1

SLEUTH Forecast for Santa Barbara Urbanization to 2050
A. Red is growth under assumption of enforced urban growth boundary.
B. Red is growth under assumption of removal of restrictions on growth.
Source: Images by Martin Herold and Jeffrey Hemphill

interpolation. To explore urban development, SLEUTH has been used to trace urban form using landscape metrics (Herold, Goldstein, and Clarke 2003); in new descriptions of urban evolution (Dietzel et al. 2005a; 2005b); and by Goldstein, Candau, and Moritz (2000), who investigated historical urban-wildfire conflicts. Judging by contacts through the discussion forum, SLEUTH applications continue, with results appearing in many dissertations, theses, and in gray literature such as planning reports.

FIGURE
3.2

Visualization of Santa Barbara Urban Status in 1997

(Higher resolution [SPOT satellite data] is urban land in 1997; lower resolution [Landsat 7] is nonurban.)

Source: Image by Martin Herold and Jeffrey Hemphill

FIGURE
3.3

Equivalent of Figure 3.2 as Forecast for 2050 Assuming Scenario of No Growth Restrictions (Image texture over newly urbanized area is simulated to give impression of urban spread.)

Source: Image by Martin Herold and Jeffrey Hemphill

FIGURE 3.4

Postcards from the Future. Visual Stimulus Concept Used to Encourage Scenario-based Thinking in Various Planning Meetings
Source: Photos and graphics by Susanna Baumgart

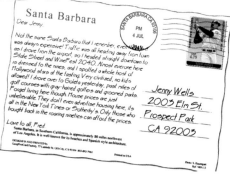
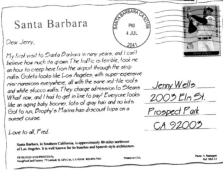

Unsolved Issues and Problems

Over time, the literature on SLEUTH has examined and conducted sensitivity tests for a large number of the SLEUTH assumptions and control parameters. For example, temporal sensitivity was examined by Candau (2002), land use class aggregation by Dietzel and Clarke (2004), and the Monte Carlo stochastic sensitivity by Goldstein, Dietzel, and Clarke (2005).

An unexamined element of the work to date is the distinction between variables and constants in the model. While the five variable parameters that are maximized through the calibration process control SLEUTH's growth and change behavior, another ten constants were arrived at through experiments and other means. First of these is the number of Monte Carlo iterations necessary for the calibration, a value initially believed to be best set high, but later shown to perform just as well when set low, which improved model performance considerably (Goldstein, Dietzel, and Clarke 2005). This research showed that almost all variance captured and measured in Monte Carlo simulation is contained in the first few iterations, and that increasing the number of iterations quickly has diminishing returns in terms of model fit.

Second, the SLEUTH scenario file that initializes the model requires the user to submit a random-number seed code. The random number generator used is ran1 (Press et al. 1992). A surprising lack of attention in spatial modeling has been paid to the idiosyncrasies of pseudorandom number generators (Van Niel and Laffan 2003). Use of this algorithm and independent specification of the seed allow a high degree of certainty in both the lack of repetitive cycling in the random numbers and the ability to replicate sequences across computational platforms.

A third constant is a set of assumptions in the land use change model about deltatron aging. A deltatron is the means by which land use persistence, or "memory," is simulated. The aging process is on CAs that exist only in change space, and the persistence is both of type (i.e., which land use transition changed to which) and time, since changes are spatially autocorrelated in time and space. How long deltatrons survive before being "killed off" by the aging process was coded by trial and error. Further research could determine the actual amount of persistence by measurement or could allow calibration of this parameter for a given landscape.

A fourth assumed constant relates to how the transportation network impacts growth. The fourth behavior type simulated is road gravity, in which new growth is attracted to and allowed to travel along the road network. In an effort to remove scale sensitivity from the model, a constant was established that is used to adjust the current road gravity value (0–100) to the size of the image in use. The constant is computed as the starting road gravity value as a proportion of the maximum (100), times the average of the map width and height divided by 8. This value is also a maximum search radius for a road when new growth takes place. Again, this value was chosen to best suit the model, and is not well tested across applications. A best value could be found through calibration or by analysis of developing transportation networks. It would be of interest to determine if the value changes over time, over space, or with transportation technology.

The slope sensitivity has a significant impact on SLEUTH growth simulations, and involves three constants. The slope coefficient is used to calculate slope weights by first calculating an exponent. This exponent is then used in a look-up table to find an actual slope resistance factor as a function from zero to the constant "critical slope." Above the critical slope value, which is left for the user to decide upon locally (often in the range of 20 to 30 percent slope), growth is excluded. At slopes below the value, the slope factor creates different shape functions based on the form in figure 3.5.

At a slope coefficient of 50, there is a linear relation between topographic slope and urbanization probability, i.e., the value used in the random number calls. Below 50, flatter slopes are favored, while above 50, midrange slopes are favored. The calibration process determines which pattern best fits the actual slopes for an application, but the shape of the curve itself, and the complete exclusion above the critical slope are assumptions. While actual cities are usually on flatter slopes, and the cost of building and risk increase with slope, the exact form of the relation could be empirically tested. Furthermore, there is clearly a scale effect with slope. Slope computed from one-meter resolution cells is very different from that at one kilometer. Computing slope directly from the digital elevation model also gives different results than averaging slope over cell areas.

The remaining four constants all determine how the model implements self-modification. Self-modification is macroscale behavior. At each time step, the model tabulates aggregate system behavior by monitoring the overall rate of growth of the urban system. Two rates (critical high and critical low) form upper and lower bounds on behavior. Above critical high, during periods of rapid

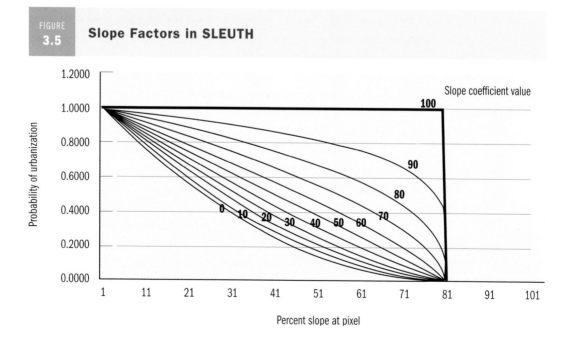

FIGURE
3.5
Slope Factors in SLEUTH

growth, several of the control parameters are multiplied by a factor greater than one (boom). Correspondingly, during periods of decline, control parameters are multiplied by a value less than one (bust).

The result of this feedback is acceleration of rapid growth and damping of decline. Self-modification was implemented to duplicate the "lazy-S" shape of system growth, with first rapid and then less rapid increase in size over time. Many cities grow little for long periods and then have short bursts of very rapid growth followed by stability. Settings for these four constants were arrived at by examining growth rates of cities over time, but are otherwise the result of trial and error. Few researchers have changed their default values, although some have chosen to disable self-modification by using artificially high or low critical values. It is possible that the study of growth rates of cities will yield considerable insight into urban process and form, as is suggested by the theoretical modeling with SLEUTH (Gazulis and Clarke 2006; Dietzel et al. 2005b).

Much work on SLEUTH has focused on improving the calibration process, and a recent publication (Dietzel and Clarke 2007), to a great extent, "solves" the problems and provides an optimal metric. This value was arrived at by conducting an exhaustive calibration, then using data reduction methods (self-organizing maps) to regionalize the multidimensional behavior space. Curiously, the research also showed that SLEUTH can suffer from overfit. The most powerful model of the future state of a system is simply the current state, and so the calibration can lead to a solution that simulates minimal or no change, a trivial outcome when growth is prevented by low values of the behavioral parameters. Conveniently, the phased exploration approach used in SLEUTH's calibration avoids this pitfall. Nevertheless, the currently high-level interest in sensitivity testing of SLEUTH's outcomes is desirable, and will hopefully continue.

Early on in SLEUTH's history, attention was paid to temporal sensitivity. Candau (2002) proved that SLEUTH gives superior results when used with short histories and shorter forecast horizons. A long history produces a less convincing short-term forecast than a short one. Other issues such as the timing of a single time step, the relation between time and study-area size, and the sequence of implementation of the four behavior types remain untested. Candau, Rasmussen, and Clarke (2000) also examined and detailed precisely the full set of interparameter interactions in SLEUTH. These were essentially fixed after version one of the model, yet were arrived at through software testing and visualization, not derived from theory. A complete derivation of the consequences for the assumed behavior interactions should be explored theoretically rather than empirically (Gazulis and Clarke 2006).

Some issues related to data and data preparation remain to be explored. Goldstein, Candau, and Clarke (2004) presented a theoretical model of uncertainty in data within SLEUTH. Just what role error in data preparation plays could be tested empirically, perhaps by using hypothetical data with controlled random perturbation. There is also scope for testing the scalability of the model further (Jantz and Goetz 2005). An early goal for SLEUTH was modeling of the whole United States urban system, something still beyond the computational power available. But is this different from aggregating models regionally? Does an application to a state produce different results than aggregating results by county? Some work has looked at land use class aggregation effects, but much work remains to be done in this regard.

Any complex software system must deal with versioning. By my count, the model has been rewritten from first principles five times, and has proven duplicable from first principles in different modeling environments. While the increments from versions one to two and two to three were tested for bitwise compatibility, and the results posted in the release, there are improvements and changes over time, nevertheless. Given the great number of improvements in calibration, an application today has superior knowledge and should produce better results than one 10 years ago. There have also been slightly different interpretations and uses of parts of the model. The essential capture of a city's growth behavior in the five parameters does allow cross-city and even cross-time comparison. Little has been done yet to compare cities in different environments— North America and Europe versus the developing world—against each other with directly similar data. The same dates, scales, resolutions, land use schema, etc., could be used so that results can be definitively compared. Such work would allow a new scientific urban geography with fully replicable outcomes.

While SLEUTH has been applied many times and become intertwined with planning support systems in the wider sense, an important purpose for modeling is to relate to policy and the decision-making process. The key issues influencing planning and local decision making today relate to sustainability of communities and to public participation. Central to the New Urbanism movement is the concept of density planning, trading development and redevelopment at the city core for more sprawl, encouraging transit-oriented neighborhoods that are accessible to public transportation nodes, and mixed-use zoning. SLEUTH is not really suited to these issues, although modifications or coupling with other models could make it more feasible. While an entropy measure for failed urbanization attempts has already been explored (Dietzel and Clarke 2007), a means of counting repeated urbanization attempts at a single location could be devised and allowed to accumulate as increased density. Thus SLEUTH could, with only minor change, output a density layer with its forecasts. Similarly, if pixels were tracked for age, as deltatrons currently are, they could become available for redevelopment as the model iterates forward.

The issue of exactly how SLEUTH and its forecasts fit into the broader planning support systems framework remains. While model results can be used effectively in scenario planning (Xiang and Clarke 2003), and indeed SLEUTH has frequently been used for scenario generation, the degree of interactivity is limited by the time needed to run the model, although in one case, SLEUTH forecasts were run overnight during a two-day planning charrette (Silva 2006).

Conclusion

All models have lifetimes, defined by the period in which they provide abstractions of the known world that have value for planning or study. Urban modeling also has had eras of models based on paradigms that have fallen into and out of favor. Cellular automata models, including SLEUTH, have been used extensively over the last decade. They have shown satisfactory performance, generated useful forecasts, and integrated well with scenario-based planning. SLEUTH can be used to generate scenarios by one or more of five methods. First, known urban plans and patterns can be placed into the future and their consequences explored (Kramer 1996). Second, the future transportation network can be modified, and the consequences determined. Third, and most usually, different zoning or planning codes are turned into weighted exclusion layers and their consequences tested. Fourth, parameters can be deliberately adjusted, to change the impact of transportation into the future, for example. This we have termed *genetic engineering* (Gazulis and Clarke 2006; Silva and Clarke 2005). Lastly, SLEUTH can be one component of a system of integrated models. The latter approach gets around the common criticism of SLEUTH that it does not include social or economic variables, and research has shown that coupled modeling is both effective and powerful.

SLEUTH has enjoyed a longer than typical lifetime as an urban model. With close to one hundred applications over more than a decade, the ultimate validation test is becoming possible. At the 2000 GIS/EM4 conference, a workshop received a challenge for modelers to openly post and share common data for a test city, to model the city 10 years hence, and to seal results for a decade to permit an eventual true test against reality. In this spirit, the 1996 UGM results for San Francisco were recovered from the author's dusty collection of data CDs, and brought into the Google Earth viewer.[4] This is the original UGM application at 600-meter resolution, with probability levels for urbanization assigned red at 90 to 100 percent, and progressively darker green down to 50 percent. While browsing the area shows many forecast errors, some related obviously to the coarseness of the slope values at 600 meters, nevertheless there are many partially correct and some perfect forecasts of urban development.

Little can be done to test the validity given these data, but in future work, tests of the decade-old forecasts against the same forecasts repeated with superior data and methods will be conducted, and real measures of SLEUTH's accuracy as a forecasting tool reported. With attention to the limitations and assumptions of SLEUTH and the other CA models, a new generation of superior urban models can arise that gain from the cumulative experience with SLEUTH and that model urbanization with completely accountable accuracy.

Endnotes

1. http://www.ncgia.ucsb.edu/projects/gig
2. http://bbs.geog.ucsb.edu
3. sleuth-users@yahoogroups.com
4. The KML file that allows anyone to see the results can be downloaded at: http://www.geog.ucsb.edu/~kclarke/GoogleEarth/UrbanGrowthSimulation.kml

Simulating Regional Futures

The Land-use Evolution and impact Assessment Model (LEAM)

Brian Deal and Varkki Pallathucheril

THE DYNAMICS OF REGIONAL PLANNING CAN BE HIGHLY COMPLEX, WITH implications and feedback that are difficult even for seasoned planners to antici-pate. Regional planning must consider the implications of unprecedented development rates and patterns in terms of their significant environmental, social, and economic consequences. A considerable challenge for regional planners is the framing of such important issues within a broad spatial and temporal context for stakeholders in the planning process. In recent years, community visioning exercises have been increasingly used toward that end, but those activities are rarely grounded in data or deep analysis; sometimes they amount to little more than wishful thinking.

During the last two decades, spatial analysis tools, geographic information systems (GIS), and remote-sensing (RS) technologies have been widely implemented to monitor, analyze, and visualize urban growth phenomena (Sun and Deal 2006). Although GIS-based tools provide useful analysis and have been widely used to assist urban planners, the static representations on which they are built are not sufficient to study the dynamics of urban growth (Klosterman 1999b; Hopkins 1999). Maps and satellite images are limited to static displays of past and current data sets. They portray the current state of a system, offering neither the reasons why things appear as they do nor projections of possible future states. The causal mechanisms associated with land use change are still not well understood, in part due to the complexity of urban systems. Consequently, policy makers and planners are often faced with the difficult task of making land use decisions without a suf-ficient quantitative basis for either analysis or forecasting.

Computer-based urban system simulation models are now being employed to forecast and evaluate land use changes (Batty and Xie 1994; Landis 1994; Engelen, White, and Uljee 1995; Wu and Webster 1998; Waddell 2002; Wad-dell, Liu, and Wang, chapter 6). Simulation models enable planners to view and analyze future outcomes of decisions and policies before they are put into action. These models, which simulate change over space and time, have the ability to help improve our fundamental understanding of land use transformation dynamics and the complex interactions between urban change and sustainable systems (Brail and Klosterman 2001; Deal 2001).

Many of these simulation models utilize cellular automata (CA). Models based on CA are both discrete and dynamic systems, the behavior of which is specified in terms of local space-time relationships. Space is represented as a regular spatial *grid* or *lattice* composed of individual *cells*, with each cell being capable of existing in any one of a finite number of *states*. The states of the cells in the lattice may change over time, and each cell is updated at each time step according to a set of local rules. The state of a cell at any given time depends not only on its local rules for change, but also on the states of its neighbors in the previous time step. All cells within the lattice may be considered interdependent relational entities. They are updated synchronously so that the visual state of the entire lattice advances in discrete time steps.

Although dozens of CA models have been proposed and built, CA-based land use modeling is still far from mature. Despite the flexibility of the CA approach, limitations remain (Torrens and O'Sullivan 2001). The visual outcomes emerging from CA models with surprisingly simple local transition rules are plausible, if not defensible. In reality, urban systems evolve in very complex ways, with layers of stochastic behaviors. Representing such complex dynamics requires that a multitude of complex rules (including some that are not yet well understood) be applied to strict CA systems in order to capture the richness of urban systems. Currently, a more feasible approach would be to extend CA techniques by loosening their strictness and integrating other models, such as traditional regional socioeconomic models (White and Engelen 1997; Wu and Martin 2002), to simulate the complex dynamics of urban growth and development.

In this chapter we describe operationalizing one regional land use model, the Land-use Evolution and impact Assessment Model (LEAM), based on a hybrid CA approach. We first describe the LEAM framework and offer a brief chronology of LEAM research. The main body of the discussion focuses on a LEAM application executed for the two-state, ten-county metropolitan region of St. Louis, Missouri. Finally, we discuss broad lessons learned in the St. Louis application and important challenges that lie ahead.

The LEAM Framework

In the modified CA approach upon which LEAM is constructed, cells evolve over a surface defined by biophysical factors, such as hydrology, soil, geology, and land forms, and socioeconomic factors, such as administrative boundaries, census districts, and planning areas. The probability of each cell change is decided not only by the local interactions of neighbor cells but also by global information available to the model. Therefore, cells within LEAM are intelligent agents that not only can capture local information, but also can sense and respond to

The LEAM Framework

Land use drivers describe the causal mechanisms of change. Spatial allocation is determined by rules applied within the land use change (LUC) model. Visual output of the land use change helps in the process of engaging stakeholders, who use the output to develop policy questions. These questions are described in the form of planning scenarios that help shape causal relationships for further simulation.

FIGURE 4.1

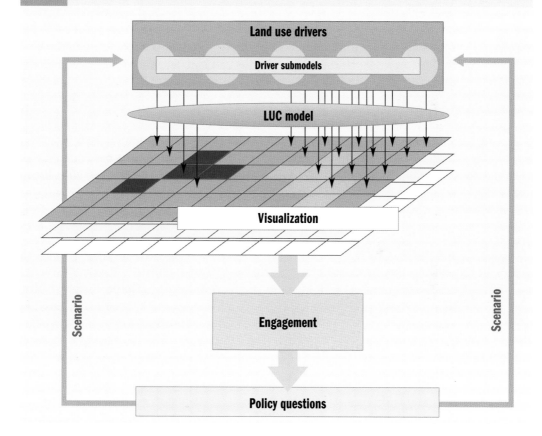

regional or global information such as social and economic trends. LEAM also has a hierarchical structure with multiple scaled models incorporated. These models are loosely coupled in a modular framework where the information can be exchanged "on the fly" through aggregate or disaggregate approaches. This design strategy enables LEAM to integrate cellular micro models and regionalized macro socioeconomic models into a single model framework.

The LEAM framework consists of two major elements: a land use change (LUC) model and urbanization impact models (figure 4.1). The LUC model is the core of LEAM. Its purpose is to determine how land use may change depending on the assumptions and policies applied. The impact models provide interpretation and analysis of the LUC model simulation results. They answer questions about what the resultant land use change patterns mean and how they affect water quality, air quality, traffic patterns, property values, etc.

A dialogue among stakeholders, planners, and policy makers completes the process by providing feedback on the value and relevance of the simulation outcomes. Dialogue and feedback are important parts of the LEAM framework, both mathematically and in local application. It has been the authors' experience that pure mathematics in complex urban dynamic models does not tell a complete story—and sometimes not even a compelling one—about the local condition. Constant internal and external review and interaction are critical for producing salient LUC output.

LEAM evaluates land use transformation potential by explicitly quantifying the forces that contribute to change. Understanding the causal mechanisms of change is critical to the success of the LUC model. That understanding provides both a better grasp of local dynamics and a framework for testing alternative scenarios. In LEAM, causal mechanisms are represented by various *drivers*. Each driver is developed as a contextually independent *submodel*. This approach allows for a first-stage calibration exercise to be completed on each submodel in order to determine its explanatory capabilities before it is run concurrently within the larger framework. At each time step, potentially developable cells are evaluated for their change potential in four transformation categories—residential, commercial/industrial, urban open space, and no change. Driver submodels are locally dependent and derived through both analysis and local stakeholder interaction. Various submodels address urban dynamics that are influenced by regional economics, social factors, transportation infrastructure, proximity characteristics, infrastructure location and availability, geographic characteristics, dynamic locational characteristics, and spontaneity. LEAM's open architecture and modular design facilitate incorporation of additional local drivers as needed to improve the explanatory power of the model.

In LEAM, a region is represented as a grid of cells, with each cell representing an area measuring 30 by 30 meters. Each cell derives its attributes from associated GIS data sets. Land use change is simulated using a hybrid approach that employs both CA and landscape-based algorithms (Wu and Martin 2002). Processes play out on a deformed, constrained surface, or probability landscape, as illustrated in figure 4.2, rather than the blank slate that is used in a pure CA model. The topographical contours or shape of the grid surface is determined by a calculated probability of land use change for each cell. It is derived by aggregating the effect of drivers (encoded into submodels) that influence location within the region. Examples of such drivers include proximity to cities, employment centers, roads, and highway interchanges; the location of wetlands, woodlands, streams, lakes, and flood plains; slope characteristics; the location of schools or health care facilities; and policy restrictions on or incentives for change. CA rules act on individual cells to modify the cumulative effect of the calculated probabilities in each time period, so the surface undergoes transformation over time. The individual calibration of each driver submodel is based on a spatial frequency approach in which the frequency of current land development is determined for each spatial and temporal value of the driver (figure 4.3).

FIGURE
4.2

The LEAM "Hilly" Constrained Surface on Which Dynamic Interactions Are Processed
(Light cells are high-probability values; dark cells are low-probability values.)
Source: LEAM

FIGURE
4.3

Spatial Frequency Approach
Source: LEAM

City accessibility

Existing development

City accessibility score map

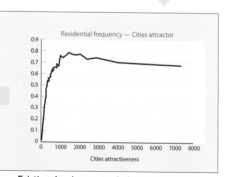

Existing development relative to accessibility

Land use transformations are simulated using a Monte Carlo experiment in which potential land uses compete for space based on probability scores and a random-number generator. In a given time step (for a specific type of land use), the regional demand for new development and the probability of land use change associated with each cell is determined regardless of whether the cell is transformed. A cell is likely to be transformed if a regional demand for new development or redevelopment exists and the cell:

- is available for development or redevelopment;

- has a high enough probability to compete successfully; or

- is randomly selected for transformation based on semichaotic occurrences that often characterize urban development (such as the construction of a house on the "back forty").

Transformation occurs if the calculated probability is greater than a random number generated for each cell, so that even cells with low scores may be transformed (figure 4.4).

The regional demand for land (residential, commercial, and open space) is a function of the generation of new households and jobs as projected over time using a regional econometric input-output model (Sarraf et al. 2005). The conversion from sector-based economic activity to households and jobs is accomplished using observed localized (county or census tract) averages for the ratio between developed land, household generation, and the types of jobs created. In lieu of subregional constraints on demand to determine spatial allocation (Wu and Martin 2002), the estimated demand serves only as a target for regional land allocation in each time period. Locations around the region compete to meet the targets, and market variables speed up or slow down development rates based on how the demand was or was not met. The final outcomes of developed cells can be described in graphs, charts, text, and map form. A typical land use change map for the greater Chicago region is shown in figure 4.5.

Environmental, economic, and social impacts of alternative scenarios involving different land use policies, growth trends, and unexpected events can be modeled and tested in the LEAM modeling environment (Deal and Schunk 2004). LEAM's visual and quantitative representation of each scenario provides both an aid to intuitively understanding policy outcomes and a mathematical basis for quantitative analysis of their implications. These representations provide an objective basis for stakeholder discussions and decision making.

LEAM Development

The LEAM laboratory at the University of Illinois at Urbana-Champaign (UIUC) has been developing and applying LEAM since 1999. LEAM has evolved along two tracks: (1) research that has focused solely on advancing the state of LEAM; and (2) LEAM applications on behalf of regional planning authorities. The applied research typically raises new research questions about

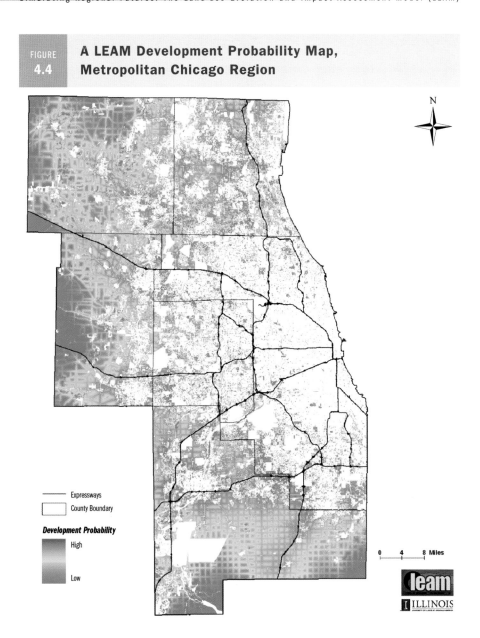

FIGURE 4.4   **A LEAM Development Probability Map, Metropolitan Chicago Region**

the model and its usefulness in urban planning, and those questions in turn serve to inform further basic research on LEAM and simulation modeling. Table 4.1 lists research projects that have contributed to the ongoing evolution of LEAM, shown in chronological order.

Model Development and Basic Research

LEAM research was initiated through a grant from the National Science Foundation (NSF) entitled "Evolving Urban Dynamics: Ecology, Modeling, and Visualization." The objective of the three-year project was to explore whether spatial dynamic methods previously used to model the behavior of ecological systems (Deal et al. 2000) could also be used to simulate the evolution of urban

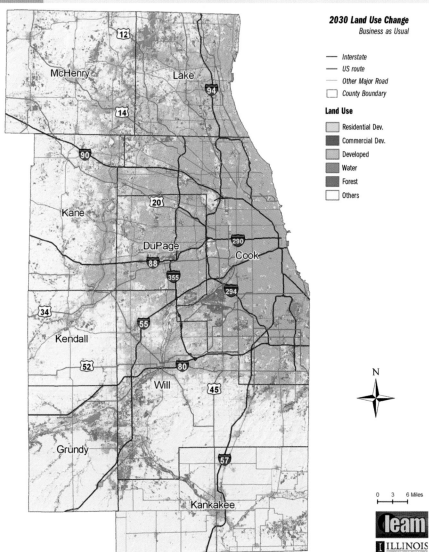

FIGURE 4.5

Typical Land Use Change Map, Metropolitan Chicago Region, 2030
(yellow areas—new residential development; red areas—new commercial development)

systems. In the initial project, the fundamental approach underlying LEAM was developed and then tested in Kane County, Illinois. Several alternative software tools, such as StarLogo, were tested for implementing the model logic. Ultimately, we combined STELLA, to model dynamic phenomena, and SME (Spatial Modeling Environment), to spatialize the STELLA models.

This approach facilitates open and modular development: Multiple sub-models can be developed separately and concurrently using STELLA and then plugged into SME when ready. Furthermore, these development tools provide

TABLE 4.1	**LEAM Research Projects**

Project Title	**Funding Agency**
An application of LEAM to South-Central Illinois	South-Central Illinois Regional Planning & Development Commission
Enabling Enhanced Protection of the Lake Michigan Coast in the Chicago Metropolitan Region	Cooperative Institute for Coastal and Estuarine Environmental Technology (CICEET)
Chicago Land Use and Transportation Evolution Project	Chicago Metropolitan Agency for Planning
LEAMplan: Planning for the Future of McHenry County	McHenry County
Development and Application of Regional Sustainability Analyses	U.S. Army Construction Engineering Research Laboratory
An Application of LEAM to Ansung-City, Kyungki-Do, Republic of Korea, and Research on Urural	Pangea21
An Application of LEAM for the Peoria Tri-County Region	Illinois Department of Transportation, Illinois Department of Natural Resources, Illinois Department of Commerce & Economic Opportunity
Local Legacy Planning for Peoria Tri-County Region	Illinois Department of Natural Resources
Application of LEAM to Kishwaukee River Watershed	Army Corps of Engineers
National LEAM	U.S. Army Construction Engineering Research Laboratory
A Dynamic Spatial Decision Support System for Sustainable Military Communities	Strategic Environmental Research and Development Program (SERDP), U.S. Department of Defense
Local Legacy Planning for McHenry County	Illinois Department of Natural Resources
Local Legacy Planning for Will County	Illinois Department of Natural Resources
Gateway Blueprint Model for St. Louis Region	East-West Gateway Council of Governments, Illinois Department of Transportation, Illinois Department of Natural Resources
NPC Common Ground	Northeastern Illinois Regional Planning Commission
Evolving Urban Dynamics: Ecology, Modeling, and Visualization	National Science Foundation

a visual representation of model logic, which facilitates direct inspection by subject experts who do not have the background to comprehend the mathematics behind the model. This approach radically differs from conventional model-building projects, in which a single individual is responsible for writing computer code on the basis of model logic articulated by the subject experts.

Because each LEAM simulation involves land use change over several years, new ways of visualizing the pertinent spatial-temporal data sets—including movie-maps and other kinds of graphic representations described in Deal and Pallathucheril (2007)—were devised and tested.

Following that initial work, significant enhancements of LEAM were developed with funding from the U.S. Department of Defense (DoD). In 2001, the DoD Strategic Environmental Research and Development Program (SERDP) issued a statement of need for proposals that would "increase the understanding of the risks to military operations and training associated with land use change outside of military installation boundaries." More specifically, the purpose was to identify and examine consequences of land use change outside military bases that might constrain DoD's operational mission in the future. A joint five-year project by the LEAM Laboratory and the U.S. Army Engineer Research and Development Center–Construction Engineering Research Laboratory (ERDC–CERL) entitled "The Evolving Urban Community and Military Installations: A Dynamic Spatial Decision Support System for Sustainable Military Communities" was funded and initiated in 2002.

The main objective of this project was to identify and address gaps in the understanding of risks to military operations associated with land use change outside the installation boundary. Outcomes from that work included enhancement of LEAM's LUC model, methods for quantifying encroachment risks, and developing a spatial decision support system. While SME is an effective platform for developing and testing models, it proved less effective in deploying the model in real-world applications. SME is intended to partition computations and run on multiple processors, but the implementation use of SME's message-passing interface (MPI) does not always work as intended. Consequently, simulation run times increase substantially when the area of the region being modeled increases. Also, SME contains many features—some experimental—that are not required in LEAM and also increase run times.

For these reasons, a new, stand-alone version of the LUC model was written. It implements the model and parallel processing more efficiently and effectively than the previous version. As part of a related project funded by ERDC–CERL, the stand-alone model was run on up to 1,024 processors, and it was found that simulation run times decreased directly in proportion to the number of processors deployed. Another LEAM enhancement involved research on calibrating this kind of hybrid CA model.

To quantify risk to military operational missions from nearby land use change, models of a variety of regional impacts were developed: water quality (LEAMwq; Wang, Choi, and Deal 2005), air quality (LEAMaq), sustainability (LEAMss), and habitat fragmentation (LEAMfrag; Aurambout, Endress, and Deal 2005). An impact model relating to a military installation's training mission (LEAMtom) was also developed at ERDC–CERL. A decision support system called SIRRA (Sustainable Installations Regional Resource Assessment), also developed at ERDC–CERL, identifies military lands at risk due to problems related to future land use change.

LEAM Applications and Applied Research

Many advances in LEAM functionality and lessons about how simulation models can be usefully integrated into regional planning have come about as a result of applying LEAM in various regions of the United States, but particularly in and around Illinois. The initial development of LEAM for Kane County prompted interest by the State of Illinois and the Governor's Cabinet Task Force on Smart Growth. That interest resulted in funding from the State of Illinois to apply LEAM to a three-county region around Peoria (Deal and Pallathucheril 2003) and then in the Metro-East portion of the St. Louis, Missouri, region. Initial results from application in the eastern portion of the region attracted interest from the region's metropolitan planning organization (MPO), the East-West Gateway Council of Governments (EWGCoG). That interest led to extension of the application to the two-state, ten-county metropolitan St. Louis region. The lessons learned from those applications prompted a further set of applications under the Illinois Local Legacy Act in McHenry County, the Peoria tri-county region, Will County, and in the Metro-East area of St. Louis. In addition to those applications sponsored by local governments, LEAM has been applied in a number of regions around the United States that host military installations, using the SERDP funding described above.

LEAM applications are tailored to meet the specific needs of the client communities, and they rely heavily on intensive interaction with multiple stakeholders throughout the subject region. Projects have typically focused on the application of LEAM to major urban and regional planning issues, including watershed and environmental planning, transportation planning, land use planning, and development in close proximity to military installations. Analyses use the results of LEAM simulations in combination with other models to assess how future land use change could affect critical economic, social, and ecological factors, including:

- population and housing change within a given geographic boundary;

- traffic congestion on a regional road network;

- watershed conditions and water quality;

- stress on natural, cultural, and agricultural resources;

- habitat fragmentation;

- infrastructure requirements;

- fiscal condition of local governments;

- regional sustainability;

- military training opportunities; and

- societal impacts.

Simulation results and impact assessments typically are made available using an easy-to-navigate, Web-based planning support system. LEAM simulation layers also can be overlaid with other relevant planning data such as administrative boundaries, infrastructure, resource data, aerial photographs, existing regional and local plans, and other data judged to be relevant by stakeholders.

Summary of LEAM Evolution and Key Developments

The list below summarizes significant research and development milestones as well as lessons learned in the course of applying LEAM for client communities in the United States and Korea:

- Peoria Pilot project. Fundamental model development and visualization work was accomplished, and the process of model feedback was begun.

- DoD SERDP project. Fundamental model development was advanced with the inclusion of an economic model and early impact models. Visualization techniques were refined, and strategies for Web-based project management were developed to facilitate work with external partners.

- DoD High-Performance Computing Modernization Program. This work resulted in the creation of a distributed model that vastly increased LEAM's potential for application to large-scale areas.

- Kishwaukee River Watershed application. This work encompassed the counties of McHenry, Boone, Winnebago, and De Kalb, Illinois, and a portion of southern Wisconsin. It explored the relationship between land use and water quality and resulted in an initial understanding of how to integrate external water-quality models into LEAM.

- St. Louis, Missouri, regional application. This work began to explore how LEAM simulations are used by the client. The first LEAM planning charrettes were convened and a model localization process was developed. Work also began on application techniques. We also began discussions on integrating transportation models and social-model development in St. Louis.

- Northeastern Illinois Planning Commission. This project improved our ability to model scenarios.

- Illinois Legacy Program. This project introduced stress analysis and the system of plans and Web interface data center concepts. Household churning techniques were also developed here and household generation begun.

- Chicago Metropolitan Agency for Planning. This project refined transportation integration. With this work, we began to modify the model to suit the Chicago Area Transportation Study transportation model.

- South Central Illinois rural application. We refined our household generation techniques and redefined some unique rural drivers.

- Strategic Sustainability Assessment (SSA) project. Develop a technique for backcasting and implication feedback. How do impact models affect land use change? Began work on the feedback between economics and land use, and began to determine sustainability indicators related to land use change.

- Korea application. This project focuses on rural integration and international data collection techniques.

Case Study: The St. Louis Planning Support System

The LEAM application made in the ten-county region around St. Louis was an important model integration effort, and the results of that work warrant some additional detail and comment.

Project Overview

Like most other older metropolitan areas, St. Louis faces the great challenge of managing sustainable growth. Even with relatively slow population growth and negative growth in the urban core, the city continues to sprawl. According to U.S. Census Bureau data, the urban population grew a very modest 7 percent between 1970 and 2000. However, the appearance of newly urbanized land mushroomed 125 percent over that 30-year period. That growth indicates that many people are moving from city neighborhoods to suburban ones. Consequently, open space and valuable farmland are consumed by urbanization while there is underinvestment in the city core. This dynamic results in a decline in the tax base, and property values likewise decline. Racial segregation and economic disparities become more severe, further aggravating socioeconomic stresses. Another result is an increase in traffic congestion and air pollution. The East-West Gateway Coordinating Council (EWGateway), the MPO, and the council of governments for the St. Louis region forecast continuing slow population growth for the region as a whole during the next 20 years, with some level of continuing decline in the core and expansion in the outlying counties.

A multitude of questions face the policy makers and planners of metropolitan St. Louis:

- Can the region afford to let growth continue in this way?

- What physical, fiscal, and governmental infrastructure will be needed to support future growth?

- What are the potential economic, social, and environmental impacts of a planning project or policy?

- How should governments encourage economic development opportunities to maintain and build healthy, high-quality communities that provide an economically and environmentally sustainable future for current and future generations?

Such questions defy easy or straightforward answers, and powerful analytical tools are essential for arriving at well-informed answers. Because LEAM has an open architecture, unlike other urban modeling tools, it is comparatively easy to incorporate multiple models and build a localized urban model. LEAM is also more open to inspection, and it can handle large regions at a very fine resolution because of its support for massively parallel computer processing. In 2003, EWGateway began to work with the LEAM research group and to use LEAM as a planning tool to help communities make decisions that affect the economic efficiency, health, and viability of the local community and the overall region (Deal 2003). LEAM also provides a framework that enables public officials and citizens to enter into dialogue with planners and to evaluate public investments through scenario exploration.

Localization of LEAM for the Study Area

Spanning both sides of the Mississippi River, the study region included the city of St. Louis and ten counties (figure 4.6)—five in Illinois (Clinton, Jersey, Madison, Madison, Monroe, and St. Clair) and five in Missouri (City of St. Louis, St. Louis, St. Charles, Jefferson, and Franklin). The study area stretches about 120 miles from east to west and about 90 miles from north to south. In LEAM, the area accounts for more than 30 million grid cells at a spatial resolution of 30 by 30 meters per cell.

As the first step the team conducted a generic LEAM run for the region. The land use simulations were generated using a limited set of drivers—those for which national data sets could be used. The parameters were either empirical or based on national averages. Although projections based on a generic simulation are not highly accurate, they serve as a starting point for public discussion of regional drivers of land use change and scenarios of interest in public workshops.

Figure 4.7 is a map illustrating the outcome of one generic LEAM simulation. New areas of development projected for 2030 appear darker, and the larger dark areas toward the center represent existing development. After input on the generic map from local planners and residents, the next step was to build a tailor-made LEAM model for the St. Louis metropolitan region that incorporated that input. To develop a localized LEAM model, a significant amount of work is required to collect relevant data and analyze the local condition.

First, a successful simulation run requires that substantial and accurate data be acquired and processed. Current and accurate land use data are critical to a LEAM simulation. Multiple data sets from various sources were used to produce a land use map for the year 2000, the inaugural year of the LEAM model.

Second, each submodel had to be refined and calibrated based on local data. For example, the input-output econometric model for projecting population and jobs had to be integrated with local data sets, and the transportation model was calibrated to emulate traffic congestion caused by bridges over the Mississippi River in order to estimate local traffic volumes.

Third, a number of new submodels had to be developed. The additional driver models were designed to capture the local urban-growth pattern, and

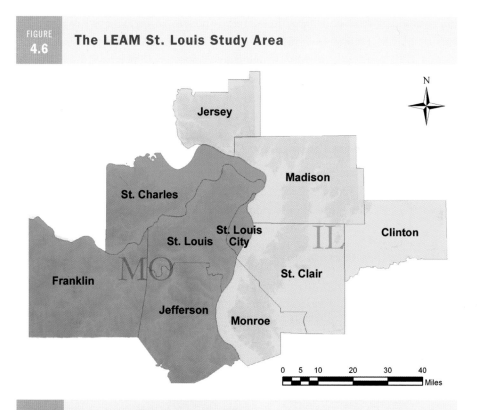

FIGURE 4.6

The LEAM St. Louis Study Area

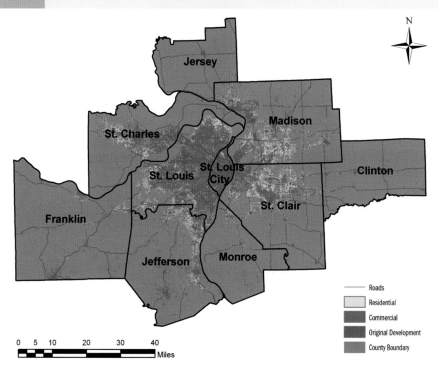

FIGURE 4.7

**Generic LEAM Simulation,
10-county St. Louis Metropolitan Region, 2030**
(yellow areas—new residential development;
red areas—new commercial development)

impact models were built to address region-specific problems. For instance, the generic LEAM simulations used proximity to city centers as a driver of land use change. Public review of these simulations suggested that land use change in the St. Louis region is likely to be driven by proximity to other centers, such as places of employment, shopping centers, health care facilities, and cultural amenities. A spatial interaction model, also called a *gravity model*, was developed based on travel time, which serves as a surrogate for proximity to these centers of gravity. In addition to adding attractor models, a *social model* was developed. The purpose of this model is to explain why certain parts of a region fail to grow and may even decline. The social model serves as a growth-repelling driver, discouraging growth based on vacancy rate, rental rate, income level, and other socioeconomic factors.

Finally, the submodels were integrated into the LEAM framework and then tested and calibrated. Because the work was part of a broader effort in the region that focused on developing a blueprint for the future, this localized model is called the LEAM Blueprint Model. It is more powerful, capable, and accurate than the initial generic model. When compared with the generic LEAM application, growth is seen to shift from Illinois to Missouri, and much less growth occurs in the urban core (figure 4.8). More detailed quantitative analysis and validation further demonstrated that the LEAM Blueprint Model produces a more realistic projection of urban growth patterns than the generic simulation.

Modeling Linkages Between Land Use and Travel Demand

Land use and transportation networks are integrally linked. Congestion in one area of a region is likely to improve accessibility in another and increase its likelihood of transformation. To improve model validity, additional information on road congestion coefficients, as calculated by a regional transportation model, was added.

In parallel with LEAM development, EWGCoG was engaged in developing TransEval, a fairly typical four-step travel-demand model. EWGCoG recognized that there are significant advantages to jointly modeling both land use and travel-demand change: The resulting simulations are more robust than they are from each individual model, and therefore they more effectively inform choices made about transportation policies and investments.

Each model can help address a limitation in the other. When computing various measures of accessibility, LEAM used posted free-flow speeds as a measure of the ease of road travel. But without coupling, those values will not change over the duration of a simulation run as a result of volumes or congestion. A travel-demand model can provide better assessments of travel speeds, and these can be continuously modified in response to changing land use conditions. TransEval uses households and jobs in traffic analysis zones (TAZs) to compute trip generation. Without coupling, however, the future value of the input parameters cannot be estimated, meaning that they do not respond to changes in the performance of the transportation network. In LEAM, socioeconomic and demographic information is available at a fine resolution. From those data, changes in households and jobs can be derived for any point in the future, for any spatial unit, including TAZs.

| FIGURE 4.8 | **LEAM Blueprint Land Use Simulation Map, Aggregated to Sections, St. Louis Metropolitan Region, 2030** |

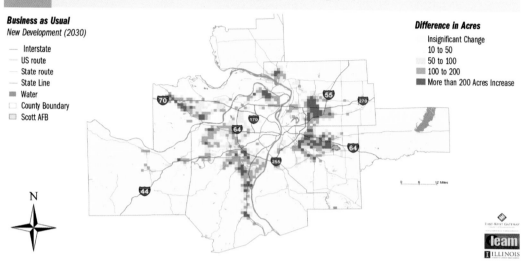

The two models were loosely coupled more or less in the manner described by Waddell et al (2007). Results from TransEval are used as inputs into LEAM, which is run for several annual time steps. The resulting land use is the basis for socioeconomic inputs back into TransEval, and the process iterates until the simulation is complete. Figure 4.9 shows a schematic of the coupling. Table 4.2 compares the acreages by county for the Blueprint and TransEval simulations.

| FIGURE 4.9 | **The Integrated Land Use–Transportation Modeling Approach** |

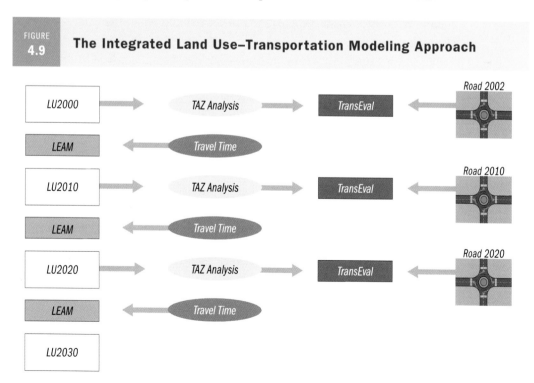

Figure 4.10 depicts the change in TAZ population between 2002 and 2010 associated with land use change modeled in LEAM. TAZs in shades of red see declining populations while those in shades of blue see increasing populations. Many TAZs within the ring of highways are likely to lose population, while TAZs at the periphery are likely to see population increases. Figure 4.11 shows changes in employment by TAZ over the same time period. Most of the job growth appears in peripheral areas and along the main highways into the city.

Figure 4.12 presents a comparison of TransEval results when socioeconomic data from LEAM are used. As a result of peripheral development, the ring of highways around the urbanized area becomes increasingly congested, with lower average speeds. One of the highways into the central business district (CBD) from the east also has lower average speeds.

Progressive changes in land use and average speeds on the road network result in different land use patterns than would occur if land use and travel demand were simulated separately. Figure 4.13 summarizes the difference between the land development pattern in 2030 as simulated without integration, called the *blueprint model run,* and the pattern simulated when the two models are coupled, called the *fully integrated run.* Sections in green show less development in the integrated run than in the blueprint run, and orange sections show more development in the integrated run than in the blueprint run. In the eastern portion of the region, coupling the two models appears to shift development closer to the CBD. A highway with increasing congestion in 2020 runs through the center and appears to push this development to the north and the south. West of the Mississippi River, the low levels of congestion in the north (St. Charles County, Missouri), which is further reduced when the bridge is added, draws development from the south.

Continuing Work

The St. Louis LEAM application is an ongoing project. More detailed calibration will be conducted, more submodels will be developed, and dozens of scenarios will be implemented for local planners to consider. Exploring these scenarios will significantly enhance planners' insights into future land use and its impact. Although LEAM will not make decisions for planners, and will not make planners smarter, it will certainly help them make smarter recommendations based on objective data, advanced simulation modeling technology, and the collective intelligence of local experts, authorities, and stakeholders.

Discussion

In the St. Louis region, questions on how and where to make critical transportation investments are an important part of the regional dialogue. Residents and stakeholders are concerned about the consequences of constructing new transportation infrastructure, including a new Mississippi River bridge. Our analysis of the potential implications of building a new bridge revealed that substantive conversations should take place in the region before any decision is made. The simulation

TABLE 4.2

Comparison of Acreage Distribution by County: Blueprint and TransEval Simulations, 2030

	Residential		Commercial	
	Blueprint	TransEval	Blueprint	TransEval
Franklin	2.5%	2.5%	2.6%	2.7%
Jefferson	13.7%	8.4%	4.3%	2.9%
St. Charles	12.6%	15.8%	17.1%	19.9%
St. Louis	34.4%	37.1%	47.6%	46.5%
St. Louis City	0.2%	0.3%	0.2%	0.2%
Missouri	**63.4%**	**64.1%**	**71.8%**	**72.2%**
Clinton	0.4%	0.2%	0.3%	0.2%
Jersey	0.1%	0.1%	0.0%	0.1%
Madison	18.0%	14.5%	13.5%	12.8%
Monroe	0.8%	0.8%	0.4%	0.4%
St. Clair	17.4%	20.2%	13.9%	14.3%
Illinois	**36.7%**	**35.8%**	**28.1%**	**27.8%**

Note: Totals may not equal 100.0% because of rounding.

FIGURE 4.10

Change in Population, LEAM–TransEval Simulation, St. Louis Metropolitan Region, 2002–2010

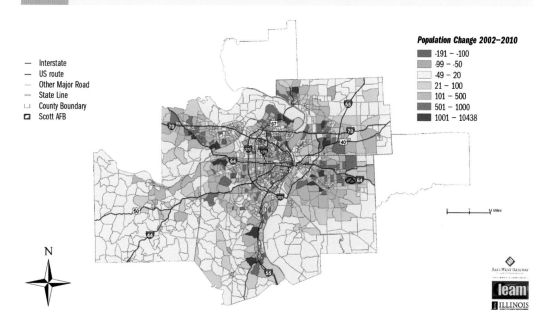

**Change in Employment, LEAM–TransEval Simulation,
St. Louis Metropolitan Region, 2002–2010**

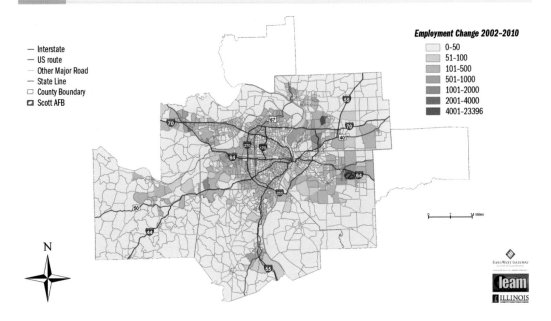

— Interstate
— US route
　 Other Major Road
— State Line
▢ County Boundary
▣ Scott AFB

Employment Change 2002-2010
▢ 0-50
▢ 51-100
▢ 101-500
▢ 501-1000
▢ 1001-2000
▢ 2001-4000
▢ 4001-23396

N

**Travel Speed Comparison, LEAM–TransEval Simulation,
2002–2010**

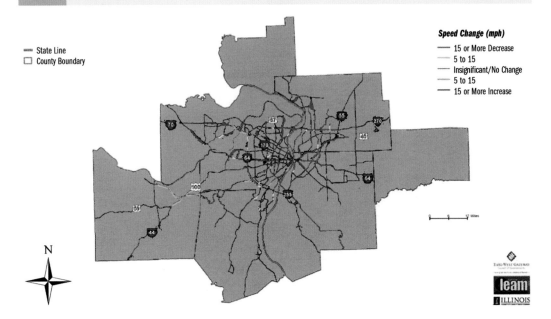

— State Line
▢ County Boundary

Speed Change (mph)
— 15 or More Decrease
— 5 to 15
— Insignificant/No Change
— 5 to 15
— 15 or More Increase

N

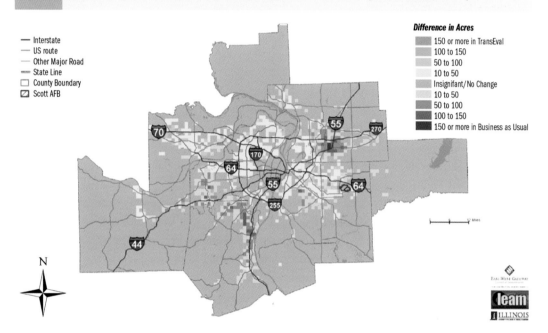

| FIGURE 4.13 | **Comparison of Projected Development, Business as Usual Blueprint Model Baseline with LEAM–TransEval Model, St. Louis Metropolitan Region, 2030**
(Green areas are highest in the base case and oranges are highest in the new travel times scenario. Note the shift from greens to oranges, which indicates decreasing developments in areas south of St. Louis and increasing to the northwest.) |

— Interstate
— US route
   Other Major Road
— State Line
☐ County Boundary
☑ Scott AFB

Difference in Acres
■ 150 or more in TransEval
■ 100 to 150
■ 50 to 100
■ 10 to 50
■ Insignifant/No Change
■ 10 to 50
■ 50 to 100
■ 100 to 150
■ 150 or more in Business as Usual

showed enough evidence of a changing dynamic between the base case and the bridge-investment scenario to suggest a pause in the decision-making process in favor of a more detailed analysis.

This ability to test important investments and policies and discuss their potential future outcomes is critical for effective planning. It also presents a unique opportunity to help reach decisions that optimize economic and environmental sustainability given a set of goals and constraints. Advanced analytical applications like LEAM can shed light on how a land use policy decision might be affected if a community knew that one investment choice (e.g., a new interstate highway interchange) and a competing investment choice (e.g., a new mass transportation line) would proffer similar results in terms of county commuting and business activity, but would lead to far different results in terms of air quality or threats to farmland, natural areas, and water resources.

The authors experienced such a case in the Peoria project. Potential scenarios preferred by regional stakeholders included farmland protection and river bluff preservation. Modeled individually, each policy was effective in its stated purpose. Farmland was preserved using a 40-acre-minimum rural zoning standard, and the bluffs were protected using a ravine overlay district that limited development in the sensitive areas. But problems arose when each was viewed in light of the other.

For example, the 40-acre-minimum rural zoning standard made bluff development more likely. By simply enacting bluff-protection policies before enacting the farmland zoning standards, bluffs were protected and rural farmland preserved. The importance of farmland protection did not change; the question became how to accomplish the goal without compromising local resources.

It must be noted that the political process can threaten to overwhelm consensus produced logically through an open, participatory decision-making process. Nevertheless, public discourse can function to demand an open accounting for the process used to make important planning decisions. Government decisions that fly in the face of valid data and public deliberation can become difficult for officials to justify.

The ability to produce multiple futures instead of a single "preferred" future also becomes relevant when discussing large-scale modeling environments. Experience shows that a collection of alternative scenarios is more valuable to decision makers than any individual scenario (Deal and Pallathucheril 2007). Although the simulations employ mathematic probabilities, no one seriously contends that simulation models can infallibly predict the future. The value of these models is to project possible outcomes and help the affected community discern the differences and potential consequences of each alternative. Because future urban development is highly stochastic and, therefore, more or less unpredictable, it is prudent to plan for many possibilities rather than just one.

In Peoria, regional planners have learned to use a collection of scenarios as a basis for working on several different regional issues rather than relying on a unitary vision for the region. For instance, land use patterns contained in the LEAM scenarios were used to identify bobcat and wood thrush habitat that requires protection from fragmentation caused by land development (Aurambout, Endress, and Deal 2005). In an environmental corridor study, planners prioritized areas to be protected based on information about the timing of future development. Habitat areas facing imminent development across a large number of scenarios were given a high priority, as were existing habitat areas threatened across multiple scenarios. The collection of scenarios has also been used in providing different forms of planning assistance to local units of government in the region (Hopkins, Kaza, and Pallathucheril 2005b).

Conclusions

Better tools are needed to manage regional dynamics, not just as economic systems or static inventories of resources, but as complex systems that are part of regional and global networks (Campbell 1996). However, effective management requires that we understand both the systems to be administered and the implications of our strategies. We have attempted here to outline an approach for understanding the dynamics of urban systems and the potential implications of urban policy and investment-management decisions. We described one modeling approach—LEAM—that utilizes cellular automata and other technological advances in spatial simulation modeling to help improve a community's ability to make ecologically and economically sound decisions. LEAM enables users to capture stochastic influences and view the reported probable consequences of intended events in a scenario-based format that is comprehensible by local experts, decision makers, and stakeholders.

The operationalization of LEAM in the metropolitan St. Louis area has been a process of gaining acceptance by the affected community and its representatives to become an integral part of the regional planning process. The process has involved persuading both the public and the relevant communities of practice that the method can be trusted, and that it can help make regional planning activity faster and more effective than previous approaches.

Through these real-world applications of LEAM, we have learned that the process of model building in a community is just as important as the model itself, if not more so. It is clear that "black box" solutions are not acceptable in the decision-making process because the affected community demands to know the hows and whys of the decisions. It is seen that participatory processes of modeling do work, and that they serve to improve the reliability and validity of modeled outcomes. It has been the authors' repeated experience that models and simulations can breathe new life into the regional planning process by providing governments and the public with visions of potential alternative futures. Simulation models cannot and need not predict the future with unerring accuracy: Their value is realized in objectively generating data-driven scenarios that promote constructive public discussion and consensus building, which can strengthen policy formation and planning decisions.

Future Applications

LEAM is a product of an academic laboratory. As such, its underlying mission is to advance the science of urban modeling and the practice of planning. By their very nature, laboratory products can be fleeting, unsupported, and difficult to maintain. In addition, repetitious applications—applications that need the same process and product previously delivered—can become tiresome and rote. For these reasons, research products, if they are to be successful, need private sector entities that can establish long-term relationships with the users, provide needed support, and apply the technology to future projects. The planners at East-West Gateway, for example, use LEAM for forecasting, travel planning, and environmental analysis. They also use it as part of their long-term transportation planning and public engagement efforts. Because it has become so endemic to their planning practices, a new private sector entity, LEAMgroup, has become their LEAM modeling provider.

The LEAM Laboratory remains dedicated to questions of urban land use change and its implications. LEAMgroup is now available to tackle service, provide long-term maintenance, and support new, simple applications. Complex problem solving, new questions, and new ideas will remain the purview of the lab. This collaborative arrangement provides a positive atmosphere for future applications, some of which are already in progress:

■ China: A LEAM application in the Jiaxing area of southern China is being negotiated.

■ Korea: Continued work on the Korean peninsula is planned with several placations and new ideas on rural technology dissemination.

■ Chicago metropolitan area: Newly connected, LEAM and the Chicago Area Transportation model are being used to test various policy-level questions in the Chicago region.

■ Peoria: New work is tightly coupling LEAM with a new regional transportation model.

■ McHenry County, Illinois: Planners are using LEAM to set up a dynamic comprehensive planning process.

■ LaSalle County, Illinois: Planners are using LEAM to update the county comprehensive plan.

A New Tool for a New Planning

The What if?™ Planning Support System

Richard E. Klosterman

WE ARE WITNESSING A SECOND REVOLUTION OF COMPUTER USE IN PLANNING. Computers first entered planning a generation ago on the crest of a widespread belief that scientific methods and computer-assisted methods could solve society's most pressing problems. This optimism was reflected in two influential issues of the *Journal of the American Institute of Planners* (Voorhees 1959; Harris 1965) and a number of ambitious, expensive, and spectacularly unsuccessful attempts to build large-scale metropolitan simulation models and urban information systems (Hemmens 1971; Webber 1965). These efforts generated an impressive body of literature (e.g., Harris 1985; Klosterman 1994b) but had little impact on planning practice.

Continued dramatic improvements in computer hardware and software have made the tools available on planners' desks faster, more powerful, and cheaper than could be imagined a decade ago. A wealth of spatially related data are becoming available, increasingly via the Web. Freely available Web-based mapping tools such as Google Earth and Microsoft® Virtual Earth™ are dramatically enhancing the public's appreciation for spatially referenced information. Perhaps most importantly, an increased concern with issues such as global warming, urban sprawl, and environmental degradation are creating an increased demand for computer-based analysis and forecasting tools. Together, these factors have stimulated a new generation of planners to develop a diverse and growing collection of computer-based tools for planning (e.g., Brail and Klosterman 2001; Geertman and Stillwell 2003b; Koomen et al. 2007).

Three Images of Planning

In this environment of exciting technological possibilities, the question should not be what kinds of models *can* we build (i.e., what kinds of tools will current technology allow us to develop) but what kinds of models *should* we build (i.e., what kinds of tools are most appropriate for planning)? The development and use of any tool implies a theory of practice that defines the contexts in which it should—and should not—be applied, the issues it addresses—and ignores—and the roles of experts and nonexperts in using the tool and its products. As a result, the current effort to develop computer-based planning support systems must consider the professional environment in which they will be used. In this regard, it is useful to consider three ideals that have shaped planning practice and education and the implications they have for computer-based planning support.

Planning as Design

Planning emerged in the United States roughly one hundred years ago as part of a broader attempt to deal with the ugliness, inefficiency, disorder, and corruption of the new industrial city. Reflecting its roots in the professional fields of architecture, landscape architecture, and civil engineering, the early profession concerned itself with the physical city and the preparation of master plans laying out a long-range, comprehensive design for the city's future form. Informed by an underlying physical determinism, the early planners assumed that social reform could be achieved by improving the physical environment and viewed the city as a collection of land uses and facilities that could be easily modified without considering the economic, social, and political structures that shaped it.

From architecture and landscape architecture the early planners adopted the perspective of "architecture writ large," the belief that the process of planning a city is fundamentally the same as the process of designing a building or a landscape. That is, it was assumed that planners could achieve in the public sector the deliberate outcomes that are readily accomplished in a private firm or a centrally controlled government enterprise. In these settings there is generally a single client with a clearly defined future, well-defined objectives, well-established means for achieving those objectives, and centralized control over the resources needed to achieve the objectives. Together, these factors allow designers to prepare blueprints that provide detailed guidance for constructing the structure or landscape that will best serve their client's needs (Webber 1969).

The early planners replaced the architect's client with the "the public" and the client's desires with their perceptions of "the public interest." The client's image of the future was replaced by the planners' projections for the city's future population, employment, land uses, and related infrastructure demands. The architect's empirically derived design principles and standards were replaced by generally accepted principles of "good professional practice." The designer's blueprints were replaced by comprehensive plans presenting images of the future city that were assumed to guide public and private actions toward a shared image of the desired future. Isolated from the give and take of politics and routine operational responsibilities by their positions with the independent planning commission, the early planners assumed that their plans were "above politics," and anyone who rejected them was either not properly informed or acting from selfish motives.

Experience has demonstrated that none of these assumptions is true. The public does not share a clearly defined set of common interests that can provide clear guidance to planners. The 20- to 30-year forecasts required for planning are difficult, if not impossible, to prepare. Norms of professional practice are inadequate for dealing with the increasingly complex issues facing planning. The urban fabric is shaped by the actions of a diverse range of organizations and groups, largely outside the control of planners. Equally important, planners have recognized for decades that their actions are inherently and inevitably political in the most fundamental sense of helping to determine who gets what, when, where, and how.

Planning as Applied Science

Planning abandoned its traditional concern with the design of the physical city in the 1950s and 1960s for a new focus on the quantitative techniques and theories of the social sciences.[1] Under this new ideal of planning as applied science, the intuitive designs of the planner-architects were assumed to be replaced by the "scientific" and "objective" methods and findings of the emerging fields of regional science, urban economics, and operations research. Computers were assumed to play a central role in the new scientific planning by improving planners' understanding of the urban development process, expanding their ability to determine the direct and indirect effects of public and private actions, and allowing them to forecast accurately future states of the metropolis (Harris 1965; Webber 1965).

Planning as Reasoning Together

The optimism of the applied science ideal was severely questioned in the 1970s and 1980s. The early attempts to develop computer-based urban models and information systems efforts of the 1960s failed miserably, due in large part to their over-ambitious goals, the inadequacies of the available technology and information, and a limited understanding of the urban development process (Lee 1973; Brewer 1973; Batty 1994). Quantitative techniques such as operations research and linear programming that were assumed to provide the foundations for the new planning were found to be inadequate for public policy issues that are poorly structured, have poorly defined goals, and no obvious technical solutions (Hoos 1972; Batey and Breheny 1978).

Together, academic theorizing and political expedience have replaced earlier ideals of professional-directed planning for the public with new images of citizen-based planning with the public. The labels for this new ideal range from civic engagement (Skocpol and Fiorina 1999) and visioning (Shipley and Newkirk 1998) to collaborative leadership (Chrislip and Larson 1994) and consensus building (Innes 1996; Klein 2000; Susskind, McKearnan, and Thomas-Larmer 1999). However, the underlying ideal is the same: Democratic ideals require new forms of governance that allow private citizens to participate more directly in the actions of government.

Public participation is hardly new. Public participation—generally in the form of public hearings—has been required for a wide range of federal, state, and local programs for decades. In all too many cases, however, the public's participation in the policy-making process has been perfunctory at best. Plans and proposals are generally prepared by a consultant or the planning staff, with minimal input from citizens or interest groups. A range of techniques may be used in an attempt to obtain public input into the planning process: Informational public meetings may be held; attitude surveys may be mailed; and volunteer working committees may be appointed.

The public's formal role is almost always limited to participating in a public hearing held to hear citizens' comments at the end of the process, just before the action or policy is approved. Minor changes may be made in response to comments made at the meeting, but the core decision concerning the issues addressed, the alternatives considered, and the criteria used in evaluating them have been made long before the public is involved. Under these circumstances, public participation is little more than a ritualistic exercise for ratifying choices made by professionals pursuing their own images of the public interest (Plein, Green, and Williams 1998; Klein 2000).

The new models of citizen participation differ from the approaches that preceded them in many fundamental ways. Unlike representative forms of governance, they involve the direct participation of spokespersons for all groups involved in the issue. Unlike traditional public hearings, citizens are involved throughout the process—reviewing past and present conditions, identifying problems and opportunities, evaluating alternatives, and attempting to make decisions they can all support. It is important to recognize, however, that the process is not a "hug fest"; getting diverse groups to set aside their differences and work together to define a common goal is a difficult, time-consuming process, requiring the assistance of trained facilitators, participant training, and carefully designed deliberative procedures (Innes 1996; Klein 2000).

New ideals of planning with the public imply fundamentally different roles for professional planners. Earlier generations of planners used their professional experience and presumably objective computer-based models and methods to identify problems, evaluate alternatives, and project a desired future, largely without involving the public. In the new model, the planners' role is limited primarily to structuring and informing a citizen-led decision process. In so doing, planners not only involve directly the people for whom the plans are being prepared; they learn from the people who know best about the realities in which the plans will be implemented.

Design Principles

These new images of planning with the public suggest that it is important to consider four principles that provide the foundation for any attempt to develop computer-based tools and techniques.[2] Their application to a particular planning support system (PSS), What if?™ 2.0, will then be considered in some detail.

Principle 1: All Models Are Wrong—Some Models Are Useful

This principle, which is often referred to as Box's Law (Box and Draper 1987), recognizes that any model is, by definition, a simplification of reality and thus inevitably is wrong in the sense that it leaves out some aspects of reality. It goes on to suggest, however, that the important question is not whether the model is correct in some absolute sense, but whether it is useful for a particular purpose. This immediately raises the question of the purpose for which a model is useful: For example, does it develop or test theory, advance basic science, impress funding agencies, or support professional practice? All of these applications are clearly valid, but our interest here is in the usefulness of computer models for supporting new ideals of citizen-based planning.

Principle 2: Prediction Is Hard, Especially About the Future

This principle, which has been attributed to both Niels Bohr and Yogi Berra, points out that it is particularly difficult to be "correct" about the future. Experience in a wide range of forecasting fields demonstrates convincingly that forecasts are inevitably wrong, often embarrassingly so. This is particularly true for planners who must prepare 20- and 30-year projections for subcounty areas.

This principle suggests that planners should abandon the unrealistic goal of exactly predicting an unknowable future and, instead, prepare a range of forecast scenarios describing a number of possible futures (see Avin 2007; Harwood 2007). In the process, they will forsake the impossible goal of precisely predicting the future for the ultimately more important objectives of informing the policy-making process, facilitating community understanding, and preparing the public to deal with an uncertain future.

Planners must also recognize that their forecasts are ultimately dependent on their underlying assumptions and will only be correct if the underlying assumptions are correct. This suggests that planning models should explicitly state their underlying assumptions concerning future trends and alternative policy choices. It also suggests that the models should allow these assumptions to be easily modified and the effects of alternative assumptions to be easily identified.

Principle 3: Keep It Simple, Stupid (KISS)

This acronym, which was used during the U.S. Apollo program in the 1960s, is particularly appropriate for computer-based tools that are used in professional practice. Planners must recognize that their models are more likely to be useful in a policy context if policy makers and the public understand and trust them. As a result, planners should attempt to develop models that are as simple—rather than as complex—as possible. While the model's detailed computational procedures will inevitably be too complex for nonexperts to understand, their underlying computational procedures should be understandable and clear. Simple models are also particularly useful in a public setting when they respond rapidly to questions and concerns raised by the public.

Principle 4: Use It Because It's BAD

This principle recognizes that while the information that is available in professional practice is always bad—i.e., incomplete and inaccurate—it is also the best available data (BAD). This suggests that computer models that are developed to support planning should not require extensive data sets that are difficult, if not impossible, to obtain. Instead they should accommodate the data that are available in a particular location and use these data as best they can. This allows the power of computer-based planning support tools to be used not only by large, well-funded agencies, but also by smaller, data-poor communities across the United States and around the world.

Implementing the Principles

These principles will now be considered with regard to an operational planning support system, What if? 2.0. The model has been used at the county, regional, and township level in the United States (Klosterman et al. 2002; Klosterman et al. 2006); Australia (Pettit 2005); Iran (Asgary, Klosterman, and Razani 2007); Korea (Kweon and Kim 2002; Kweon, Kim, and Choi 2004); and is currently being applied in a number of communities in the United States, Australia, China, Italy, Korea, Malaysia, Spain, and the United Kingdom.

IMPLEMENTING PRINCIPLE 1: ALL MODELS ARE WRONG—SOME MODELS ARE USEFUL
What if? reflects the first design principle by abandoning the effort to develop a complex and all-encompassing, theoretically rich model that attempts to capture the complexity of the urban-development process. Instead, it provides an understandable, easily used, and fully operational model that helps community leaders and the public understand their present, consider their future, and evaluate alternative policies for achieving their collective goals.

IMPLEMENTING PRINCIPLE 2: PREDICTION IS HARD, ESPECIALLY ABOUT THE FUTURE
As its name suggests, What if? implements the second principle by not attempting to predict precisely an unknowable future. Instead, it is an explicitly policy-oriented model that suggests *what* might happen in the future *if* clearly specified public policies are adopted and assumptions about the future are correct. Policy choices that can be considered in the model include the staged expansion of public infrastructure, the implementation of alternative land use plans or zoning ordinances, and the establishment of farmland and open space protection programs. Assumptions about the future that can be considered in the model include future population and employment trends, household characteristics, and development densities.

IMPLEMENTING PRINCIPLE 3: KEEP IT SIMPLE, STUPID (KISS)   What if? incorporates the KISS principle by providing a relatively simple, rule-based model that does not attempt to duplicate the complex spatial interaction and market-clearing processes that shape the urban fabric. Instead, it incorporates a set of explicit decision rules for determining the relative suitability of different locations, projecting future land use demands, and allocating the projected demands to the most suitable sites. These concepts and their implementation can be readily understood by planners, elected officials, and the public.

IMPLEMENTING PRINCIPLE 4: USE IT BECAUSE IT'S BAD   What if? implements the fourth principle of using the best available data by accommodating the variety of data sets that are available for different areas around the world. Thus, for instance, it can accommodate up to 30 different land uses, 20 suitability factors, and an unlimited number of policy options. This allows the model to be applied to states, multicounty regions, counties, and subcounty areas almost anywhere.

What if? also provides four analysis options to accommodate very different levels of available information. The Suitability option produces maps and reports showing the relative suitability of different locations for accommodating future land uses. This option only requires GIS layers for the current land use/land cover and for the natural and man-made features to be considered in the suitability analysis. The Land Use option projects up to thirty land uses for five projection years and for buildout. This option requires the GIS information for the Suitability option and current and projected information on the study area's residential population and employment.

The Land Use/Population option projects the following variables for five projection years and for buildout: (1) total population; (2) group quarters population; (3) number of households; (4) number of housing units; (5) number of vacant housing units; (6) vacancy rate; and (7) average household size. The projections are reported for the entire study area and for user-defined areas such as census tracts, political jurisdictions, and traffic analysis zones (TAZs). This option requires all of the information for the previous analysis options and current population and housing information for census enumeration districts.

The Land Use/Population/Employment option projects the employment, by place of work, for up to 20 employment sectors. This option requires all of the information for the previous analysis options and current employment information for census enumeration districts. The required population and employment information for 20 NAICS (North American Industrial Classification System) employment categories is available for all block groups in the United States from readily available commercial sources.

Using What if?

What if? 2.0 includes seven options. The File option can be used to open, add, copy, move, and delete previously created projects. The Help option provides interactive online access to the *What if? User's Guide* via the table of contents, index, and full-text search. The Project option is used to specify non-GIS information used by the program. The Current option can be used to view maps and reports describing current conditions in the study area and any user-defined subareas. The other three options are described briefly below.

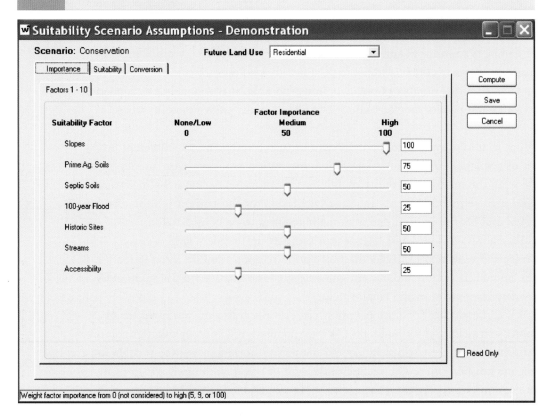

FIGURE
5.1

What if? Importance Sheet
Source: What if? Inc.

Suitability Option

The Suitability option can be used to prepare scenarios that determine the relative suitability of different locations for accommodating the projected land use demands. As shown in figure 5.1, the Suitability scenario assumptions form contains three tabbed sheets, labeled Importance, Suitability, and Conversion.

The Importance sheet provides slider bars that can be used to specify the user's assumptions concerning the relative importance that each suitability factor (i.e., slopes, prime agricultural soils, etc.) should play in locating a particular land use demand.[3] Thus, for example, importance values of 100 for slopes and 50 for septic soils for the residential land uses in figure 5.1 indicate that slopes are assumed to be twice as important as septic soils for locating new residential development. Importance values of 0 can be used to designate factors that should not be considered in locating a particular land use.

Similarly, the Suitability sheet provides slider bars that can be used to specify the user's assumptions concerning the relative suitability of the different suitability factor types (e.g., different slopes for the slope factor) for accommodating each land use demand. The values on a slider bar range from a low value of 0 to a high value of 100. Suitability values of 0 can be used to identify areas from which development is to be excluded, regardless of their ratings on other factors.

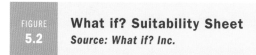

FIGURE
5.2

What if? Suitability Sheet
Source: What if? Inc.

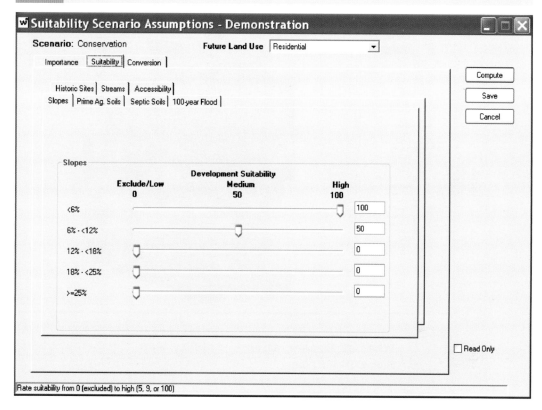

Thus, for instance, the 0 values for slopes greater than or equal to 12 percent for the residential land uses in figure 5.2 indicate that residential development will be excluded from all areas that have slopes of 12 percent or more. The Conversion sheet is used to identify land uses that can be converted from their current use (e.g., agriculture) to another use (e.g., residential) during the land use allocation process.

After specifying the factor-importance weights, suitability ratings, and conversions, the user can click on the Compute button to compute the suitability scores used to determine the relative suitability of all locations for each future land use. The suitability scores are computed by multiplying the importance weight for each suitability factor by the suitability ratings for a particular location and summing the products. The scores are displayed in the Suitability maps and reports and used to allocate the projected demand for different land uses to the most appropriate sites in the Allocation portion of the analysis.

As shown in figures 5.3 and 5.4, the Suitability maps show each location's suitability for a particular scenario and land use, scaled from low (light green) to high (dark green). The map also identifies areas that are not developable (in dark grey), not suitable for development (in yellow), and not convertible from their current use (in light grey).

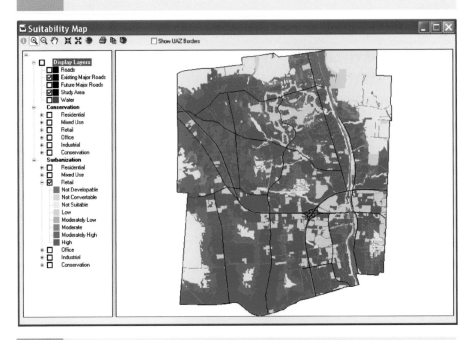

FIGURE 5.3

What if? Development Suitability Map
Source: What if? Inc.

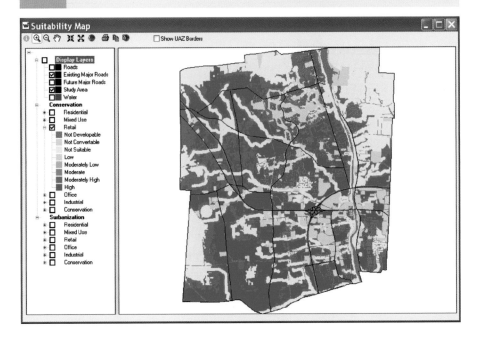

FIGURE 5.4

What if? Conservation Suitability Map
Source: What if? Inc.

The map in figure 5.3 shows the suitability of different locations for new retail land under a scenario that only considers the physical constraints on development. In contrast, the Suitability map for retail development in figure

5.4 has significantly less suitable land because it also prohibits development in environmentally sensitive areas near streams. What if? also generates reports that specify the number of acres or hectares within each suitability class for all land uses for a specified Suitability scenario and all of the assumptions that were specified for a particular Suitability scenario.

Demand Option

The What if? Demand option is used to prepare scenarios that project the future demand for residential, employment-related, preservation, and local land uses. As shown in figure 5.5, the Residential sheet contains three tabbed sheets that are used to specify the information that determines the projected demand for residential land. The first Residential sheet, labeled Projections, is used to specify the study area's projected population, group quarters population, and average household size. The second Residential sheet, labeled Housing Units, is used to specify the future breakdown by housing type and the future housing densities, vacancy rate, and infill percentage for each type of residential housing. The third Residential sheet, labeled Group Quarters, is used to specify the projected population living in group quarters such as nursing homes and college dormitories.

FIGURE 5.5	**What if? Residential Demand Form**
	Source: What if? Inc.

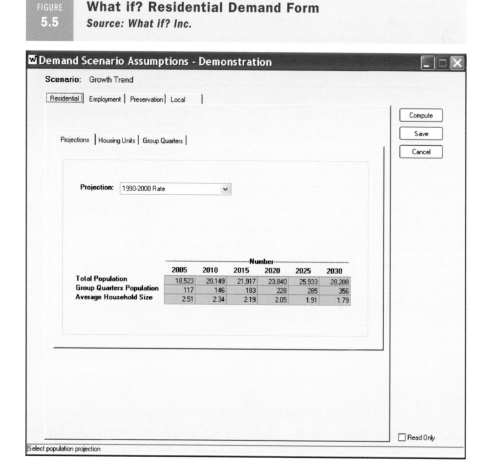

The Employment sheet is used in a similar way to specify the assumptions to be used in computing the future demand for employment-related land uses. The Preservation sheet can be used to specify the amount of new land that should be set aside for agriculture, conservation, or open space/environmental protection in each projection year. The Local sheet is used to specify the quantity of land that will be required per thousand new residents in each political jurisdiction for locally oriented land uses such as local parks and recreation facilities, the location and size of which are dependent on the local (e.g., municipal) population.

After all of the demand assumptions have been specified, the user can click on the Compute button to compute the projected land use demand by type in each projection year. The projected values and the assumptions underlying a particular demand scenario are provided in written reports.

Allocation Option

The Allocation option is used to specify the assumptions that will be used to project the study area's future land use, population, and employment patterns. The Allocation scenario assumptions form contains four tabbed sheets. The Allocation Order sheet is used to specify the order in which projected land use demands are to be allocated in each projection year—i.e., the land use demand to be satisfied first, the demand to be satisfied second, and so on. The Infrastructure Controls sheet is used to specify the influence that different kinds of infrastructures will have on the allocation process. Thus, for example, the user may specify that new industrial development requires sewer and water service and new commercial development must be located near major highways. The Land Use Controls sheet is used to select land use plans or zoning ordinances specifying where the various land uses may be allocated. The Growth Pattern sheet is used to specify the general spatial pattern for future growth—i.e., the areas to be developed first, those to be developed second, and so on, other things being equal.

What if? projects future land use, population, and employment patterns by allocating the projected land use demands from a Demand scenario to different locations based on their relative suitability as defined by a Suitability scenario, subject to the allocation controls specified in an Allocation scenario. For instance, the projected residential land use demand in a projection year will first be allocated to the most suitable sites for residential development, then to the second most suitable residential sites, and so on, until all of the projected residential demand in each projection year has been satisfied. The projected demand for employment-related, preservation, and local land uses are allocated in an identical way. If desired, the allocation process can be guided by user-selected public policies such as the implementation of a land use plan, zoning ordinance, or infrastructure expansion plan. Thus, for example, the user can specify that new industrial development can only be allocated to areas that are planned for industrial uses and have sewer and water service in a particular year.

As shown in figures 5.6 and 5.7, the What if? Allocation maps display the projected land uses in each projection year for each Allocation scenario. Figure

5.6 shows the current land uses in Dublin, Ohio. The map shows a substantial quantity of vacant land (shown in green) in the western part of the community, residential development (shown in yellow) in the center, and industrial and

FIGURE 5.6	**Land Use Map for Dublin, Ohio, 2006**
	Source: What if? Inc.

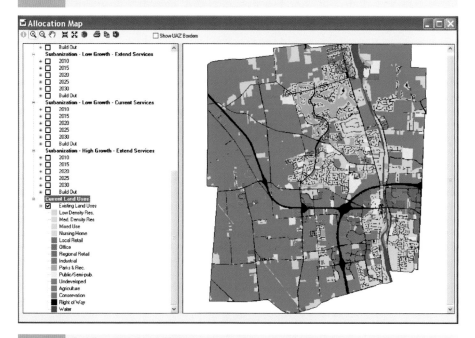

FIGURE 5.7	**Projected Land Use Map for Dublin, Ohio, in 2030**
	Source: What if? Inc.

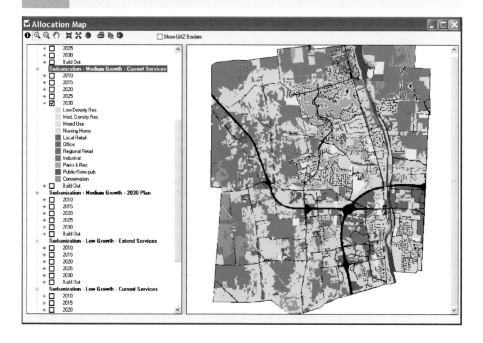

commercial uses located near the interstate bypass (shown in purple and red). Figure 5.7 shows the projected land uses in 2030 in Dublin for a scenario that assumes the development suitability scenario, a moderate growth scenario, and no controls on future development. As the map clearly indicates, under these assumptions, substantial portions of the community's vacant land will be converted to residential use in less than 25 years. Other allocation maps show the implications of alternative suitability assumptions, growth projections, and public policies for controlling growth.

The allocation reports record the projected quantity of land, population, housing, and employment in each user-defined subarea for all projection years. This option also produces GIS layers (shapefiles) reporting the projected land uses, population, housing, and employment in each subarea in all projection years. These data can easily be loaded into GIS packages such as ESRI's ArcGIS™ or into specialized packages for transportation and other analyses. The assumptions that underlie an Allocation scenario are recorded in the allocation assumptions report.

A Possible Future

All too often contemporary planning practice has abandoned the pursuit of a better future for routine tasks of reviewing development proposals, implementing regulations, and administering state- and federally mandated programs. At the same time, planners' methods and models are used too frequently to forecast the future, as if it were an inevitable reality, beyond our ability to control. Instead, planners should recognize that a range of alternative futures are possible and a variety of public policy tools are available for helping shape the future. They should reclaim their role as visionaries who dream of a better world and help design and implement the programs and policies needed to achieve it (Isserman 1985; Brooks 1988; Myers and Kitsuse 2000; Myers 2007).

In so doing, planning must not abandon its foundations in design, science, and citizen involvement. Rather, the profession should expand and enrich its appreciation for the role its members can play in professional practice and education. "Design" must not be seen as merely the solitary concern of individuals working out their personal visions of a desired future. Instead, it should be seen as an inherently social process in which members of the relevant public work together to define their common future (Forester 1983).

The planning profession also must not abandon science and rationality; rather, it should extend them beyond the unnecessarily constrained views that underlay much of contemporary social science. In particular, planners should abandon their naïve attempts to use "scientific" methods to forecast an unknowable future and avoid "value" questions of defining what the future should be. Instead, they should view planning as a process of public debate, argument, evaluation, and justification in which questions of value can be dealt with just as rationally as questions of fact (Klosterman 1978; 1980; 1983).

Most importantly, planners must abandon the paternalistic ideals of planning for the public that underlie the profession's design tradition and the false posturing of the applied science ideal. Instead, they should adapt the insights of the design and applied science perspectives to new ideals of planning with the public and create new models, methods, and procedures that can help the public define and achieve its vision for the future. In this way planning support systems such as What if? may help the planning profession use the lessons of its past to guide its future.

Endnotes

1. For a further discussion of the applied science ideal and its limitations see Klosterman (1997, 47–50).
2. The discussion in the following section draws on Klosterman (2007, 200–201).
3. Note: The suitability factors, land uses, and all other variables used in a particular study are specified by the user as part of the What if? setup process. The information shown in figure 5.1 and the other examples in this chapter were defined for a particular What if? application.

Moving from Region to City

UrbanSim

An Evolving Planning Support System for Evolving Communities

Paul Waddell, Xuan Liu, and Liming Wang

PLANNING SUPPORT SYSTEMS ARE GAINING CONSIDERABLE ATTENTION AND interest from a variety of potential users and for a wide array of applications. Planners in cities, counties, and metropolitan planning agencies need to use the best available information technology to attempt to inform major infrastructure investments and land use plans. Citizens and advocacy groups interested in promoting transit or bicycling, preventing loss of farmland and other open spaces and sensitive habitats, or improving or expanding existing infrastructure also want access to information technology to aid them in becoming more effective advocates for their respective causes. Community and regional visioning efforts such as the Envision Utah process have attempted to bring together stakeholders from across the community or region to generate consensus about the broad goals, objectives, and strategies for shaping communities over coming years, rather than allowing dissonant choices made by uncoordinated actions of individuals and agencies to produce ever more sprawling and auto-dependent development.

In response to the growing interest, new planning support systems (PSS) have emerged rapidly over the past decade. PSS cover a broad spectrum. They may be: (1) visualization tools that make it possible to get a 3D, visual sense of what one alternative future or another might look like; (2) sketch-planning tools that allow users to enter rules and then to visualize the outcome of those assumptions; or (3) simulation systems that attempt to model the behavior of urban agents and the potential effects of alternative policy actions. These actions might include building more freeways, adding congestion tolls, adding transit capacity and bicycle lanes, implementing urban growth boundaries or policies, or encouraging mixed-use development in more walkable urban centers, among others. UrbanSim falls in the third category of PSS, but attempts also to provide accessible visualization and stakeholder interaction.

This chapter describes UrbanSim and how it addresses some of the challenges and opportunities presented by the current interest in using information technology to enable more effective community visioning and decision making regarding issues related to land use, transportation, and the environment—issues that are inherently controversial and often politically intractable.

UrbanSim is an urban simulation model system that has been evolving continuously since it began as a project in the late 1990s. It was developed by the Center for Urban Simulation and Policy Analysis at the University of Washington, and over the years numerous individuals have contributed to its development. It originated as a project to address what was considered a major oversight in metropolitan planning for transportation: Land use effects of highway and transit projects were being systematically ignored. After legislation such as the Clean Air Act Amendments of 1991 and related transportation legislation clarified that metropolitan transportation planning must be coordinated with land use planning, a mandate to address this need arose. UrbanSim was developed to model the land use patterns in urban areas in a way that would support more coordinated planning of land use, transportation, and the environment—especially as it affected air quality.

The need to promote consistency among land use, transportation, and air quality planning has motivated a substantially different approach to planning than that which characterized these efforts in previous decades. Transportation planning, perhaps through the 1970s, was preoccupied with reducing congestion through capacity increases. The secondary effects of transportation on land use and the resulting induced congestion and consequent increase in emissions from the new expansion of capacity had been well and widely documented (e.g., Downs 1992). But these ideas did not impact the planning practice in most metropolitan areas until the passage of federal legislation mandating that these interactions be considered in transportation planning. In the early 1990s, the Sierra Club and Environmental Defense Fund initiated a lawsuit in the San Francisco Bay Area taking on the metropolitan transportation planning process and sending a wake-up call to metropolitan planning organizations (MPOs) across the nation (Garrett and Wachs 1996). A similar lawsuit in Salt Lake City over a major highway project led to a settlement that included using UrbanSim to address the coordination of land use and transportation (Waddell et al. 2007).

Supporting the coordination of land use, transportation, and environmental planning at various scales remains the primary focus of the UrbanSim project, but the potential to use the model system for evaluating a wide variety of policies affecting urban development and infrastructure has led to a rapid evolution of the system to make it adaptive to rapidly changing environments and needs. It has been a decade since the first version of UrbanSim was released as open source software on the Web in 1998. Since the time it was first released, it has been put into use in a variety of communities in the United States and around the world, with places as divergent as Amsterdam, Brussels, Detroit, Honolulu, Houston, Paris, Rome, Salt Lake City, San Francisco, Seattle, Seoul, Taipei,

Tel Aviv, Turin, and Zurich. With extensive support from the National Science Foundation in addition to funding related to working directly with several of these applications, the UrbanSim system has been able to continue developing the models and supporting software to refine the system and make it more robust and accurate as well as more sensitive to the policies users wish to examine.

Anyone who has been involved in developing software will recognize how difficult it is to implement a system that can be maintained easily and adapted over time to new applications. Considerable effort has gone into the software engineering of UrbanSim to ensure that it is efficiently designed. Professional development and testing techniques and a modular approach were used. The system has, in fact, been reengineered several times over the past decade in order to improve its performance, modularity, flexibility, and transparency to users. The most recent reengineering began in 2005 and led to the development of a new Open Platform for Urban Simulation (OPUS), first released in 2006. This chapter describes key aspects of the software platform and the UrbanSim model system as currently implemented in OPUS.

The next section is an overview of the design of UrbanSim and its software implementation (see Waddell 2000; 2002; and Waddell et al. 2003; 2007). This is followed by a review of some of the applications of UrbanSim and ways the model system has been adapted to deal with differing circumstances. The following section provides an in-depth examination of one case study, the application of UrbanSim in the Detroit metropolitan area by the Southeast Michigan Council of Governments (SEMCOG). The chapter closes with an assessment of the current state of the system and plans for further development.

Design of UrbanSim

UrbanSim was developed in order to respond to a variety of needs for assessing the possible consequences of alternative transportation, land use, and environmental policies in order to better inform deliberation on public choices with long-term, significant effects. The principal motivation was that the urban environment is complex enough that it is not feasible to anticipate the effects of alternative courses of action without some form of analysis that can reflect the cause and effect interactions that could have both intended and possibly unintended consequences.

Consider a highway expansion project, for example. Traditional civil engineering training from the mid-twentieth century suggested that the problem was a relatively simple one: Excess demand meant that vehicles were forced to slow down, leading to congestion bottlenecks. The remedy to ease the bottleneck was added capacity, thus restoring the balance of capacity to demand. Unfortunately, as Downs (1992; 2004) has articulately explained and most of us have directly observed, once capacity is added, it rather quickly gets used up, leading some to conclude that "you can't build your way out of congestion."

The reason things are not as simple as the older engineering perspective would have predicted is that individuals and organizations adapt to changing circumstances. Once the new capacity is available, vehicle speeds do increase initially, but the drop in the time cost of highway travel allows drivers taking other routes to change to this now-faster route, change their commute to work from a less convenient shoulder of the peak time to a mid-peak time, or switch from transit or car pooling to driving alone. These all add demand at the most desired travel time. Over the longer term, developers take advantage of the added capacity to build new housing and commercial and office space, and households and firms take advantage of the accessibility to move farther out, to a place where they can acquire more land and sites are less expensive. In short, the urban transportation system is in a state of dynamic equilibrium, and when you perturb the equilibrium, the system—or more accurately, all the agents in the system—react in ways that tend to restore equilibrium. If faster travel speeds to desired destinations are to be found, people will find them.

The highway-expansion example illustrates a broader theme: Urban systems that include the transportation system, housing market, labor market (commuting), and other real estate markets for land, commercial, industrial, warehouse, and office space are closely interconnected, much like the global financial system. An action taken in one sector ripples through the entire system to varying degrees, depending on how large an intervention it is and what other interventions are occurring at the same time.

A second broad theme is that interventions are rarely coordinated with each other and often are conflicting or have unintended consequences. This pattern is especially true in metropolitan areas consisting of many local cities and possibly multiple counties, each of which retains control of land use policies over a fraction of the metropolitan area, and none of which has a strong incentive, or generally the means, to coordinate their actions. It is more often the case that local jurisdictions are taking actions in strategic ways that will enhance their competitive position for attracting tax base–enhancing development and residents. It is also the case that transportation investments are usually evaluated independently of land use plans and the reactions of the real estate market.

UrbanSim was designed to attempt to reflect the interdependencies in dynamic urban systems, focusing on the real estate market and the transportation system initially, and on the effects of individual interventions and combinations of them on patterns of development, travel demand, and household and firm location (Waddell et al. 2007b). Several sets of goals have shaped the design of UrbanSim and emerged through the past several years through seeing it tested in the real world.

Outcome Goals

- Enable a wide variety of stakeholders (planners, public agencies, citizens, and advocacy groups) to explore the potential consequences of alternative public policies and investments using credible, unbiased analysis.

- Facilitate more effective democratic deliberation on contentious public actions regarding land use, transportation, and the environment, informed by the potential consequences of alternative courses of action that include long-term cumulative effects on the environment, and distributional equity considerations.

■ Make it easier for a community to achieve a common vision for its future and its broader environment and to coordinate their actions to produce outcomes that are consistent with this vision.

Implementation Goals

■ Create an analytical capacity to model the cause and effect interactions within local urban systems that is sufficiently accurate and sensitive to policy interventions to be a credible source for informing deliberations.

■ Make the model system credible by avoiding bias in the models through simplifying assumptions that obscure or omit important cause and effect linkages at a level of detail needed to address stakeholder concerns.

■ Make the model design behaviorally clear in terms of representing agents, actions, and cause and effect interactions in ways that can be understood by nontechnical stakeholders while making the statistical methods used to implement the model scientifically robust.

■ Make the model system open, accessible, and transparent by adopting an open source licensing approach and releasing the code and documentation on the Web.

■ Encourage the development of a collaborative approach to development and extension of the system, both through open source licensing and Web access and by design choices and supporting organizational activities.

■ Test the system extensively and repeatedly, and continually improve it by incorporating lessons learned from applications and from new advances in methods for modeling, statistical analysis, and software development.

The original design of UrbanSim adopted numerous elements to address these implementation goals, and these elements have remained foundational in the development of the system over time. They include:

■ the representation of individual agents—initially households and firms, and later, persons and jobs;

■ the representation of the supply and characteristics of land and of real estate development, at a fine spatial scale—initially a mixture of parcels and zones, later grid cells of user-specified resolution;

■ the adoption of a dynamic perspective of time, with the simulation proceeding in annual steps and the urban system evolving in a path-dependent manner;

■ the use of real estate markets as a central organizing focus, with consumer choices and supplier choices explicitly represented, as well as the resulting effects on real estate prices. The relationship of agents to real estate tied to specific locations provided a clean accounting of space and its use;

■ the use of standard discrete-choice models to represent the choices made by households and firms and developers (principally location choices). This has relied principally on the traditional multinomial logit (MNL) specification, to date;

■ integration of the urban simulation system with existing transportation model systems to obtain information used to compute accessibilities and their influence on location choices and to provide the raw inputs to the travel models; and

■ the adoption of an open source licensing for the software, written originally in Java, and recently reimplemented using the Python language. The system has been updated and released continually on the Web since 1998 at www.urbansim.org.

The model is novel in that it departs from prior operational land use models based on cross-sectional, equilibrium, aggregate approaches to adopt an approach that models individual households, jobs, buildings, and parcels (or grid cells) and their changes from one year to the next as a consequence of economic changes, policy interventions, and market interactions (see Hunt, Miller, and Kriger 2005).

The components of UrbanSim are models acting on the objects in figure 6.1, simulating the real-world actions of agents in the urban system. Developers construct new buildings or redevelop existing ones. Buildings are located on land parcels that have particular characteristics such as value, land use, slope, and other environmental characteristics. Governments set policies that regulate the use of land through the imposition of land use plans, urban growth boundaries, environmental regulations, or pricing policies such as development-impact fees. Governments also build infrastructure, including transportation infrastructure, which interacts with the distribution of activities to generate patterns of accessibility at different locations that, in turn, influence the attractiveness of these sites for different consumers. Households have particular characteristics that may influence their preferences and demands for housing of different types at different locations. Businesses also have preferences that vary by industry and size of business (number of employees) for alternative building types and locations.

These urban actors and processes are implemented in model components that are connected through the software implementation shown in figure 6.2. The diagram reflects the interaction between the land use and travel model systems, and between the land use model and the GIS used for data preparation and visualization.

FIGURE
6.1   **Object Diagram of UrbanSim**

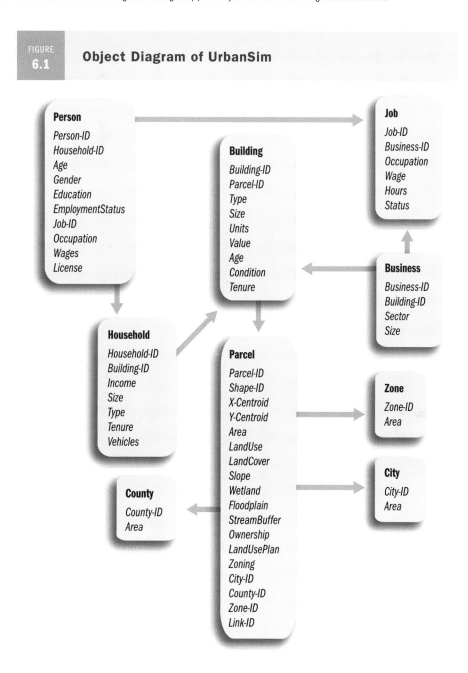

UrbanSim predicts the evolution of these objects and their characteristics over time, using annual steps to predict the movement and location choices of businesses and households, the development activities of developers, and the impacts of governmental policies and infrastructure choices. The land use model is interfaced with a metropolitan travel–model system to deal with the interactions of land use and transportation. Access to opportunities, such as employment or shopping, are measured by the travel time or cost of accessing these opportunities via all available modes of travel.

FIGURE
6.2   **Data Flow in UrbanSim**

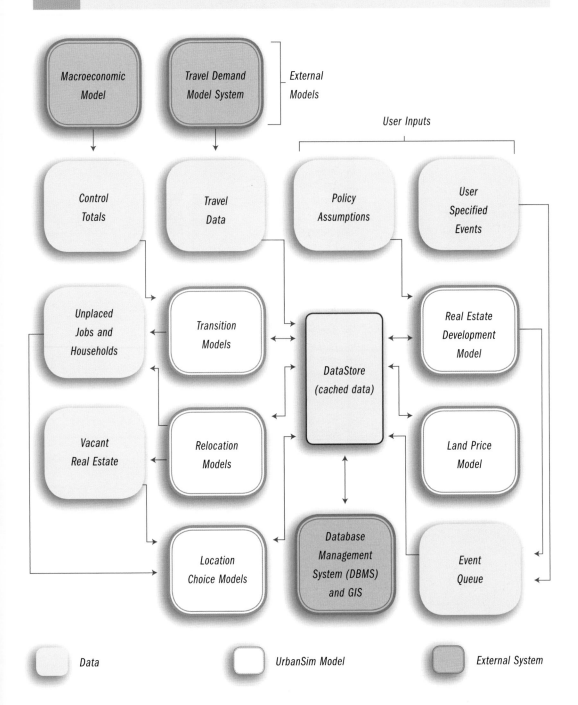

The key factors considered in the household- and business location–demand functions are shown in box 6.1. The influence of these factors on household and business location and building-type choices are estimated through a calibration process, with different parameters estimated for significantly different subgroups of households or businesses. Common elements considered in both include accessibility to population or employment at each location, density of development, and the age of the development. Prices that each subgroup would be willing to pay for each alternative are estimated and form the basis for predicting which consumer type will outbid others for a particular site. The probabilities of

---

BOX 6.1 **Factors Considered in Location Demand Components**

Household Demand for Housing Types and Locations
- *Housing type: Single family, Residential with 2–4 units, or Multifamily*
- *Accessibility to total employment*
- *Accessibility to retail employment*
- *Net density in units per acre of a particular housing type in a zone*
- *Number of housing units of a particular type in the zone*
- *Average age of the buildings of a type in a zone*
- *Percent of households in a zone in the lowest income group*
- *Percent of households in a zone in the second lowest income group*
- *Percent of households in a zone in the highest income group*
- *Percent of households in a zone that have one or more children*
- *Percent of developed land in the zone that is in industrial use*
- *Percent of developed land in a zone that is in residential use*
- *Travel time to the central business district (CBD), in minutes*

Business Demand for Building Types and Locations
- *Building type: Industrial, Warehouse, Retail, Office, or Special Purpose*
- *Accessibility to total population, total employment, and high-income households*
- *Basic employment in a zone per square mile*
- *Retail employment in a zone per square mile*
- *Service employment in a zone per square mile*
- *Accessibility to basic, retail, and service employment*
- *Total square feet of commercial space of a particular type*
- *Building age*
- *Net density of the building type in a zone*
- *Percent of developed land in a zone in industrial use*
- *Percent of developed land in a zone in retail use*
- *Travel time to the CBD, in minutes*
- *Presence of a highway in a zone*

choosing a particular site and of being the highest bidder for it are simulated by a competitive process.

The factors considered in determining development of land parcels are shown in box 6.2. These factors are combined to estimate the profitability of land development on each parcel of land, for all permitted development types. The assumption that drives the development component of the model is that the most profitable sites and uses will have the highest probabilities of development. The model operates at the level of the individual land parcel to provide behavioral realism and the ability to incorporate and test spatially explicit policies. It should be obvious, however, that the specific timing and location of major development projects are patently impossible to predict. The model system attempts to predict tendencies and patterns, but predictions on specific projects at a precise location should be interpreted as a probability and not overinterpreted.

It is recommended generally that results be aggregated to a higher level of geography and that the uncertainty of model results be communicated to avoid potential misinterpretation. Nonetheless the model provides useful information

---

| BOX 6.2 | Factors Considered in Land Development and Redevelopment Component |

Expected Revenue
- *Current market price for type of development at zonal location*
- *Quantity and type of development feasible under development rules*

Expected Costs for New Development
- *Land cost*
- *Hard construction costs (replacement cost of structure)*
- *Soft construction costs (development impact fees, infrastructure costs, taxes, or subsidies)*

Density of Development
- *Regulatory constraints (land use plan, urban growth boundary, environmental constraints)*
- *Land value*
- *Land use*

Filter for Considering Developed Parcels for Redevelopment
- *Improvement to land value ratio of parcel*

Additional Costs for Redevelopment
- *Current building improvements*
- *Demolition costs*

about what types of development patterns are likely to occur as a result of policy interventions. Thus, for example, the quantity of greenfield development, infill, and redevelopment that occurs in different scenarios can be compared as can the distribution of densities and property values in new development.

The model system includes a means of incorporating local knowledge about developments that are in progress, such as a building that has obtained plat approval and permits or a business location decision that has been announced. These kinds of user-specified events can be put into input data to be used by the model as events to introduce at specific locations and times. The model then reacts to these exogenous events. Note that this capability can also be used to examine the consequences of a siting decision, such as a major big-box retail project.

In order to reconcile the demand and supply components of the local real estate markets, the model implements a market-clearing and price-adjustment mechanism. This is similar to the stock-adjustment model (DiPasquale and Wheaton 1996) and is based on the use of structural or normal vacancy rates as market signals that trigger new construction and price adjustments. Movers and new migrants are assigned to the available vacant space in each year on the basis of their consumer surplus for each alternative. New construction decisions then instigate developments for additions to the building stock in the following year. Vacancy rates at the end of the year are used to make adjustments that influence location choices at the beginning of the following year. Over the period of one year, this model sequencing provides a dynamic process that reflects the tendency of real estate development to respond to market signals and strive to achieve equilibrium.

The data inputs and outputs for operating the UrbanSim model are shown in box 6.3. Developing the input database is a difficult challenge owing to its detailed data requirements. A GIS is required to manage and combine these data into a form usable by the model; it can also be used to visualize the model results. Once the database is compiled, the model equations must be calibrated and entered into the model. A final step before actual use of the model is a validation process that tests the operation of the model over time and makes adjustments to the dynamic components of the model. Ideally, this will be done with historical data over a fairly long period of time, such as is now being done in the Eugene-Springfield area for 1980 to 1994.

The policy instruments that can be incorporated into an UrbanSim scenario are summarized in box 6.4. Several land use policy instruments are available in addition to the transportation system assumptions regarding route capacity, level of service, and pricing. These policy instruments include a comprehensive land use plan, minimum and maximum density constraints, and possibly pricing instruments, such as development impact fees and infrastructure costs. Other available instruments include regulatory overlays such as the rules regulating development outside urban growth or urban service boundaries, on environmentally sensitive lands, or within any special planning overlays designated by the user. Several of these rules, including the allowed land use conversions, soft

| BOX 6.3 | Data Inputs and Outputs from UrbanSim |

UrbanSim Inputs

- *Employment data, in the form of geocoded business establishments*
- *Household data merged from multiple census sources*
- *Parcel database with acreage, land use, housing units, nonresidential square footage, year built, land value, improvement value, city, and county*
- *Land use plan*
- *GIS overlays for environmental features such as wetlands, floodways, steep slopes, or other sensitive or regulated lands*
- *Traffic analysis zones*
- *GIS overlays for any other planning boundaries*
- *Travel model outputs*
- *Development costs*

UrbanSim Outputs (by traffic analysis zone)

- *Households by income, age, size, and presence of children*
- *Businesses and employment by industry*
- *Acreage by land use*
- *Dwelling units by type*
- *Square feet of nonresidential space by type*
- *Land values per acre by land use*
- *Improvement values per unit or square feet by land use*

Travel Model Outputs (zone-to-zone)

- *Travel time by mode*
- *Composite utility of travel using all modes*

development costs, and density constraints, can be varied between counties, cities, and specific overlays. That is, different regulatory and pricing policies can be applied to each county, city, and overlay area if needed. This offers a high degree of flexibility in reflecting the character of local land policies.

The decision to develop the OPUS platform grew out of interactions with research groups developing transportation and land use models in North America, Europe, and Asia, all of which needed to develop their own software applications and found that they were spending far too much time on developing and debugging software and far too little on developing models, applications, and new research. Following a meeting in Toronto in January 2005, an initiative emerged to develop an open platform that could be shared among researchers and practitioners for land use and transportation–model

BOX 6.4	**Policy Instruments Incorporated in UrbanSim Scenarios**

Transportation (from travel model)
- *Transportation capacity: highway, arterial, bus, rail, and HOV*
- *Transit level of service*
- *Pricing: tolls, gasoline tax, etc.*

Land Use
- *Land use plan: restrictions on conversion of land to alternative urban land uses*
- *Density constraints: minimum as well as maximum density by land use*
- *Soft construction costs: development impact fees, infrastructure costs, taxes, or subsidies*

Policy Overlays (can affect land uses allowed, density, soft development costs)
- *Urban growth boundary*
- *Environmental restrictions*
- *Other policy overlays (special planning areas designated for exceptional policies)*

development, thus allowing people to more easily leverage the work of others and to make their own investments more effective. The OPUS architecture is intended to facilitate collaborative development and contributions of packages by a community of users and developers.

The University of Washington team has led the development of OPUS and has ported UrbanSim to it. This effort was completed in 2006, though some work remains to refine documentation and to create a graphical user interface (GUI). Current efforts are focused on developing an interface to GIS for data manipulation and visualization and on developing a GUI for the model system. These should improve the ease of use of the model system considerably. An international working group has been established to further develop and refine OPUS and to begin to provide a stable, shared laboratory for collaboration and for rapid development, testing, and comparison of alternative algorithms and models.

The OPUS architecture is three-tiered, with the Opus Core forming the foundation, a set of OPUS packages extending this, and a set of external libraries that provide access to functionality in external systems and languages. OPUS packages are all implanted in Python, but external libraries may be in C, C++, or FORTRAN. Interfaces to a range of databases and flat files are available, including MySQL, MS SQL Server, Postgres, SQLite, DBF, CSV, and tab-delimited ASCII files. Geoprocessing and visualization is being integrated with ArcGIS™, and the open source PostGIS and Quantum GIS (QGIS) applications.

Applications of UrbanSim

UrbanSim has been developed with a combination of federal, state, and local support and has been applied in a variety of contexts to date. This section briefly reviews some of these applications, principally to highlight the adaptations that have been involved in making a model system such as this relevant and useful in widely varying contexts.

Honolulu, Hawaii

The initial design of the UrbanSim model was funded by the Oahu Metropolitan Planning Organization as part of a larger effort to undertake the development of new travel models. Oahu presents a highly unusual location for development of land use and transportation models for several reasons. First, it more closely approximates a closed system than any metropolitan area on the mainland United States, thus eliminating some of the boundary conditions that plague analysis of many mainland metropolitan areas. Second, the use of land is highly constrained by water, mountains, and policy. Approximately 4 percent of the land area is designated for urban uses, with the vast majority of land on the island assigned to agricultural and watershed preservation areas. Development is highly regulated and the city and county are consolidated, eliminating the jurisdictional fragmentation that characterizes most mainland metropolitan regions. These factors, coupled with high density, extremely high housing prices, and high transit ridership required developing a model design that would reflect the interactions of the real estate market, the natural physical environment, and local development policies. These considerations heavily influenced the initial implementation planning for the model system. The model has been calibrated and integrated with the transportation model system used in Honolulu. This application, like the majority of the later applications, used grid cells of 150 by 150–meter resolution as the basic unit of analysis.

Eugene-Springfield, Oregon

In 1996, the Oregon Department of Transportation (ODOT) launched an ambitious project to support growth management policies within the state. The Transportation and Land Use Model Integration Project (TLUMIP) sought to develop analytical tools to support both statewide and metropolitan-scale land use and transportation planning. The key policy concerns motivating the Oregon project relate to the effects of different growth management policies on a series of outcomes of interest and the interaction between land use and transportation initiatives. For example, what effect would an overly restrictive urban growth boundary in Portland have on the potential relocation of businesses and households into other metropolitan areas in the Willamette Valley, such as Salem? If this effect were substantial, it might seriously undermine the original objectives of growth management, promoting long-distance commuting on an already congested Interstate 5. Other questions concern the effects of the urban growth boundary on housing densities and housing costs. Critics of the urban growth boundary complain about its effects on housing prices, but there is little compelling evidence in either direction on these questions.

The prototype metropolitan land use model was based on the UrbanSim design developed in Honolulu, which was extended and fully implemented as an operational prototype software system within TLUMIP. The model was calibrated for a case study in Eugene-Springfield using principally cross-sectional data. The model was calibrated and validated to examine its dynamic behavior over the period from 1980 to 1994 during which it was initially completed, and later this calibration approach was made significantly more sophisticated by using advanced statistical methods to calibrate the model from 1980 to 2000 (Ševčíková, Raftery, and Waddell 2007).

Seattle, Washington

Washington is also a growth management state, though with perhaps less stringent application than in Oregon. Much of the control for implementing the Growth Management Act remains in the control of local governments, and there has been relatively little evaluation of compliance to date. The Puget Sound Regional Council (PSRC), the MPO for the Seattle-Tacoma-Everett metropolitan area, develops a regional vision—the current plan under review is Vision 2040—and oversees the coordination of local land use plans with the Growth Management Act. The PSRC has invested in the development and application of UrbanSim in the region, and has participated as a partner in the evolution of the model system to address needs in the region.

The most recent innovations of the model system for application in the Seattle area include a new approach to modeling real estate development, which reconciles developer and land owner perspectives and adopts the use of development templates that describe projects in terms of their spatial scale, land use composition (including mixed use), density, and cost. Individual parcels are evaluated and the projected return on investment is compared among those development projects that would be feasible according to local land use policies. This project is at the stage of undergoing extensive testing in preparation for operational use.

Houston, Texas

UrbanSim has been adopted by the Houston-Galveston Area Council, the metropolitan planning organization for the Houston-Galveston area, as its land use model system to support regional planning. The agency was creative in overcoming inconsistencies in its data availability and integrated a variety of data sources to create a usable database. Due to the size of the region, the model was run separately by county and has been used in operational planning for support of the regional transportation planning process. A grid of 1,000 by 1,000 feet was adopted for the geographic basis of the model.

Salt Lake City, Utah

In Utah, the Governor's Office of Planning and Budget coordinated a technical process in close cooperation with a community visioning process titled Envision Utah. The Envision Utah process engaged community leaders from the public and private sectors to assess alternative visions of how the community might wish to evolve over the next several decades in the face of unrelenting population growth that threatens the region's environmental amenities and quality of life. Peter Calthorpe and John Fregonese were engaged to lead this public visioning process and have raised community awareness of more transit-oriented, dense, and walkable urban neighborhoods as an alternative to continued sprawl.

Utah provides a fascinating political testing ground for the growth management debate. Environmental groups are very active and concerned about the potential damage from both continued sprawl and large-scale infrastructure such as the Legacy Highway, proposed to be built through some of the region's prime wetlands. The highway project led to a lawsuit by the Sierra Club and Utahans for Better Transportation, and an eventual settlement of the lawsuit included a component requiring the Wasatch Front Regional Council to test UrbanSim in coordination with its transportation models and, if the testing was successful, to bring the model into its operational planning process for regional transportation planning. The testing was done over approximately one year, and eventually did lead to the adoption of the model for operational planning purposes (Waddell et al. 2007).

Paris, France

The regional planning agency for the Paris metropolitan region, IAURIF, in coordination with the University of Cergy-Pontoise, developed a project to apply UrbanSim to the Paris region. It is the largest application of the model system to date, with 11 million inhabitants in the region. The model required several adaptations to address the available data and other aspects that were remarkably different from the previous applications in U.S. cities. Among the obvious, notable differences was the prominence of the historic city of Paris, with a ubiquitous metro system and extremely walkable environment. The transit ridership and extremely low auto ownership rates stand in stark contrast with most newer cities in North America. The suburban development around Paris is much more auto-oriented, and growth in auto travel is increasing at a much faster rate than transit, according to recent travel surveys.

Due to limited data on land and buildings, the model system was developed using *communes* (approximately municipalities) outside of Paris and *arrondisements* within Paris. The resulting 1,300 zones provided the geographic basis for the model. IAURIF later developed additional data and implemented the model system using a grid of 500 by 500 meters. One of the research programs developed as part of this project focused on an analytical method for estimating the model parameters by separating the effects of housing-supply constraints from household preferences (de Palma, Picard, and Waddell 2007).

San Francisco, California

The San Francisco County Transportation Authority (SFCTA), in coordination with the City and County of San Francisco Planning Department, has adopted UrbanSim as the land use model for undertaking a variety of planning applications, ranging from interacting with the activity-based travel model developed by SFCTA, to redevelopment planning in the core of San Francisco. This application has been in progress approximately one year, and the model system has been calibrated and is undergoing final testing before operational use. The San Francisco model uses individual parcels, buildings, and business establishments (Waddell, Wang, and Charlton 2008).

Numerous other applications of UrbanSim are at varying stages of development. In the next section, we use the Southeast Michigan Council of Governments (SEMCOG) application of UrbanSim as a case study in the application of the model system, with extensive visual documentation of the process.

Case Study: The SEMCOG Application of UrbanSim

SEMCOG is the designated MPO in southeast Michigan. Established in 1968 as a regional planning partnership, SEMCOG provides planning services for the overlapping jurisdictions in the southeast Michigan region that encompasses Livingston, Macomb, Monroe, Oakland, St. Clair, Washtenaw, and Wayne counties. SEMCOG supports local government planning in the areas of transportation, environment, community and economic development, and education. SEMCOG is the primary resource for data about southeast Michigan, gathering and analyzing information for public and private sector decision making on the region's economy and quality of life.

Scope of the Project

The planning area of SEMCOG is a very large, diverse, and complex region centered on the City of Detroit. The region currently has a population of almost 4.9 million and supports approximately 2.7 million jobs. Its economic origins date to the birth of the automobile era, and it has seen significant decline in its industrial base over a prolonged period. The central city and some older suburbs of the region contain significant concentrations of poverty and a predominantly minority population. The population and economy of Detroit have been declining for many years, especially in the manufacturing sector. At the same time, many of the suburban communities in the region have been growing rapidly. Despite the declining economy and population of Detroit, in recent years there has been a significant increase in residential and commercial redevelopment in its downtown core. The complex dynamics of decline and revitalization and the problems associated with extensive patterns of segregation by race and income present a challenging context for planning and for forecasting changes in land use to support these planning activities.

Over its 40-year history, SEMCOG has produced an update of the regional development forecast (RDF) approximately every five years. The forecast provides a long-range and comprehensive view of future demographic, socioeconomic, and land use changes. It provides base data for updating the regional transportation plan and for other regional planning activities of the agency. Member communities use the data in planning for infrastructure and other needs. After SEMCOG completed its 2030 forecast in 2001, it began searching for a next generation model that could not only forecast population, households, and jobs by small area with reasonable accuracy, but also would have capacity to analyze the dynamics of real estate development and the impacts of alternative land use and transportation policies in this complex region.

After examining the available decision support systems to address its needs, SEMCOG adopted UrbanSim as its analytical tool to produce long-range forecasts and support its varied planning efforts in the region. Key aspects of UrbanSim that led to this choice were the behavioral realism of the model, its adaptability, and a substantial and growing community of users. Over the past several years of using the system at SEMCOG, it has been extended in several ways to address the needs of the region, such as handling declining areas, infill and redevelopment, and the use of user-provided information about major events such as business closures or major development projects.

The following sections provide a more in-depth examination of the application of UrbanSim by SEMCOG, supported by graphics demonstrating the application of the model in two pilot applications and now in a regional-scale effort that is in its early stages.

Pilot Projects

WASHTENAW COUNTY   SEMCOG initially implemented UrbanSim in a pilot study in Washtenaw County, containing the City of Ann Arbor and the University of Michigan. Considerable data were available from the county, and interesting land use planning policies were in place for both the city and the county. SEMCOG staff, coordinated by Xuan Liu, led the development of the database and model application. Paul Waddell provided technical support and advice throughout the process.

Figures 6.3 and 6.4 show the geographies used in the Washtenaw County pilot project. These include minor civil divisions, cities, parcels, and 150 by 150–meter grid cells. Data were compiled from parcel-level assessor files, census data, and ES202 state unemployment insurance records for employment data. Additional information on local land use plans and environmental features were integrated as well. Figure 6.5 shows the spatial distribution of housing units in 2000. Nonresidential square feet, obtained from the parcel data and converted to grid cells, is shown in figure 6.6. Figure 6.7 shows how these quantities of housing units and nonresidential square feet were subsequently converted to development types, and the resulting land values per grid cell are shown in figure 6.8. Finally, figure 6.9 shows the housing age distribution

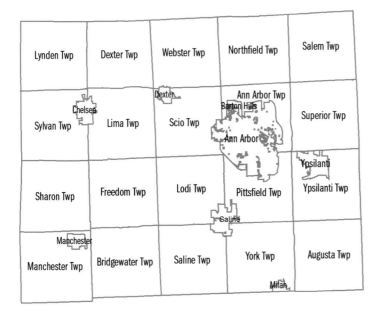

FIGURE 6.3

Geographic Units in Washtenaw County
Source: SEMCOG

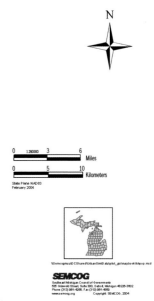

FIGURE 6.4

Grid Cells, Central Ann Arbor, Washtenaw County
Source: SEMCOG

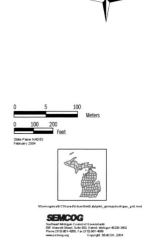

FIGURE 6.5

Housing Units per Grid Cell, Washtenaw County
Source: SEMCOG

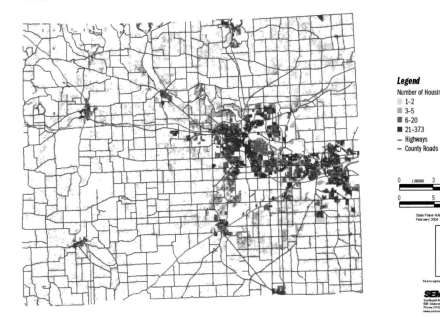

Legend

Number of Housing Units

- 1-2
- 3-5
- 6-20
- 21-373
— Highways
— County Roads

State Plane NAD83
February 2004

FIGURE 6.6

Square Feet per Grid Cell, Washtenaw County
Source: SEMCOG

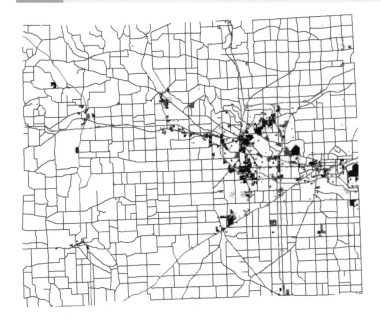

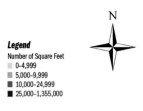

Legend

Number of Square Feet

- 0-4,999
- 5,000-9,999
- 10,000-24,999
- 25,000-1,355,000

— Highways
— County Roads

State Plane NAD83
February 2004

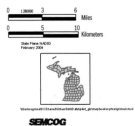

FIGURE
6.7

Development Types per Grid Cell, Washtenaw County
Source: SEMCOG

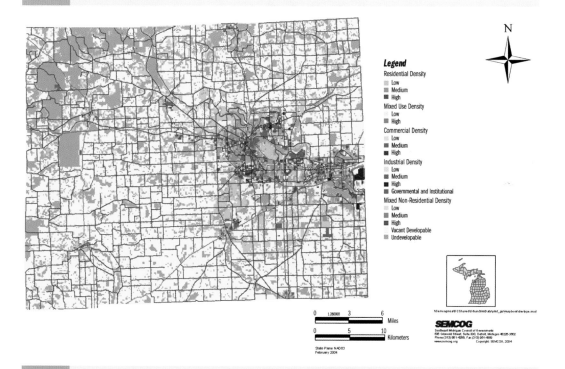

Legend

Residential Density
- Low
- Medium
- High

Mixed Use Density
- Low
- High

Commercial Density
- Low
- Medium
- High

Industrial Density
- Low
- Medium
- High
- Governmental and Institutional

Mixed Non-Residential Density
- Low
- Medium
- High
- Vacant Developable
- Undevelopable

N

0   1,280000   3   6
        Miles
0   5   10
        Kilometers

State Plane NAD83
February 2004

SEMCOG
Southeast Michigan Council of Governments
535 Griswold Street, Suite 300, Detroit, Michigan 48226-3602
Phone (313) 961-4266, Fax (313) 961-4869
www.semcog.org   Copyright SEMCOG, 2004

FIGURE
6.8

Land Value per Grid Cell, Washtenaw County
Source: SEMCOG

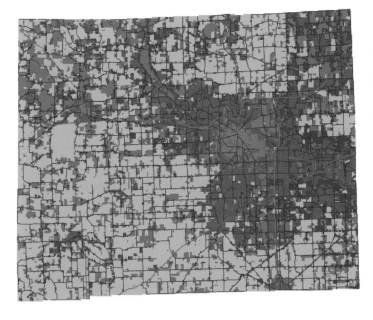

Legend

Land Value
- 0–19,999
- 20,000–49,999
- 50,000–99,999
- 100,000–999,999
- 1,000,000–19,342,808

— Highways
— County Roads

N

0   1,280000   3   6
        Miles
0   5   10
        Kilometers

State Plane NAD83
February 2004

SEMCOG
Southeast Michigan Council of Governments
535 Griswold Street, Suite 300, Detroit, Michigan 48226-3602
Phone (313) 961-4266, Fax (313) 961-4869
www.semcog.org   Copyright SEMCOG, 2004

Year Built of Housing, Washtenaw County
Source: SEMCOG

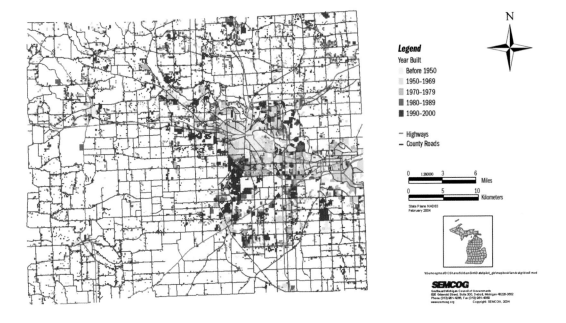

Distribution of Most Common Nonwhite Race, Washtenaw County
Source: SEMCOG

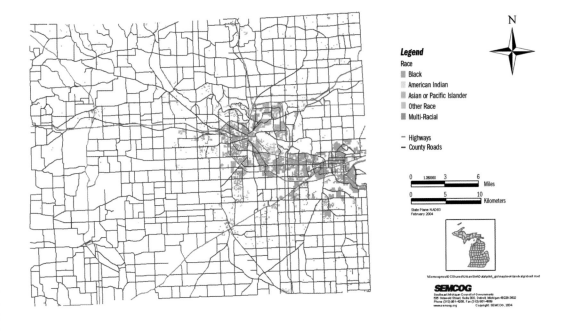

and figure 6.10 displays the concentration of ethnic groups within neighborhoods in Washtenaw County.

Once the data were compiled and models estimated, SEMCOG developed a baseline scenario that included the most likely transportation and land policy assumptions. An alternative scenario was constructed to evaluate the possible effects of a greenbelt policy. Figure 6.11 outlines the greenbelt region and figure 6.12 details selected areas. Parcels were selected for greenbelt designation based on such criteria as proximity to Ann Arbor (figure 6.13) and to recreational areas (figure 6.14). The resulting differences in residential land development between these two scenarios are shown in figures 6.15 (no greenbelt) and 6.16 (greenbelt).

Land policy analysis also included modeling the impact of a county master plan that calls for high density and mixed uses in areas adjacent to developed places and other transportation hubs. UrbanSim results show significant savings of additional land to be developed over 30 years if such a plan can be implemented.

FIGURE 6.11

Greenbelt Region, Washtenaw County
Source: SEMCOG

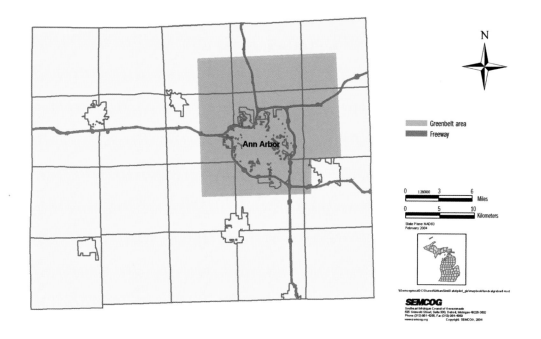

FIGURE
6.12
Selected Greenbelt Parcels, Washtenaw County
Source: SEMCOG

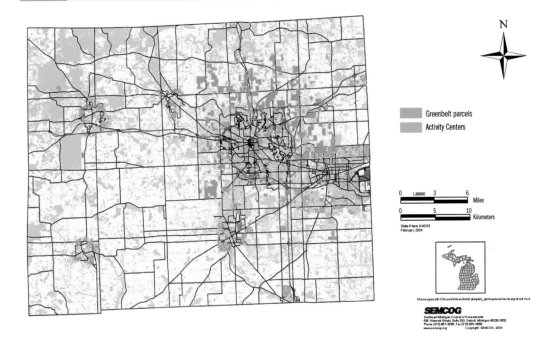

FIGURE
6.13
Proximity of Greenbelt Parcels to Ann Arbor
Source: SEMCOG

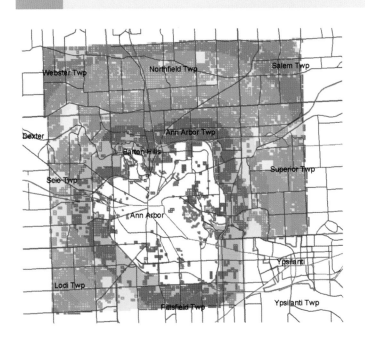
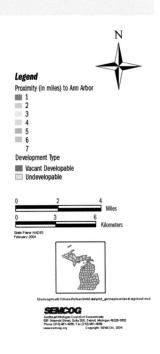

FIGURE
6.14
Proximity of Greenbelt Parcels to Recreational Areas
Source: SEMCOG

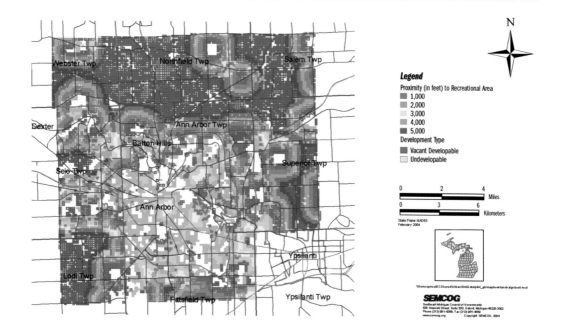

FIGURE
6.15
Residential Land Development Without Greenbelt
Source: SEMCOG

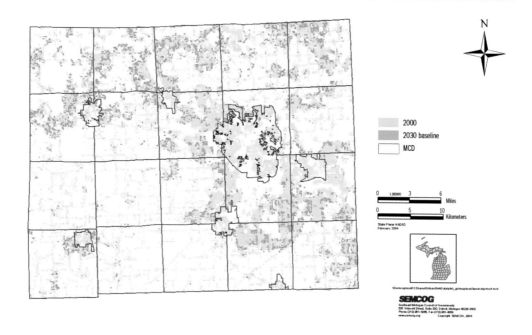

Residential Land Development with Greenbelt
Source: SEMCOG

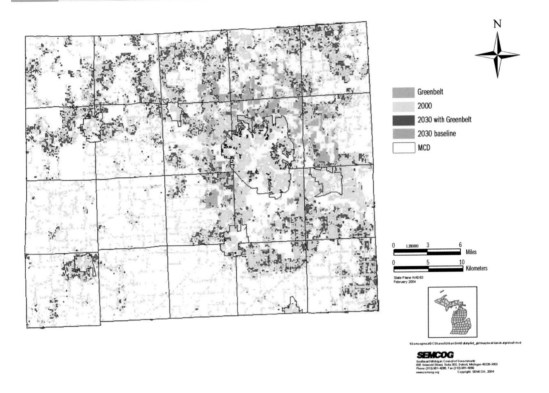

ST. CLAIR COUNTY   Following the Washtenaw County pilot study, SEMCOG undertook a second pilot study to apply UrbanSim in St. Clair County, which is more rural in character. This project was developed to assist in the countywide planning process by providing views of future land development patterns. The base year for this model was 2000. Post-2000 building permits were geocoded to parcels and converted to grid cells. They were used as development events to guide allocation of new households over the first simulation years. As part of the validation process, figures 6.17 and 6.18 were compared, and they showed a close match of the simulation results from UrbanSim to the changes reflected in the census and SEMCOG estimation from 2000 to 2005.

The St. Clair County pilot study also explored modeling development capacities and "refill development" (redevelopment and infill development). It was discovered that initial model runs overdeveloped the built areas by adding housing units and nonresidential square feet to some unrealistically high densities allowed in master plans. SEMCOG studied refill development potentials by comparing land value and improvement value by grid cell. By limiting refill development potential to areas where improvement value is less than land value, UrbanSim produced a more realistic land use forecast based on past trends and current policies in this rural county.

**New Households from Census and SEMCOG Data,
St. Clair County, 2000–2005**
Source: SEMCOG

FIGURE
6.17

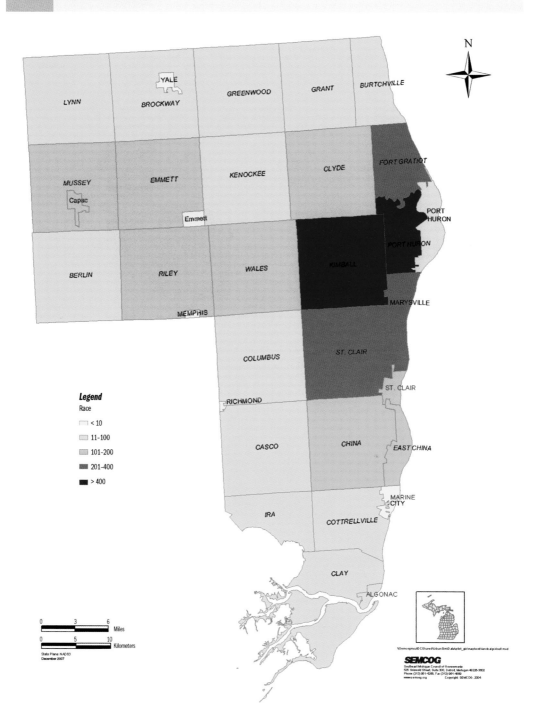

FIGURE
6.18
New Households, UrbanSim Simulation, St. Clair County, 2000–2005
Source: SEMCOG

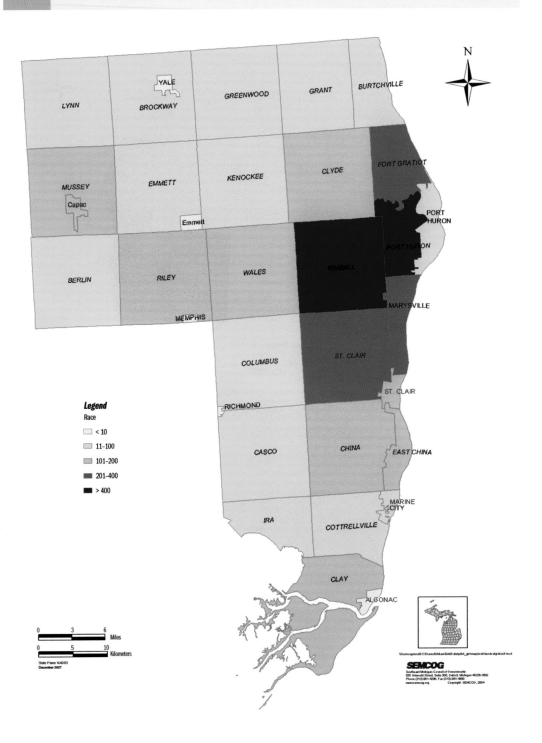

Legend

Race

⬜ < 10
⬜ 11–100
⬜ 101–200
⬛ 201–400
⬛ > 400

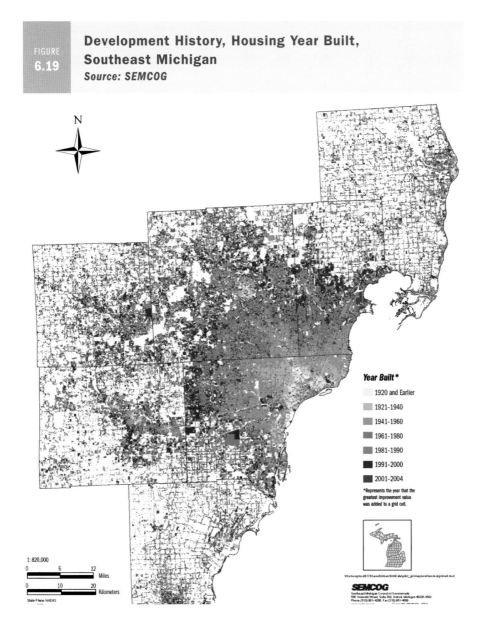

FIGURE 6.19

Development History, Housing Year Built, Southeast Michigan
Source: SEMCOG

Year Built*
- 1920 and Earlier
- 1921-1940
- 1941-1960
- 1961-1980
- 1981-1990
- 1991-2000
- 2001-2004

*Represents the year that the greatest improvement value was added to a grid cell.

Regional Short-term Forecast

SEMCOG is now embarking on a regional application, as shown in figure 6.19. This process will produce a 2035 forecast of population, households, employment, and land use. It includes extensive meetings with local planning officials in the region to incorporate local input on land use plans and development events and local review of the model results. This is an ongoing effort, scheduled for completion in 2008.

Southeast Michigan is undergoing some fundamental transformations. The dynamics of its economic and demographic changes are very complex. As the domestic automobile industry continues to decline, the region has been losing jobs since 2000. Its economy is expected to stabilize in the next few years, led by increases in health care and service industries. On the other hand, out-migration accelerated a few years after jobs started declining. Residential construction activities have slowed down dramatically. Despite these very complex circumstances, SEMCOG has been able to use UrbanSim effectively to simulate the real estate market and assist in communities searching for solutions.

Figure 6.20 shows the land development patterns predicted by UrbanSim in Wayne County, the largest county in the region. It indicates that the additional land developed in the second five years of the decade is only about a quarter of the land developed in the previous five years, which is consistent with the dynamic lag observed in the slowdown of population growth.

Figures 6.21 through 6.24 show employment and household changes by community. Figures 6.21 and 6.22 show employment change during the 2000 to 2010 period by five-year increments. Figures 6.23 and 6.24 display household change. Many communities that lost jobs significantly in the first five years of the decade have large amounts of vacant commercial and industrial spaces. This situation becomes an advantage in attracting jobs when the overall economy improves in the second five years. However, more communities are losing more or gaining fewer households in the second five years, reflecting the lag between population and household decline and the economic downturn.

| FIGURE 6.20 | Land Development, UrbanSim Simulation, Wayne County, 2000–2010 |

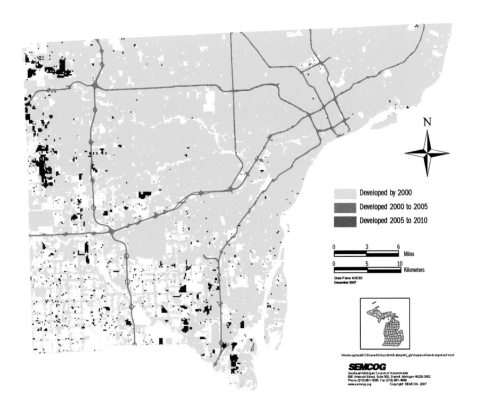

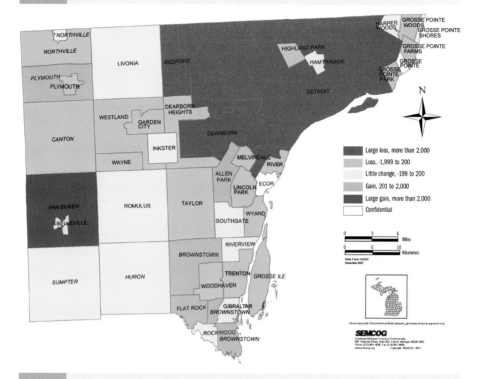

FIGURE 6.21 Employment Change, UrbanSim Simulation, Wayne County, 2000–2005

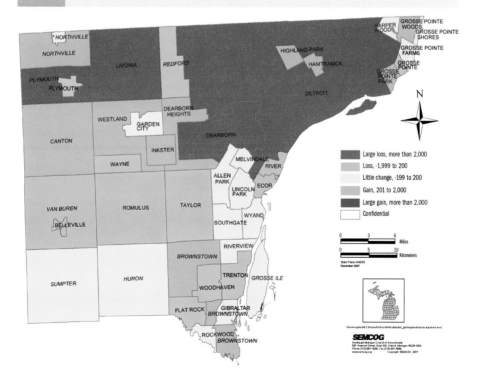

FIGURE 6.22 Employment Change, UrbanSim Simulation, Wayne County, 2005–2010

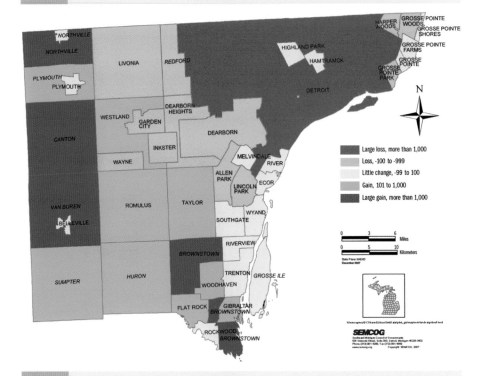

FIGURE 6.23 Household Change, UrbanSim Simulation, Wayne County, 2000–2005

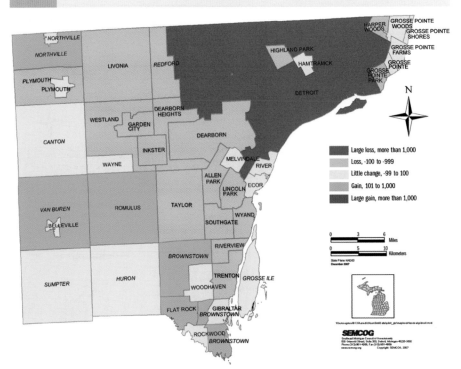

FIGURE 6.24 Household Change, UrbanSim Simulation, Wayne County, 2005–2010

Although southeast Michigan operates as an economic region, each county is substantially different. To reflect this phenomenon, the UrbanSim model has been run with subregional (i.e., county) control totals. Regional accessibility, such as travel time and other generalized travel costs, use data for the entire region. But location choices by households and businesses are constrained to match the county control totals within each county. Vacancy rates for housing and nonresidential buildings also vary from place to place. SEMCOG's experience indicates such improvements as subregional controls and vacancy rates make the analysis more accurate than running one regional model.

The SEMCOG model also has the capability to include user-specified events to add or delete specific businesses as well as housing units and nonresidential buildings. Typically, a model such as UrbanSim is designed to analyze overall trends and forecast general development patterns. It is not designed to predict large-scale individual events such as the closure of a major business. However, there are major events such as a proposed large subdivision or a planned closure of a plant that are anticipated by planners. Being able to incorporate such events into the model makes the analysis and forecasting more accurate using data collected by continuous development monitoring and by meetings with local officials and planners.

Community Meetings

SEMCOG is accountable to local governments who join as members. Local elected officials, ensuring that regional policies reflect the interests of member communities, make all SEMCOG policy decisions. Although SEMCOG is still in the early stages of applying the UrbanSim model to the region, it has held a meeting with elected officials, planners, and the public in each one of its seven counties. The idea is to have communities involved in the process as early as possible. At these meetings, SEMCOG staff first presented the big picture of the region and its overall 30-year forecast generated using UrbanSim. Then community-level analysis and short-term forecasts are presented. Meeting attendees have the opportunity to discuss the analysis and its results as well as to provide more information to SEMCOG based on their local knowledge.

A more important part of the discussion at these meetings is the exploration of solutions to solve the problems revealed by the analysis. Topics discussed at the meetings include the following.

- Can communities take advantage of the slowdown in growth to better plan and protect their quality of life?

- How can older developments be revitalized in a slow-growth environment?

- Are the economic development strategies up to the challenge of a restructured economy?

- What can be done to respond to the continued loss of manufacturing jobs?

- Are communities prepared for the increasing service needs of the elderly population?

- How consistent are county plans or other strategic initiatives with the new economic and demographic realities?

- Can form-based planning, zoning, and urban design help create the environment that attracts young people and serves the increasing elderly at the same time?

Refining the SEMCOG UrbanSim Application

SEMCOG is receiving additional comments and input from local communities. In addition to incorporating such additional information into the model, SEMCOG is considering ways to improve the analysis in the following areas.

INTERACTION WITH TRAVEL MODEL   SEMCOG has worked with UrbanSim and TransCAD model developers to develop an automated link between its land use model and travel demand–forecast model. This utility controls the sequence of running UrbanSim annually and TransCAD every five years as well as the flow of data between the two models. This link is essential to model impacts of land use on transportation and vice versa. SEMCOG is planning to run the two models interactively in producing the next forecast as well as analyzing alternative transportation and land use policies.

REDEVELOPMENT AND INFILL DEVELOPMENT   Many redevelopment and infill development possibilities exist in southeast Michigan. The current model specification of UrbanSim in the SEMCOG model is perhaps more suitable for modeling greenfield development than redevelopment and infill. SEMCOG will continue to explore methods of analyzing redevelopment and infill development. Besides comparing land values and improvement values, analysis on prevailing rent and necessary subsidies in stressed areas could expend the model's capabilities to assess urban policies. In addition, a new version of the UrbanSim real estate development model that addresses directly the problems of infill and redevelopment is currently being tested in the Puget Sound region and could be used by SEMCOG in the future.

MORE LOCALIZED VACANCY RATES   Presently, residential and nonresidential vacancy rates vary only at the large-area level, such as county, in the current version of UrbanSim. However, vacancy rates vary significantly from community to community in a complex region such as southeast Michigan. In addition, many communities in the region, especially communities near the Great Lakes or rivers, have a high percentage of vacation homes. It is important to represent accurately the supply of housing and nonresidential spaces in the model. This refinement is scheduled for short-term model improvement.

CLUSTERING DEVELOPMENT   As shown in the Wayne County developed-land map (figure 6.20), the current UrbanSim model specification tends to predict a scattered development pattern. A more desirable implementation should predict a range of development projects including larger clusters of residential development such as subdivisions or large apartment complexes.

The new version of the real estate development model under testing in the Puget Sound region uses development templates that explicitly simulate a variety of types of development such as different densities of single-family subdivisions, multi-family complexes, and other types, which directly addresses this clustering pattern.

Summary

SEMCOG has been able to internalize the development and maintenance of the data and model estimation process, and this implementation has required additional adaptations. These include tailoring the specification to appropriately reflect the mix of greenfield development and redevelopment, and the need to include user-specified events for addition or loss of real estate and economic activity. Other changes include the use of subregional vacancy rate targets and control totals for population and employment.

SEMCOG also developed its own data preparation utilities, such as a tool to synthesize household data from the census. The application of the UrbanSim model at SEMCOG has helped the region in its planning work. The experiences of SEMCOG in applying UrbanSim may not be directly transferable to other places, but do indicate the degree to which the model system can be adapted to conditions that vary from one region to another, and even within a region.

Status, Limitations, and Plans for Further Development

The objectives laid out here are ambitious. The echoes of Lee's "Requiem for Large-Scale Models" (Lee 1973; 1994) still resonate today, providing a still-relevant caution against unguarded optimism for the potential for such models. Much more remains to be done. Recent research has focused on improving the capacity to estimate flexible models with interdependent, nonnested choice dimensions such as residence and workplace (Waddell et al. 2007). Work is nearing completion on a major new release of OPUS and UrbanSim that will include a GUI, integration with GIS, and more user-friendly documentation and tutorials. New projects are under way to develop integrated activity-based travel models that are more realistic than current four-step models, and to add more environmental impact model components to deal with greenhouse gas emissions, land cover change, biodiversity, and consumption of water and energy. In order to improve the feasibility of model development by new model users, we are creating project templates and tools to facilitate data development and integration. Finally, efforts to enable collaborating users and developers to augment and extend the system are under way through an international working group initiated in 2007.

Acknowledgments

This research has been funded in part by National Science Foundation grants EIA-0121326 and IIS-0534094, by EPA grant R831837, and by previous support from the Federal Highway Administration, the Puget Sound Regional Council, the Southeast Michigan Council of Governments, Maricopa Association of Governments, and Pima Association of Governments. OPUS and UrbanSim have been developed by the Center for Urban Simulation and Policy Analysis at the University of Washington.

Clicking Toward Better Outcomes

Experience with INDEX, 1994 to 2006

Eliot Allen, AICP

Origins and Goals of the Tool

INDEX IS A STATIC, RULE-BASED GEOGRAPHIC INFORMATION SYSTEM (GIS) TOOL with a menu of indicators that can be applied to user-created scenarios to gauge achievement of user-defined goals. The tool was introduced in 1994 to support land use and transportation practitioners who work in local and regional agencies on plans and development reviews. This chapter is an account of a small consultancy's experience developing and applying the tool during the ensuing 13 years.

INDEX was conceived as a business decision with two motivations: (1) greater productivity for the consultancy's community planning practice; and (2) a perceived market opportunity among local and regional planning agencies interested in innovation by using planning support systems (PSS). In contrast to more elaborate, dynamic forecasting tools such as UrbanSim, INDEX was designed to be a simple scenario generator and scoring device for agencies making decisions with limited time and technical resources. The target audience was moderate-sized jurisdictions of roughly 50,000 to 500,000 persons, as opposed to larger jurisdictions with abundant in-house resources or smaller jurisdictions where no resources usually exist for PSS. The tool was also purposely aimed at current planning work as opposed to advanced or long-range activities, since a large majority of such agencies' work deals with processing current development projects.

Why INDEX?

The following conditions and perceptions were important contributors to the tool's focus:

LARGE NUMBERS OF SMALL DECISIONS BEING POORLY MADE   Roughly 40,000 agencies in the United States are charged with land use and transportation responsibilities (figure 7.1). Once or twice a month, year in and year out, these entities render tens of thousands of incremental decisions that profoundly affect built and natural environments for decades. These actions include plan amendments, zone changes, subdivision plattings, and a wide variety of site permitting. The enormous volume and limited consideration these actions receive results in decisions that are often environmentally and economically adverse. There is ample evidence of the detrimental consequences of poorly considered land use and transportation actions (U.S. Environmental Protection Agency 2001), and targeting this large class of actions offered major promise for a PSS tool.

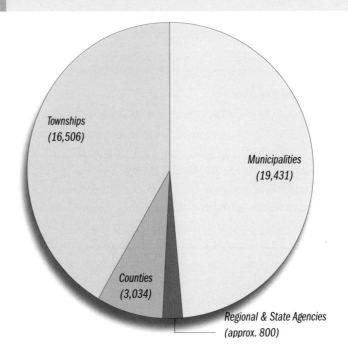

FIGURE 7.1

Organizations with Land Use and Transportation Responsibilities in the United States, 2007
Source: U.S. Census

Townships
(16,506)

Municipalities
(19,431)

Counties
(3,034)

Regional & State Agencies
(approx. 800)

UNTAPPED GIS POTENTIAL FOR PSS APPLICATIONS   After permit-tracking software, the most common PSS in most local planning agencies is GIS. Most local GIS were (and still are) significantly underutilized in community decision making. GIS are often treated simply as libraries of cartography instead of engines for community design and evaluation. Some have argued that GIS data are often so backward looking that they present a distraction and are off message for planning the future (Myers 2007). In 1994 the forward-looking power of GIS was going largely unused and INDEX was seen as a way to tap into this power.

INTRODUCTION OF DESKTOP GIS   The introduction in the early 1990s of portable GIS such as ESRI's ArcView® and Caliper's Maptitude created unique opportunities for portability and interaction with citizens in their neighborhoods. For the first time, PSS tools could travel by laptop to venues in stakeholders' literal backyards, significantly improving access to, and the convenience of, participation in community planning.

The Goals for INDEX

With these circumstances in mind, the following goals were set for INDEX at the outset of its development and deployment:

MORE OBJECTIVITY IN DECISION MAKING   The tool's primary function was to score scenarios with indicators. The intent was to apply a goal-relevant set of quantitative indicators to planning and implementation actions over time in a jurisdiction and thereby instill greater rationality, consistency, and accountability in its decisions.

GREATER INTEGRATION OF LAND USE, TRANSPORTATION, AND ENVIRONMENTAL ISSUES   The tool was purposely designed to describe scenarios in both land use and transportation terms and to evaluate them with an interdisciplinary set of indicators that could reveal the connectedness of community elements. With INDEX, users would immediately see the travel behavior and greenhouse gas effects of land use changes, for example.

SUPPORT FOR THE ENTIRE PLANNING AND IMPLEMENTATION PROCESS   As conceptualized in figure 7.2, INDEX was designed to underpin the complete cycle of community planning and implementation. Ideally, the tool could serve as an institutional memory bank whose long-term use in an area would increase

FIGURE 7.2

INDEX Integration with Local Planning and Implementation Process
Source: Criterion Planners

The Community Planning Process

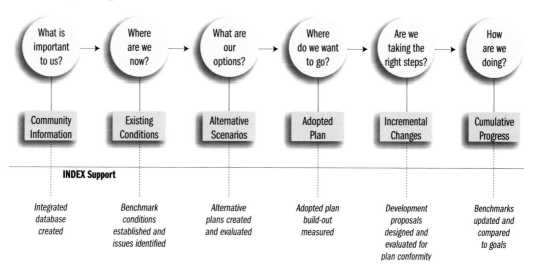

goal achievement and accrued benefits. Even though an adopted plan might be five years old, and current elected officials were therefore unfamiliar with it, the tool could reach back and gauge decision-making consistency against original objectives.

REAL-TIME INTERACTIVITY FOR PROCESS PARTICIPANTS   By giving citizens control of the mouse, it was believed that a wider range of ideas could be generated, a greater sense of process and product ownership would occur, and ultimately more people would become involved because participation would be recognized as more engaging and meaningful.

SENSITIVITY TO SMART GROWTH AND SUSTAINABLE DEVELOPMENT POLICIES   The 1990s saw the emergence of smart growth, new urbanism, green buildings, and similar initiatives devoted to greater sustainability in community development. Local and regional practitioners faced these ideas unequipped to test and evaluate new policies, and INDEX indicators were specifically focused to fill this gap. Particular attention was given to characterizing the built environment's suitability for multimodal travel at the neighborhood level.

In sum, INDEX was to be a yardstick that practitioners and citizens could use for engaging the future in a modest but useful manner. It sought the iterative kind of thinking in calculations and images that are essential to inventiveness, effectiveness, and persuasive collaboration (Hopkins and Zapata 2007a). With sufficient institutionalization over time, and enough applications across a region's geography, it was hoped that the tool could ultimately support the kind of performance-based design and environmental transect shown in figure 7.3, and by doing so, validate the regional and local benefits of PSS.

FIGURE 7.3 Regional Design and Environmental Performance Transect
Source: INDEX output for Sacramento, California, region

Design Context

	Rural	Urban
Residential Density (net DU/ac)	0.10	35.00
Open Space (% total land area)	20.00	5.00
Employment Proximity (jobs w/i 1 mi.)	10.00	30,000.00
Street Density (centerline mi./sq.mi.)	1.00	25.00
Transit Proximity (avg. ft. DU–closest stop)	25,000.00	400.00
Auto Use (total VMT/capita/day)	35.00	10.00

Environmental Performance

	Rural	Urban
Land Consumption (gross ac/capita)	5.00	0.01
Domestic Water Use (gal/capita/day)	200.00	50.00
Energy Use (MMBtu/capita/yr)	200.00	100.00
Imperviousness (impervious ac/DU)	0.10	0.03
Nonpoint Source Pollutants (kg/capita/yr)	0.04	0.01
Criteria Air Pollutants (lbs/capita/yr)	800.00	200.00
Greenhouse Gases (tons/capita/yr)	12.00	4.00

Tool Description

INDEX is a proprietary software application for assessing current land use and transportation conditions and evaluating alternative courses of action in a neighborhood, community, or region. As shown in figure 7.4, it is essentially a spatial spreadsheet that scores user-created scenarios with indicators to gauge and rank scenario performance relative to user-defined goals. It is intended to perform the following support duties for local and regional practitioners: (1) create or update plans that involve alternative scenarios; (2) process current development proposals that need plan-compliance reviews; and (3) populate regional transportation models with land-use scenarios. It is also designed for real-time citizen use in creating and evaluating scenarios.

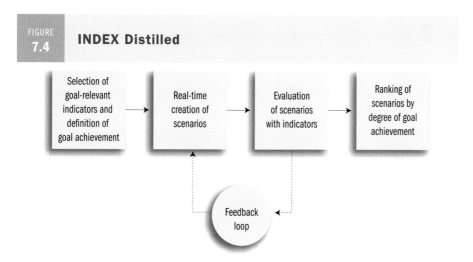

FIGURE 7.4   INDEX Distilled

Software Requirements

INDEX is an ArcMap extension that runs with ESRI's ArcGIS™ products and the Microsoft® Windows operating systems (Criterion Planners 2007). It is built with ArcObjects and Visual Basic components that allow operation with either ArcView®, ArcEditor™, or ArcInfo®, and optionally, with ArcScene and ArcIMS®. In addition to one of the ArcGIS platforms, INDEX requires Microsoft Access. INDEX is available in two forms: a parcel-level version called Plan-Builder®, and a traffic zone or raster cell version called Paint the Region. INDEX accommodates three levels of users: (1) software stewards or administrators who need advanced ArcGIS experience to maintain the tool; (2) general users (practitioners) who have completed some minimal ArcGIS training and experience; and (3) citizens with basic computer literacy.[1]

Primary Functions

The tool performs five primary duties for practitioners and citizens.

1. *Assess Community Conditions.* This benchmarking of existing conditions identifies an area's strengths and weaknesses, provides input into the formulation of goals, and establishes a baseline for gauging change in future scenarios and for periodically updating cumulative progress toward long-range goals.

2. *Design Future Scenarios.* This interactive, digital charretting function allows drawing and "painting" of land use and transportation scenarios in real time. Scenarios are informed by indicator scores and maps describing existing conditions (Where are we now?) and the build-out of applicable current plans (Where are we headed?).

3. *Measure Scenarios.* Once created, scenarios are evaluated with indicator scores and maps to reveal areas of strong and weak performance that can be considered in the next iteration of scenario fine tuning.

4. *Rank Scenarios.* When multiple scenarios are created, they can be ranked by degree of overall goal achievement and by individual indicator objectives using a rating and weighting function that holds user-defined thresholds of success.

5. *Monitor Implementation.* Once a preferred scenario is adopted as a formal plan, each implementation step (development proposal) can be measured to gauge conformity with adopted goals. Periodically, cumulative progress can be measured and the existing-conditions baseline updated.

Application Steps

As shown in figure 7.5, the application of INDEX is normally done in two stages: installation and set up for a user jurisdiction, such as a city or region; and preparation of "studies" of the jurisdiction or any subpart (e.g., a neighborhood). Studies are prepared using the following steps:

FIGURE
7.5
Application Process

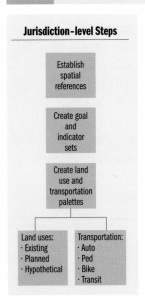

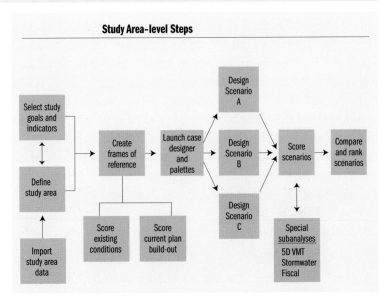

DELINEATION OF A STUDY BOUNDARY AND SELECTION OF RELEVANT INDICATORS
Boundaries can be custom drawn by users, or relevant features can be adopted by reference (e.g., watershed boundary). A menu of 75 or more indicators is available for calculating land use, housing, employment, transportation, and environmental metrics (table 7.1).

TABLE 7.1	**INDEX Indicators** (partial list)

Indicator	Units
Demographics	
Population	residents
Employment	employees
Population density	residents/gross acre
Land Use	
Study area acreage	total acres
Average parcel size	avg square feet
Use mix	0–1 scale
Use balance	0–1 scale
Development footprint	net acres/1,000 residents
Housing	
Dwelling density	DU/gross acre
Dwelling unit count	total DU
Student enrollment level	% student capacity used
Residential footprint	net acres/1,000 residents
Single-family parcel size	avg square feet
Single-family dwelling density	DU/net acre
Multifamily dwelling density	DU/net acre
Single-family dwelling share	% total DU
Multifamily dwelling share	% total DU
Amenities adjacency	% pop w/i user buffer
Amenities proximity	avg walk ft to closest
Transit adjacency to housing	% pop w/i user buffer
Transit proximity to housing	avg walk ft to closest stop
Wastewater generation	gallons/day
Solid waste generation	lbs/day
Structural energy use	MMBtu/yr/capita
Residential water consumption	gallons/day/capita
Employment	
Jobs to housing balance	jobs/DU
Employment density	emps/net acre
Commercial building density	avg FAR

INDEX Indicators (partial list)   *continued*

Indicator	Units
Employment (continued)	
Transit adjacency to employment	% emps w/i user buffer
Transit proximity to employment	avg walk ft to closest stop
Recreation	
Park/schoolyard space supply	acres/1,000 persons
Park/schoolyard adjacency to housing	% pop w/i user buffer
Park/schoolyard proximity to housing	avg walk ft to closest park/schoolyard
Environment	
NOx pollutant emissions	lbs/capita/yr
HC pollutant emissions	lbs/capita/yr
CO pollutant emissions	lbs/capita/yr
Greenhouse gas emissions	lbs/capita/yr CO_2
Open space share	% total net area
Open space connectivity	$0-1$ scale
Stormwater runoff	cu ft/acre/yr
Nonpoint pollution	kg/acre/yr
Imperviousness	% of total net land area
Floodplain encroachment	% study area w/i floodplain
Land suitability	% net vacant land developable
Travel	
Internal street connectivity	cul-de-sac/intersection ratio
External street connectivity	avg ft between ingress/egress streets
Street segment length	avg ft
Street centerline distance	total ft
Street network density	centerline mi/sq mi
Transit service coverage	stops/sq mi
Transit service density	vehicle route mi/sq mi
Transit-oriented residential density	DU/net acre w/i user buffer of stops
Transit-oriented employment density	emps/net acre w/i user buffer of stops
Light rail boardings	avg persons/day
Heavy rail mode shift	avg daily VT/capita shifted
Pedestrian network coverage	% of streets w/sidewalks
Pedestrian crossing distance	avg curb-to-curb ft
Street route directness	walk distance/straightline ratio
Pedestrian setback	avg commercial bldg setback ft
Pedestrian accessibilities	% origins w/i 15 min walk of destinations
Bicycle network coverage	% street centerline w/i bike route

Indicator	Units
Travel (continued)	
Residential multimodal access	%DU w/3+ modes w/i 1/8 mi
Home-based vehicle miles traveled	mi/day/capita
Nonhome-based vehicle miles traveled	mi/day/capita
Home-based vehicle trips	trips/day/capita
Nonhome-based vehicle trips	trips/day/capita
Personal vehicle energy use	MMBtu/yr/capita
Parking requirements	total spaces required

DEFINITION OF RESULTS THAT CONSTITUTE SUCCESS   Users determine the desired direction of indicator scores, acceptable minimum and maximum scores, and indicator weighting with the software dialogue shown in figure 7.6. These definitions of goal achievement are calculated for all indicators to arrive at an overall scenario score or degree of goal achievement, as shown in table 7.2.

FIGURE 7.6   **Dialogue for Defining Goal Achievement by Indicator**
Source: INDEX

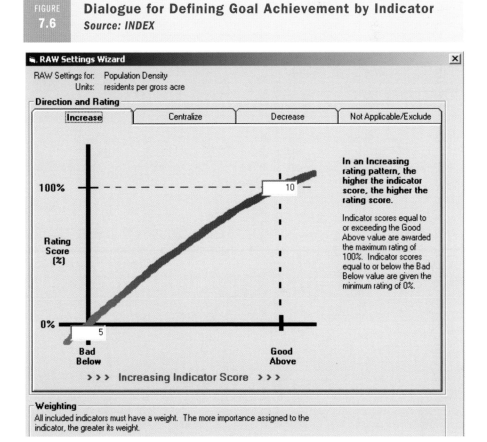

TABLE 7.2

Sample Goal Definition and Achievement Calculation for a Scenario

| GOAL-RELEVANT INDICATORS | Weighting | | DEFINITION OF GOAL ACHIEVEMENT | Rating | | | Indicator Score | | Equivalent Rating (0 to 1) | x | Indicator Weight | = | Indicator RAW Score |
	Overall Topic Importance	Allocation to Indicators	Positive Movement of Score	Worst Indicator Scores (Get 0)	Mediocre Indicator Scores (Get 0.5)	Best Indicator Scores (Get 1)							
Housing	50	–											
Dwelling density	–	20	Up	10–	15	20+	16	↑	0.6	x	20	=	12
Distance to transit	–	30	Down	2,640+	1,170	300–	1,250	↑	0.4	x	30	=	12
Employment	25	–											
Employee density	–	10	Up	20–	35	50+	37	↑	0.6	x	10	=	6
Distance to transit	–	15	Down	2,640+	1,170	300–	863	↑	0.2	x	15	=	4
Parks	25	–											
Distance to housing	–	25	Down	2,640+	1,170	300–	2,300	↑	0.9	x	25	=	21
	100	100											55

GOAL ACHIEVEMENT CALCULATION

Rated and Weighted Scenario Score (0–100 scale)

ASSEMBLY OF A LAND USE AND TRANSPORTATION PALETTE   Users can select these features when sketching scenarios. The features can represent land use classes and transportation standards already adopted by a jurisdiction, or they can simulate new concepts being tested. Up to 250 land use types can be defined by household characteristics, jobs, density, parking, property value, energy and water use, stormwater runoff, and other descriptors (figure 7.7).

FIGURE
7.7

Dialogue for Defining Land Use Paints
Source: INDEX

INTERACTIVE DRAWING AND PAINTING OF SCENARIOS   Scenarios can be sketched by staff in advance of public meetings (figure 7.8) or they can be created in real time with citizens participating in digital charrettes (figure 7.9). The tool allows any number of scenarios to be created in a given study. Users paint parcels with land use types selected from the palette by clicking on the parcel and thereby editing its attributes.

FIGURE 7.8   **Real-time Drawing and Painting of Scenarios**
Source: Criterion Planners

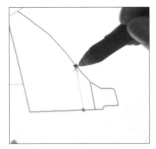      

Drawing blocks and parcels   *Designing streets*   *Painting land uses*

FIGURE 7.9   **Digital Charrette Set-up for a Small Group**
Source: Criterion Planners

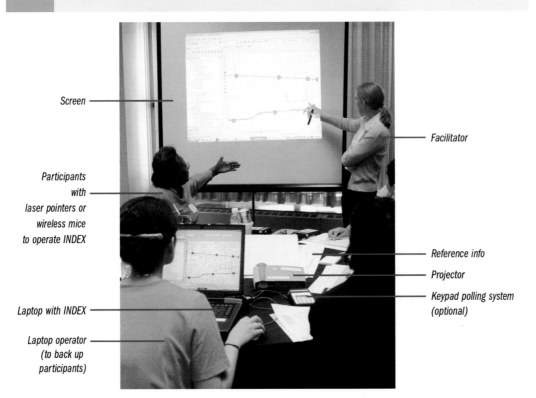

Screen

Facilitator

Participants
with
laser pointers or
wireless mice
to operate INDEX

Reference info

Projector

Keypad polling system
(optional)

Laptop with INDEX

Laptop operator
(to back up
participants)

SCENARIO TRACKING WITH A PAINT CALCULATOR   As painting occurs, this function simultaneously tabulates how much of a development program or growth forecast has been painted or allocated and how much remains to be painted (figure 7.10).

| FIGURE 7.10 | Painting Calculator
Source: INDEX |

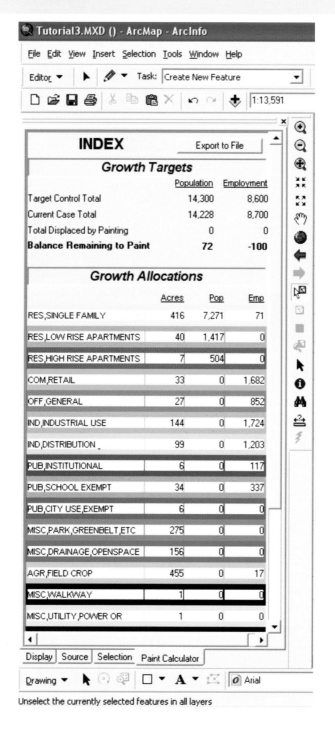

Indicator Maps
Source: INDEX

Housing Proximity to
Amenity (grocery)

Feet
- 0–300
- 330–660
- 660–1,320
- 1,320–1,980
- 1,980–2,640
- 2,640 +

Housing Proximity to
Transit Stops

Feet
- 0–300
- 330–660
- 660–1,320
- 1,320–1,980
- 1,980–2,640
- 2,640 +

Use Mix

0 – 1 scale
- 0–0.25
- 0.25–0.5
- 0.5–0.75
- 0.75–1

Pedestrian Route
Directness

Walk distance versus
straight line distance

INDICATOR SCORING FOR FEEDBACK ON GOAL ACHIEVEMENT With indicator scores and maps (figure 7.11), users are able to diagnose scenario strengths and weaknesses as a charrette unfolds and then iterate to the most robust variations.

SCENARIO RANKING BY GOAL ACHIEVEMENT As shown in figure 7.12, when multiple scenarios have been created they can be ranked according to the degree of overall goal achievement using the stakeholders' definitions of success set earlier.

Installation

Installing and setting up an INDEX base case of existing conditions for a moderate-sized local or regional agency usually takes one to three person weeks of labor depending on staff experience and data conditions. Following base case preparation, scenarios can be built and scored in minutes or hours depending on their size, complexity, and the number and type of indicators selected.

Indicator selection also drives data requirements. When operated at the parcel level, the tool's minimum requirements are parcels attributed with dwelling unit type and count, job type and count, and a fully connected street centerline

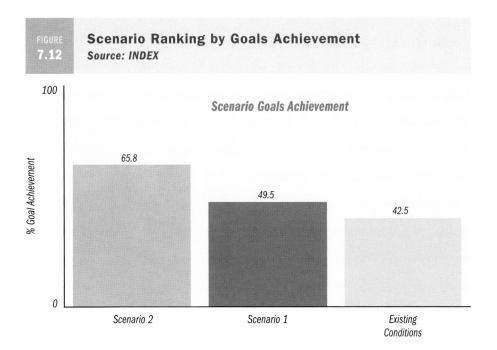

FIGURE 7.12 Scenario Ranking by Goals Achievement
Source: INDEX

network attributed by street class type. Investigation of specific policy topics, such as walkability or stormwater management, requires additional data to support indicator calculations. The tool's user documentation contains an indicator dictionary that details each calculation and the requisite data. As with many PSS, INDEX is intolerant of poorly built data files, and a certain amount of labor is usually required for data clean up prior to runs.

If INDEX is used in a digital charrette, several additional person days of labor will be required for extra preparation, equipment set up, and execution of the charrette itself. For example, citizens working at tables will need laptop operators with ArcGIS and INDEX experience, tool projection on table screens, and tool-savvy facilitators with scenario-building experience, who are familiar with the study area's existing conditions and applicable goals.

Experience from 1994 to 2006

During the period from 1994 to 2006, INDEX was developed and released in five versions, which kept pace with ESRI's evolving ArcGIS platforms. INDEX has been marketed commercially in three ways: (1) as a generic version licensed to user organizations; (2) in custom versions built according to the unique specifications of user organizations; and (3) as consultant applications of the tool for organizations that desired the tool's analysis, but not the software.

Application Locations

Over the years, INDEX was applied in the United States at 690 locations in 36 states and the District of Columbia, as shown in figure 7.13. It was also applied at locations in Australia, Canada, China, Japan, and Spain.

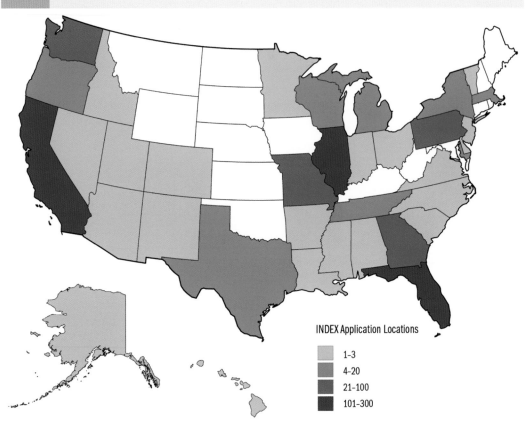

FIGURE 7.13 **Application Locations in the United States, 1994–2006**

INDEX Application Locations

- 1–3
- 4–20
- 21–100
- 101–300

In the United States, Illinois, Florida, and California have had by far the greatest number of application locations. INDEX was applied in 283 locations in Illinois, including all municipalities in the six-county region surrounding Chicago, where it was used as part of a regional growth–planning process. It was applied in 116 locations in Florida as part of a state-sponsored PSS program to assist local and regional planning. In California, of the 101 locations in which it was applied, the majority were in the Sacramento region due to the tool's adoption by nearly all planning agencies in that area. A large majority of the U.S. locations were urban and suburban settings, often in large metropolitan areas. INDEX has rarely been used in small towns or rural areas because of its advanced user-skill requirements, data intensity, and the urban orientation of its indicators.

Users

During this period, the software was licensed to a total of 157 user organizations the largest of which were local governments and regional planning agencies (figure 7.14). Most local government users were municipalities and counties with populations greater than 50,000. Most regional user organizations had populations of 200,000 or more.

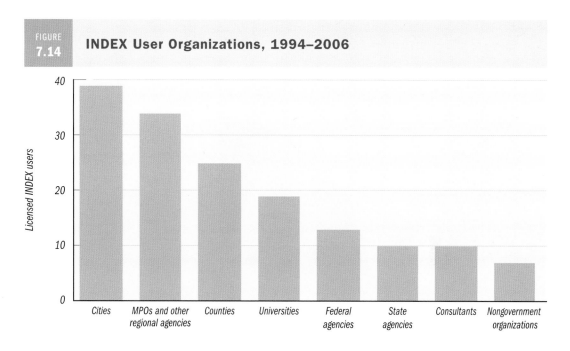

FIGURE 7.14 **INDEX User Organizations, 1994–2006**

State and federal agency users have been concerned with land use, transportation, and environmental protection. The U.S. Environmental Protection Agency's smart growth program has been a major user, as has the Florida Department of Community Affairs, which oversees local land use planning statewide. Nineteen universities use the tool for instruction and research, most in urban and regional planning graduate programs. The tool has also been licensed to land development design consultants and nongovernmental organizations advocating smart growth and sustainable development.

Formal INDEX training has been given to approximately 470 persons in user organizations. A majority of the trainees have been GIS technicians working in the planning or information technology sections of the organizations. It is worth noting that these tool operators were often organizationally removed from the planning staff that conceived the need for INDEX and used its output.

Approximately 2,000 citizens used INDEX in several dozen real-time digital charrettes between 1994 and 2006. Typically, 20 to 60 citizens participated in sessions devoted to neighborhood design, comprehensive planning, or regional-growth visioning. Charrette sessions ranged from two to six hours, and often a series of sessions were conducted in multiple locations in a jurisdiction or in stages according to a process.

Applications and Scenarios

INDEX has been applied to a wide variety of planning projects (figure 7.15). The most common have been community- and neighborhood-level analyses of land use and transportation scenarios. The average size of neighborhood studies has been approximately 500 acres. (The minimum land area that makes an application worthwhile is roughly 100 acres.) Frequently investigated concepts include

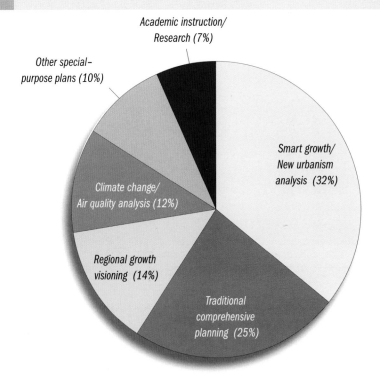

FIGURE 7.15

Application Subjects, 1994–2006

Academic instruction/ Research (7%)

Other special-purpose plans (10%)

Smart growth/ New urbanism analysis (32%)

Climate change/ Air quality analysis (12%)

Regional growth visioning (14%)

Traditional comprehensive planning (25%)

smart growth plans and new urbanist designs, particularly pedestrian and transit-oriented concepts; and sustainable development practices, such as energy- and water-efficiency measures, and stormwater pollution prevention. Climate change mitigation applications have increased markedly in recent years.

After communities and neighborhoods, a large number of INDEX applications have been regional in scope. Averaging approximately 5,000 square miles, these have been multijurisdiction applications, which were often conducted by metropolitan planning organizations (MPOs). INDEX has been used to build land use scenarios for export to regional travel-demand models in cases where staff or citizens painted spatial concepts, as opposed to populating the travel models with forecasting output from tools such as UrbanSim.

During the period from 1994 to 2006, approximately 4,100 scenarios were created and scored by users and Criterion staff at the 690 locations described above. Typically, anywhere from two to six scenarios would be drawn, and the most commonly varied parameters were land use type, density, and mix, and improved transportation facilities, including changes to street networks and pedestrian, bicycle, and transit features.

Case Studies

This section describes two INDEX applications that are typical of the tool's use at the neighborhood and region levels. The work was performed for the Florida

Department of Community Affairs, which has distributed INDEX to local and regional agencies for assistance in the preparation of comprehensive plans, growth visions, and special-purpose plans. Tampa Heights in the city of Tampa is a typical neighborhood-scale application, and the four-county Emerald Coast region of northwestern Florida is given as a regional example.

Tampa Heights, Florida

In contrast to the popular image of prosperous suburban growth, Florida's older, larger cities are saddled with economically depressed inner neighborhoods, where diminishing services and deteriorating building stock are barriers to redevelopment and infill growth. Situated next to downtown Tampa, the neighborhood of Tampa Heights is an example of these conditions. The 700-acre area, which is home to 4,000 persons, is burdened by low incomes, high unemployment, and a patchwork of vacant lots and abandoned buildings that undermine property values. On the positive side, however, the neighborhood has superior regional transportation accessibility, and is characterized by a small-block pattern and high connectivity, which offer "good bones" for walkability and small businesses. It also has been designated a historic district, which can be leveraged to improve the neighborhood's identity and property appeal.

To capitalize on these land use and transportation advantages, the city's planning division convened a group of neighborhood stakeholders, who worked in partnership with the local community development corporation (CDC). This group decided to focus on redevelopment of the neighborhood center as a prominent catalyst feature that could stimulate surrounding public and private improvements. INDEX PlanBuilder was selected to inventory existing conditions and provide a platform for digital charretting of alternative scenarios for the center.

The City and CDC prepared a base case of existing conditions, in which parcels available for redevelopment in the focus area were identified as were deficiencies in pedestrian, bicycle, and transit facilities. Using the existing-conditions case to inform their approach, the stakeholders conducted two digital charrettes to create four redevelopment scenarios for the center (figure 7.16).

FIGURE 7.16

Tampa Heights Neighborhood Center Concepts
Source: City of Tampa, Florida

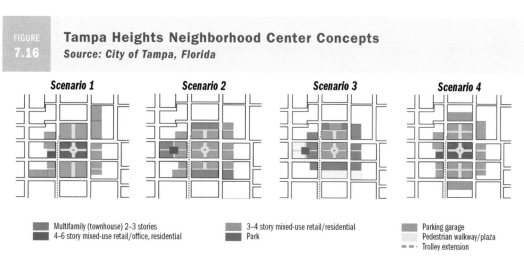

Scenario 1   Scenario 2   Scenario 3   Scenario 4

Multifamily (townhouse) 2-3 stories
4-6 story mixed-use retail/office, residential

3-4 story mixed-use retail/residential
Park

Parking garage
Pedestrian walkway/plaza
Trolley extension

TABLE 7.3	**Tampa Heights Goals and Scenario Scores**
	Source: INDEX

Indicator	Units	Existing Conditions	Goals	Scenario 1	Scenario 2	Scenario 3	Scenario 4
Demographics							
Population	residents	817	open	2,256	1,752	1,367	2,267
Employment	employees	513	open	1,215	971	608	1,316
Population density	residents/ gross acre	7.07	open	19.54	15.17	11.84	19.64
Land Use							
Average parcel size	avg square feet	9,425	none	10,557	10,502	10,545	10,555
Use mix	0–1 scale	0.37	0.50 or more	0.54	0.50	0.44	0.54
Use balance	0–1 scale	0.73	0.80 or more	0.72	0.75	0.72	0.71
Development footprint	net acres/ 1,000 residents	95.1	60.0 or less	33.9	44.1	57.1	33.6
Housing							
Dwelling density	DU/gross acre	3.00	5.00 or more	8.28	6.43	5.02	8.32
Dwelling unit count	total DU	346	none	956	742	579	961
Amenities proximity	avg walk ft to closest grocery	1,244	800 or less	975	934	979	875
Transit proximity to housing	avg walk ft to closest stop	622	500 or less	483	479	509	453
Employment							
Jobs-to-housing balance	jobs/DU	1.48	0.90 to 1.10	1.27	1.31	1.05	1.37
Employment density	emps/net acre	21.44	25.00 or more	41.91	35.46	26.62	40.89
Transit proximity to employment	avg walk ft to closest stop	553	500 or less	480	458	523	442
Recreation							
Park/schoolyard space supply	acres/1,000 persons	3.8	4.0 or more	1.5	2.0	2.5	1.5
Park/schoolyard proximity to housing	avg walk ft to closest park/schoolyard	1,306	800 or less	893	921	978	880
Travel							
Transit service coverage	stops/sq mi	122.0	130.0 or more	127.5	127.5	127.5	127.5
Home-based vehicle miles traveled	mi/day/capita	18.0	15.0 or less	13.8	14.2	14.9	13.6
Environment							
Greenhouse gas emissions	CO_2 lbs/capita/yr	8,395	7,000 or less	6,415	6,644	6,933	6,361

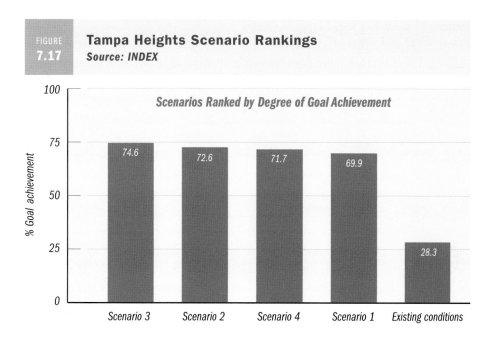

FIGURE 7.17 **Tampa Heights Scenario Rankings**
Source: INDEX

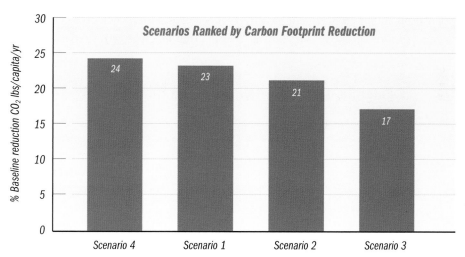

The scenarios were scored with indicators and compared against stakeholder-defined goals (table 7.3) and then ranked by overall goal achievement and by key issues such as carbon-footprint reduction (figure 7.17).

Feedback from the stakeholders about the value of INDEX support was positive. Having had no previous measurement of neighborhood characteristics, they appreciated the frame of reference provided by the existing condition scores and mapping. They felt comfortable with the scenario rankings because their own definitions of success were being used in the ranking. And they believed strongly enough in the outcome to request that the next stage of municipal assistance focus on the two top-ranked scenarios. The final preferred scenario will become a priority in the CDC's economic-development strategy and capital-improvement program.

Emerald Coast, Florida

Outside of older, distressed neighborhoods like Tampa Heights, in recent years other parts of Florida have been growing at some of the nation's fastest rates. Much of this growth has occurred in rural regions where land and housing prices have been relatively affordable. Northwestern Florida, known as the Emerald Coast, is an example of such a region, which is experiencing rapid urbanization and suburbanization. The Emerald Coast covers 3,700 square miles along the Gulf of Mexico, and currently has a population of 668,000 and a workforce of 277,000. The area, which is already facing major constraints of water availability and auto dependency, is forecasted to grow by as much as 100 percent over the next 30 years.

In this application, INDEX Paint the Region was used by the West Florida Regional Planning Council to support the creation and evaluation of alternative regional growth scenarios. In its Paint the Region configuration, INDEX offers a "growth canvas" on which future population and employment can be allocated or "painted." Painting is guided by the location of community centers, transportation corridors, and conservation areas (figure 7.18).

To allocate growth, Paint the Region simulates "paper chip" or "Lego stacking" exercises by offering their digital equivalents. Users select an increment of population and/or employment growth to allocate, and then click on a cell or traffic analysis zone on the growth canvas to assign that much growth to that location.

FIGURE 7.18   **Emerald Coast, Florida, Scenario Components**
Source: INDEX

Growth Canvas
Local comprehensive plans

Centers
Street grids supporting multimodal travel and urban infrastructure

Corridors
Major regional travel corridors

Conservation Areas
Protected/ nondevelopable lands

By repeatedly clicking on a spot, the user "stacks" growth at that location. Figure 7.19 illustrates this process with the optional use of ArcScene that extrudes growth in 3D heights equivalent to painted headcounts.

In the Emerald Coast process, INDEX provided a base case of existing conditions and digital charrette support that produced two scenarios: business as usual versus sustainable (figure 7.20). Using stakeholder-selected indicators and

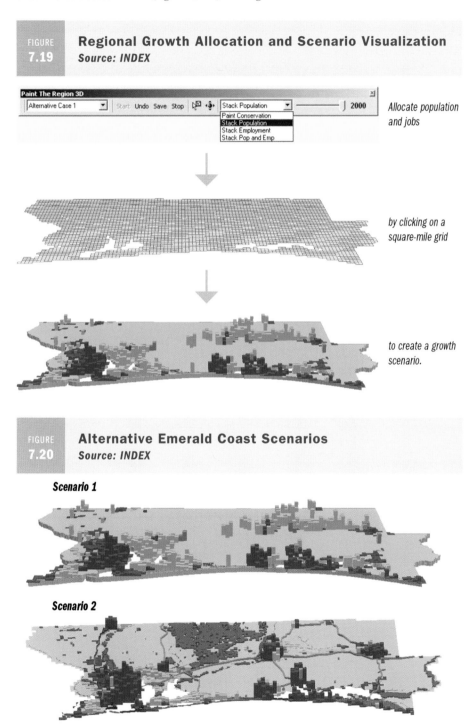

FIGURE 7.19 **Regional Growth Allocation and Scenario Visualization**
Source: INDEX

Allocate population and jobs

by clicking on a square-mile grid

to create a growth scenario.

FIGURE 7.20 **Alternative Emerald Coast Scenarios**
Source: INDEX

Scenario 1

Scenario 2

objectives, the tool scored and ranked the alternatives, showing that the sustainable alternative achieves a much larger share of stakeholder goals (figure 7.21).

With the demonstration of benefits from the sustainable alternative, stakeholders are now fashioning action measures that will bring local plans and infrastructure improvements into conformity with the preferred regional vision. Of the four counties in the region, two have acquired the parcel-level version of INDEX in order to apply regional policies at the community and neighborhood levels.

<table>
<tr><td>FIGURE
7.21</td><td>Scoring and Ranking of Emerald Coast Scenarios
Source: INDEX</td></tr>
</table>

Scenario 1 Indicator Scores

Indicators	Scores
Demographics	
Population	1,000,005
Employment	500,020
Population density	0.39
Land use	
Development footprint	553.6
Housing	
Dwelling density	0.12
Dwelling unit count	317,394
Suburban dwelling density	0.53
Urban dwelling density	0.69
School adjacency to housing	21.2
Transit adjacency to housing	30.7
Employment	
Jobs to housing balance	1.58
Employment density	1.11
Transit adjacency to employment	34.9
Environment	
Open space share	2.0

Scenario 2 Indicator Scores

Indicators	Scores
Demographics	
Population	1,000,030
Employment	499,956
Population density	0.39
Land use	
Development footprint	551.7
Housing	
Dwelling density	0.12
Dwelling unit count	317,404
Suburban dwelling density	0.41
Urban dwelling density	0.80
School adjacency to housing	28.8
Transit adjacency to housing	40.7
Employment	
Jobs to housing balance	1.58
Employment density	1.17
Transit adjacency to employment	63.0
Environment	
Open space share	11.9

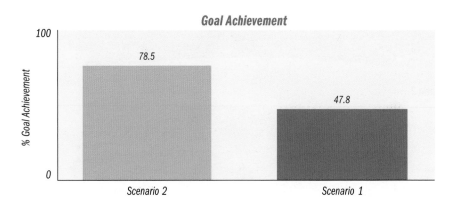

Goal Achievement

Conclusions

General Environment for PSS

Based on the author's experience, the adoption and use of PSS in moderate-sized local and regional agencies remains relatively limited because practitioners either do not have sufficient tools expertise or must rely on others, often in settings with equipment and data limitations. The burdens incurred in implementing PSS are often seen to outweigh the benefits, particularly by information technology (IT) specialists who are usually called upon to apply a tool like INDEX on behalf of practitioners.

The only PSS that are widely and regularly used in local and regional agencies are permit tracking, simple GIS mapping, traffic-impact modeling at the site level, and stormwater-runoff modeling at the site level. With few exceptions, all other tool use in moderate-sized agencies remains episodic, if it occurs at all.

When PSS are used, it is almost always as the result of one or a small group of champions who push for tool use. Interestingly, these champions usually occupy positions at the top or bottom of an organization's hierarchy; rarely are they in the middle, where most practitioners are laboring on the largest amount of work. Not surprisingly, when a top-level champion imposes a tool on an organization, the tool often ends up being resisted or ignored by practitioners and IT technicians, who perceive it as an uninvited burden. Sometimes champions emerge at the lower levels of an organization where IT expertise is usually most abundant. In these cases, however, the tool innovators are often bureaucratically disconnected from the practitioners who could benefit from it and skeptical supervisors who need to approve its use. The best situations are those where all levels of an organization are enthusiastic and committed to the use of PSS, but those occur infrequently.

Tool Impact

After 13 years, some of the original goals set for INDEX have been achieved to modest degrees, and in some cases the tool has missed the mark. Achievements under the original goals include:

MORE OBJECTIVITY IN DECISION MAKING　The tool's scenario scoring with indicators has been well received by practitioners and the general public. Having a consistent yardstick that produces insightful measurements has been a notable asset for working planners sorting through options and claims. In many cases, indicator scores have been a deciding factor in screening scenarios and making land use decisions that were more environmentally conscious. In particular, indicator scores have contributed to better factual evaluation of the pedestrian environment and the transit orientation of urban designs.

GREATER INTEGRATION OF LAND USE, TRANSPORTATION, AND ENVIRONMENTAL ISSUES　INDEX's integrated assessment of land use and transportation impacts to the environment has proven to be an effective educational device and eye opener for citizens and elected officials. As an example, one of the tool's most frequently used features is the "5D method," which estimates vehicle miles traveled and pollutant emission changes resulting from land use alterations and transportation facility improvements.

SUPPORT OF THE ENTIRE PLANNING AND IMPLEMENTATION PROCESS   Except for the Sacramento, California, region, this has not happened to any appreciable degree. The tool's use remains episodic and focused primarily on the front end of long-range processes rather than regular, day-to-day use during postadoption implementation, e.g., development reviews.

REAL-TIME INTERACTIVITY FOR PROCESS PARTICIPANTS   When resources have been sufficient to conduct digital charrettes, this has been one of INDEX's most popular capabilities. Participants have found the quasitactile sketching using clicking and dragging for scenario building to be highly engaging. Using citizen definitions of success has enabled a high degree of buy-in of outcomes.

SENSITIVITY TO SMART GROWTH AND SUSTAINABLE DEVELOPMENT POLICIES   This is where INDEX may have achieved most in terms of raising consciousness and steering practitioners and citizens toward planning practices generally. The tool has contributed to the research documenting the environmental benefits of smart growth and new urbanism (Allen 1999; 2000a; 2000b; U.S. Environmental Protection Agency 2001; Natural Resource Defense Council 2000; 2003), and has been used by design teams to help optimize the sustainability of some of America's premier smart growth projects, such as Atlantic Station in Atlanta. Its indicators can provide a detailed, parcel-level audit of the built environment's sustainability.

Nonetheless, these achievements have been relatively modest because INDEX's use and impact remains largely dependent upon champions within user organizations. As with PSS generally, there have simply not been enough adopters to tip the balance toward more mainstream use. When and how PSS enters the mainstream is a question that deserves attention given the magnitude of environmental and economic damage being done by ill-considered land use and transportation decisions.

Obstacles Encountered

The INDEX experience has largely validated many of the PSS impediments already cataloged in the literature (Hunt 2005; Waddell 2005). Significant barriers encountered in moderate-sized local and regional planning agencies include:

STAFF LIMITATIONS IN USER ORGANIZATIONS   The single greatest impediment to wider and more effective INDEX use has been user organization staffing. This problem manifests itself in several ways: lack of staff time for learning and applying new tools; turnover that eliminates advanced users and mentors; lack of familiarity with urban morphology, transportation, and environmental metrics used in modeling scenarios; and inexperience applying tools in real time with live audiences.

Perhaps most disappointing is the tendency within agencies for tools expertise to be pigeonholed and seen as a narrow, dead-end career track in contrast to other career options that are perceived to be wider and more upwardly mobile.

STOVEPIPE BUREAUCRACY   Effective tool use is often impeded by organizational structures that separate land use planning from transportation planning and those two functions from IT. When GIS is housed in a separate IT department, it has been difficult to penetrate the IT "work order" atmosphere to get the kind of commitment, creativity, and spontaneity needed for successful PSS use in planning processes.

EQUIPMENT LIMITATIONS   Local governments, particularly small and moderate-sized jurisdictions, often do not possess state-of-the-art computer hardware and software and public presentation hardware. In many cases, insufficient laptop capacity has prevented or curtailed tool use at public meetings. Some agencies still lack equipment as basic as computer projectors.

PRICE RESISTANCE   The cost of third-party application software, on top of ESRI's ArcGIS license fees, can be a serious hurdle for many agencies. Although tool costs are gradually diminishing, they still remain a significant consideration for many local government budgets.

LIMITED POLITICAL SUPPORT   Elected and appointed officials serving on planning and governing bodies sometimes resist tools because of concerns about giving up control to "black boxes." Absent some political understanding and leadership that telegraphs a PSS endorsement to staff, it can be very difficult to get tool traction inside an organization.

DATA   No list of PSS barriers would be complete without pointing a finger at data. Although conditions have improved in the past decade, many planning agencies still have difficulty fully describing their current conditions and future plans in digital terms. In particular, employment locations, pedestrian environments, and urban morphology in general are often unavailable. What is available is often of such poor quality that basic analysis cannot be supported without first doing clean-up work.

Remedies

No "silver bullets" will revolutionize PSS use in local and regional planning. Instead, phased technology advancements will make tools more accessible and relevant, and more tool adoption will gradually happen for common, repetitive chores. These trends should accelerate with the coming of Web-served software, touch-sensitive "surface" computers, and audience-polling innovations. All of these will enable wider and friendlier access to more powerful PSS at less cost. Even with these positive trends, however, tool use by the large majority of midsized local and regional agencies could still lag without more concerted efforts by PSS supporters to advance best practices. Five proposals outline a potential way to proceed.

SIMPLER TOOLS   The most important thing that tool designers can do to mitigate agency-user problems is to create simpler tools that require less staffing and less advanced technical skills. A huge constituency of midlevel practitioners only have the time and skills for simple tools. This is not to say that tools can ignore the complexities of community planning, but rather their modeling complexity must operate beneath a simple interface that can be used rapidly.

PRACTITIONER SKILLS   Higher and continuing education programs in urban and regional planning need to equip students better with the ability to apply tools analytically, interpret results knowledgeably, and use them effectively in real time with the public. Tools expertise must be seen as an attractive career path, not a geeky dead end.

GREATER REAL-TIME PUBLIC USE   Once citizens have seen the power and immediacy that tools can bring to a process, their enthusiasm will help accelerate tool adoption generally. The retrofitting of America's planning commission hearing rooms with something as simple as real-time access to local GIS would be an enormous step toward PSS mainstreaming, not to mention better decision making.

DATA STANDARDS AND DEVELOPMENT   The time may have come for legislating certain minimum data standards, as has been done in a handful of states including Oregon, Florida, and Wisconsin. This could be especially effective when done for policy reasons, such as California's Assembly Bill 1020 which would require that MPO data and models be sensitive to smart growth policies (California Legislature 2005). A comparable approach could focus on the minimum data needed to support land use and transportation planning that mitigates climate change.

COMPARATIVE EVALUATION OF TOOLS   To help prospective users sort through tool choices, independent, rigorous evaluation of tool capabilities and performance is needed. Such a service, performed by a qualified academic or nonprofit professional group, could accelerate tool adoption by reducing uncertainties and risks that new users face when selecting tools and by encouraging tool developers to pursue best practices.

With these ideas, and suggestions from others in the field, a PSS "mainstreaming" agenda can and should be assembled and acted upon. To do otherwise would be to ignore the consequences of ill-informed land use and transportation decisions that are continuing to undermine the planet's sustainability.

Endnote

1. The tool's calculation methods and application process are fully documented and downloadable at www.crit.com/documents/planuserguide.pdf.

Communities in Control

Developing Local Models Using CommunityViz®

8

George M. Janes and Michael Kwartler

Urban Modeling Context

SINCE THE ADVENT OF COMPUTERS, URBAN PLANNERS AND COMPUTER scientists have been developing models of urban growth. While many models have been developed and applied over the past 40 years, the environment for new large-scale urban models remains a rich area of study. DRAM/EMPAL, METROPILUS, POLIS, MEPLAN, and notably UrbanSim, among others, have continued their development and, at times, implementation in regions across the country.[1] While much attention is paid to the development and implementation of these models, for the vast majority of planners, elected officials, and planning commissioners the utility of these models to their daily decisions is limited at the present time.

Implementation of a complex model of urban growth is not only inappropriate for the vast majority of local governments, it is also impractical considering the limited resources available. Yet, in the United States, virtually all development regulations are made by local governments. Indeed, they are often made by members of planning commissions and boards, who are citizen planners living in the community and volunteering their time to make decisions regarding development regulations in the community. But if these citizens are not using our large-scale urban models to support their decisions, how are these decisions being made?

Clearly, professional planning staff support these commissions and boards, but in many communities the entire planning staff consists of one or two people, if any full-time staff are employed at all. It appears that a disconnect between the study and implementation of urban models and the need for practicing professional and citizen planners has evolved.

In part to address this need, over the past several years decision support systems have been developed and applied in many communities across the country. These systems are designed to support decision making and tend to be simple, easy both to apply and understand, and are transparent and customizable to the needs of a community. This chapter briefly describes the planning support system CommunityViz®, its evolution, and current status as an applied planning support tool. It also presents a case study of South Kingstown, Rhode Island, to demonstrate how this small local government addressed their needs for quantitative models using CommunityViz's Scenario 360™.

CommunityViz and Its Origins

Lyman Orton, the proprietor of the Vermont Country Store, volunteered his time as a citizen planner in Vermont. Orton had a strong commitment to the landscape and rural way of life common in Vermont. In the mid-1990s, Orton and his friend Noel Fritzinger decided that citizen planners who try to help in their communities by serving on planning commissions needed to have better tools to help them make better land use decisions. The Orton Family Foundation, a not-for-profit operating foundation based in Vermont, was started to help fund an effort to develop such a tool.

After a few years of investigating how to realize this vision, the foundation hired a group of consultants to develop the tool that would become CommunityViz. Until its first commercial release, CommunityViz was functionally defined by the Environmental Simulation Center, which also managed a software development team consisting of:

- Foresite Consulting for the Scenario Constructor™ module;

- Multigen Paradigm for the SiteBuilder™ module; and

- PricewaterhouseCoopers's Emergent Solutions Group for the Policy Simulator™ module.

Scenario Constructor extended the functionality of ESRI's ArcView® geographic information system (GIS) by allowing users to develop formulas and indicators so that options about land use and other scenarios for the future could be evaluated and compared (Wendt 2002). Both conceptually and architecturally, Scenario Constructor was at the center of CommunityViz and was built as an extension to ArcView GIS version 3. Scenario Constructor provided the essential infrastructure from which the other two modules of CommunityViz were called and could be used independently or in conjunction with the other modules.

SiteBuilder was a real-time, visual-simulation environment that allowed users to visualize their communities in three dimensions using topographic information from the town's GIS as well as three-dimensional buildings modeled with photorealistic facades. This kind of information allowed users to evaluate the future not only using maps, indicators of performance, and charts and graphs, but also experientially in three dimensions.

The Policy Simulator made it possible for users to forecast change in their community using an agent-based land development model. It was designed with a policy construction template so that users could implement various land use policies, either singly or in conjunction, and see how they would affect forecasted change in the community. The Policy Simulator was perhaps the most far-reaching element of CommunityViz and was certainly the most data- and computation-intensive component (Kwartler and Bernard 2001; Bernard 2001).

CommunityViz Today

While CommunityViz is still controlled by the Orton Family Foundation, CommunityViz operations are now run by Placeways, LLC, a Colorado-based concern that markets and improves the tool, with support from the Orton Family Foundation. What is now known as CommunityViz consists of two major modules: Scenario 360, an improved version of Scenario Constructor that can be used with ESRI's ArcGIS™ version 9; and SiteBuilder, which is largely unchanged since its initial release. The Policy Simulator module was dropped in 2003 since it was considered too difficult for most users to implement.

Scenario 360 is now clearly the most important module of CommunityViz. It also shows the most utility as a comprehensive planning decision support system. With the improvements to the formula, build-out, and suitability wizards, along with sketch planning functions and the ability to export scenes to Google Earth or simple HTML reports, the Scenario 360 component has matured into a comprehensive, easy-to-use planning support system.

CommunityViz is designed for use by planning practitioners who wish to extend their knowledge and capabilities by combining their professional expertise with the data that exists in a community's GIS. For those who develop spatial models, it remains perhaps the most important platform, as it can be used for the development and implementation of complex quantitative geographic models that use GIS data and functions natively. Consequently, models that consider distances (either straight-line or network) or use conditional proximities can call those GIS functions in ArcGIS and build them directly into the model algorithms. Since these functions are native to ArcGIS, when data are updated they do not need additional processing for use by the model. In a planning office, where data may change constantly, this is the only practical way to ensure that quantitative models are using the most current data.

CommunityViz's SiteBuilder module, while in the process of becoming redundant with the advent of a variety of other visual simulation environments, still retains some value. In the opinion of many, its motion model remains the most intuitive of all 3D environments, and its close integration with ArcGIS allows the development of 3D environments that are entirely consistent with ArcGIS data in a community's GIS. As of this writing, however, further development of the SiteBuilder module has been suspended, which brings into question its long-term viability.

Unlike other planning support systems, CommunityViz is not a model. Rather, it is a platform that allows the development of planning models. To illustrate the breadth of this functionality, the following case study demonstrates how a planning office can develop an interactive model wholly customized to the specifics of its own community.

Case Study: South Kingstown, Rhode Island

South Kingstown is a semirural New England town in southern Rhode Island bordering the Atlantic Ocean. The town has about 30,000 residents and occupies 56.8 square miles of land and 6.1 square miles of water. It includes a portion of the Great Swamp, an ecologically important forested wetland. The main campus of the University of Rhode Island occupies another part of the town. Settled for over 300 years, the town features a variety of housing types and lot sizes. It has some seasonal housing, mostly small beach bungalows on tiny lots. Only portions of the town have sewer service.

Administratively, South Kingstown is notable for its active planning staff, a first-rate GIS and GIS manager, and a town manager who has provided the community with strong leadership over many years.

The Town has a mechanism in its zoning ordinance that places a limit on building permits as a part of its growth management program. It sets a two-year maximum quota for new residential building permits, and that quota cannot be more than one-third of the Town's six-year housing capacity. As a consequence of this ordinance, the Town's housing capacity needs to be known. In 2001, the Town calculated this internally using GIS queries that summarized conditions and fed into a spreadsheet that applied density assumptions to the data. The Town made a major methodological update to its model in 2004, but in that same year it also decided it needed a build-out system that would be more flexible, repeatable, and easier to maintain and update every year.

In 2005 South Kingstown engaged the Environmental Simulation Center (ESC) to develop such a system. The scope of work for what became an in-depth process had three major parts: (1) replication of the Town's previous method and output; (2) model design and implementation; and (3) installation of the model and training of the South Kingstown staff on operations.

Task 1: Replicating the Town's Previous Method and Output

Considerable time and effort went into re-creating the Town's homegrown build-out model. The first task in developing a new model was to capture as much of the knowledge gained in that previous work as possible. This involved reviewing the Town's build-out method and then replicating the results using the same data to ensure that the method and data were understood by the ESC and Town staff. The purpose of this exercise was threefold. First, it required that the ESC understand how the Town had previously implemented build-out, which would inform subsequent model design. Second, it required the ESC to work with the Town's data thoroughly so it could understand the data's limitations, strengths, and weaknesses. Third, this exercise required the development of a model that generated results similar to current operational practices.

After months of communication with South Kingstown, the ESC was finally comfortable that it fully understood the Town's previous method, the data which informed it, and that it could reliably implement the original version of the Town's model. The exact same results could never be reproduced, however.

Regardless, the result of this exercise was quite close to what the Town had produced and the goal of the task—understanding the Town's previous method and data environment—was met.

Task 2: Model Design and Implementation

Design and implementation was an iterative process. A model was designed and implemented and the results were analyzed and evaluated with Town staff several times before the final model results were produced. Much was learned through understanding previous versions of the model and through interviews with Town staff. Even more important, these preliminary results inspired the professional staff to provide very detailed comments on how and why development will and will not happen in the community. With each iteration the model was improved to incorporate this knowledge within the system.

The final version of the model is described here; components that were implemented but ultimately dropped are, for the most part, not documented here. Furthermore, this design is presented to help tell the story of this one community and its challenges, rather than to be a model to be followed for other communities. The value of developing a method for use in a single community is that it can be custom designed to the needs and requirements of that place and take into account variations that make the place unique. Any community developing its own model should look inward at how development in that community happens and how data describing the community are organized, rather than using the framework outlined below directly.

SOFTWARE ARCHITECTURE   Difficulties replicating the Town's already complex method informed the ultimate design of the system. Because of the amount of data involved and the processing required for its use, it was clear that any system needed to include an automated data processing model. Such a model would eliminate the need for multiple, order-dependent queries, and also reduce much of the potential error that is introduced in such processing. In discussions with the Town it also became clear that the ability to change assumptions and edit any method developed was desirable for planning purposes beyond growth management, and that this flexibility should be relatively simple to implement.

Importantly, the Town used the ArcGIS system. With ArcGIS two desirable software elements became available to address the major requirements of the system. The first is ESRI's ModelBuilder™ extension, and the second was CommunityViz's Scenario 360 extension. Each of these tools loads directly into ArcGIS, which minimizes data processing/data extraction, simplifies implementation, and ultimately reduced the time required to train South Kingstown staff in model operations.

The ModelBuilder extension allows the construction of complex data models, which can be edited, viewed, and saved in a graphical user interface. The result is more than just a picture since ModelBuilder generates and stores geoprocessing workflows and scripts, which speeds the design and implementation of complex

The Build-out Model Flowchart Shows the Conceptual Design of the Model and the Division of Functions Between ModelBuilder and Scenario 360 Components of the Model

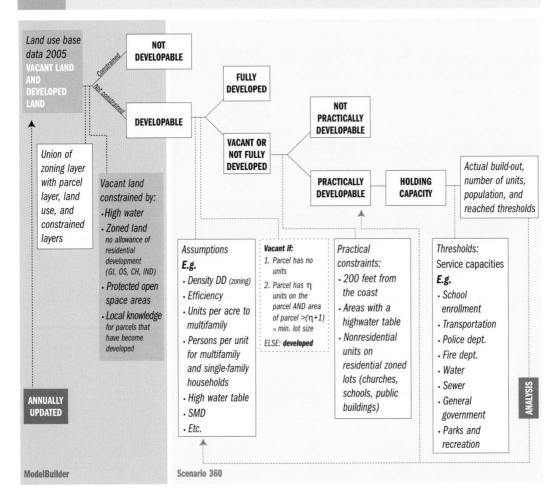

ModelBuilder

Scenario 360

geoprocessing models. Data models are developed as flow diagrams that connect functions and data. Consequently, all data queries required for the build-out model could be predefined and saved and then run with a few simple commands.

Conceptually, Scenario 360 can best be described as a spatial spreadsheet. Like a spreadsheet it allows for computing formulas and calculations, but it can perform these calculations on spatially related data and can include formulas that call standard GIS functions. There is, by definition, no "black box" element to a model defined in Scenario 360. Each formula, assumption, and dependency is viewable and editable. A model developed in Scenario 360 shares a genetic heritage with those described in the classic *Spreadsheet Models for Urban and Regional Analysis* (Klosterman, Brail, and Bossard 1993), rather than the large-scale urban models mentioned earlier. As discussed later, transparency and the ability to edit formulas and alter assumptions became one of the major strengths of the system developed.

MODEL DESIGN In consultation with Town staff, the ESC first created a conceptual framework for model function and data processing and sketched out what would eventually become the flowchart shown in figure 8.1, which describes the entire build-out model in a two-part process. The first part—labeled Model-Builder—unions land use, parcels, and constraints to prepare the data for use in the build-out model. The second part—labeled Scenario 360—describes a decision tree for each parcel that produces holding capacity and ultimate build-out.

THE MODELBUILDER COMPONENT Input data for ModelBuilder are shapefiles. Outputs from ModelBuilder are newly created shapefiles. Input shapefiles (land use, zoning, parcels, local knowledge, and the constraint layers) are all combined using ModelBuilder and produce data used in the Scenario 360 model. This portion automates GIS queries and unions that had been done manually and produces three shapefiles:

1. a union of the constrained shapefiles—protected open space, land use (wetlands and water), zoning (nonresidential land), high water table, local knowledge (developable parcels about which the Town has knowledge that they will not be developed);

2. a union of the parcel and zoning shapefiles; and

3. a union of all the input layers.

The final ModelBuilder model is shown in figure 8.2. The initial build-out model developed during the iterative process described earlier did not have a local knowledge layer. During model development it was determined that many

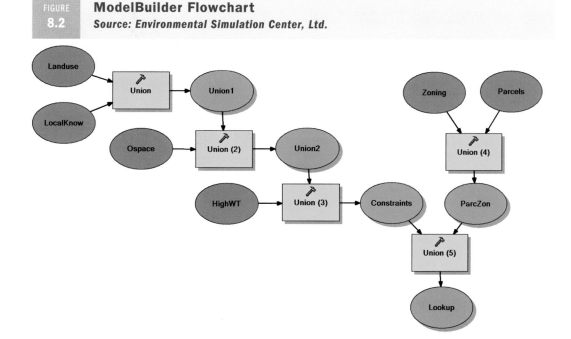

FIGURE 8.2 **ModelBuilder Flowchart**
Source: Environmental Simulation Center, Ltd.

unusual situations and odd quirks pertained to specific parcels. The Town needed to develop a new data layer that would utilize this local knowledge about the land and inform the build-out model. Ultimately, this was called the local knowledge layer. It includes elements such as cemeteries, which are theoretically developable, but for the purposes of build-out identified as undevelopable. Other examples included parcels recently built out by recent subdivision approvals, but which do not show up on any other data source.

While it would have been ideal to have represented all of these elements in original data layers, there were so many unique or unusual cases that the only practical solution was to have this layer summarized as local knowledge that exists outside the base data.

THE SCENARIO 360 COMPONENT   Models built in Scenario 360 can read spatial and tabular data, use a host of traditional as well as spatial functions, and can be built with easily manipulated assumptions that can test the impacts of policy decisions. Scenario 360 was used to construct, store, modify, and apply the build-out model and its assumptions and produce holding capacity and ultimate build-out.

Two primary types of input data are required to run the model: geographic data necessary to calculate the build-out, and the assumptions that drive the

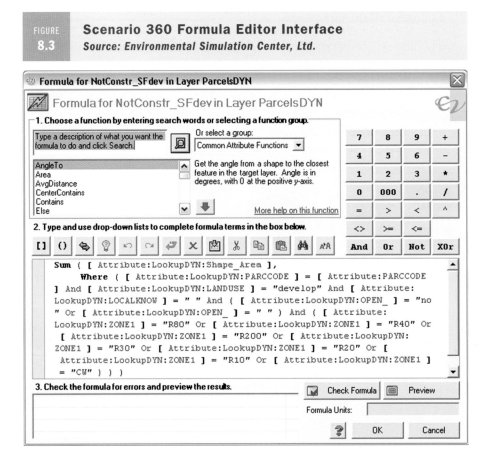

FIGURE 8.3   **Scenario 360 Formula Editor Interface**
Source: Environmental Simulation Center, Ltd.

model. The model itself is a series of simple arithmetic equations, all of which are stored in Scenario 360. While simple mathematically, formulas that make up the final build-out model take up 10 pages in the appendix of the user documentation. It was possible to create and manage such a system because of Scenario 360's formula editor, which not only assists in the construction, display, and editing of the formulas, but also keeps track of dependencies, keeping all components of the model in sync. A snapshot of the formula editor with the equation that calculates the amount of developable land for single-family units on each parcel is shown in figure 8.3.

DEVELOPABLE AREA ON THE PARCEL   Build-out calculates residential holding capacity for each parcel. Fundamental to this calculation is identifying vacant land available for development. Developable land is run through a series of formulas to determine if parcels are already fully developed, are vacant, or are partially vacant. Vacant areas are then run through practical constraints and a calculation of vacant holding capacity by parcel is produced. Calculations are made per parcel and the lookup table is used for calculating the developable area on a parcel. Box 8.1 describes how developable land is identified.

BOX 8.1	**Calculating Developable Area on a Parcel**

An area is developable using the following criteria.

LAND USE IS VACANT OR DEVELOPED. *The land use layer was defined as four uses: water, wetlands, vacant, and developed. The data are based upon aerial photography interpretation, which does not necessarily correspond to actual land uses, zoning districts, or allowable densities. For example, areas marked as developed are often not fully built out under current zoning densities. The build-out model includes vacant developable parcels, and calculates the undeveloped capacity of developed and partially developed parcels. Wetlands and water are never developable.*

REMOVE PROTECTED OPEN SPACE. *Like wetlands and water, protected open space is not developable.*

SELECT AREAS THAT ALLOW RESIDENTIAL USE. *Only areas zoned for residential use are developable. In South Kingstown, these are zoning districts R10, R20, R30, R40, R80, R200, RM, MU, CW, CN, and CD.*

IMPLEMENT PRACTICAL CONSTRAINTS. *The model includes practical constraints to development. Practical constraints include high water table, which makes some parts of South Kingstown difficult to develop, and conforming nonresidential uses on residentially zoned parcels. Typically these are churches, schools, and other institutional developments that are permitted in residential districts. The model was developed so that the user can choose if these areas are buildable or not, and in case of areas covered with a high water table, the user can choose the percentage that reduces the development capacity of this land.*

Assumptions in the Model

Build-out is an assumption-driven model, and any of the assumptions in the model can be changed. When an assumption is changed, all formulas within the scenario that use that assumption are automatically recalculated. Parameters that were set up as assumptions are summarized in box 8.2.

BOX 8.2 **Parameters Set up as Adjustable Assumptions**

ASSUMED PARAMETERS

ALLOWABLE DENSITIES *The densities of current zoning districts are built as assumptions in the model. When combined with developable area, they produce holding capacity. When a user varies these assumptions, the model will show how changing zoning density in a particular district would impact total build-out.*

PERSONS PER UNIT FOR MULTIFAMILY AND SINGLE FAMILY *To calculate total population at build-out, assumptions have been created to vary the number of persons per unit in multifamily and single-family units. The default value is 2.56 for single family and 1.25 persons per unit for multifamily, based upon 2000 Census data for South Kingstown.*

NUMBER OF UNITS PER YEAR *This assumption allows the user to estimate the average number of building permits issued in any given year, allowing a calculation of an estimate of the number of years left until ultimate build-out is reached.*

APPROVED UNITS FOR MULTIFAMILY AND SINGLE FAMILY *This assumption allows Town staff to override certain components of the build-out model with exogenous information. Staff members calculate the number of units that have been approved or are in the approval process and then input that number as an assumption. Entries for both multifamily and single-family units may be made. Parcels under development are included in the local-knowledge layer and removed from the build-out model. They are added back into the total number of units at the end of the analysis.*

ACTUAL NUMBER OF UNITS AND ACTUAL NUMBER OF PEOPLE *These assumptions allow the user to calculate the number of housing units and the population at build-out. The default values are 12,633 units and 30,269 people. This is a 2005 estimate from tax assessor's data using a housing unit method.*

SUBDIVISION EFFICIENCY FACTOR FOR VACANT AND DEVELOPED LAND *The efficiency factor reflects the amount of developable land that is lost to roads and inefficient lot splits during subdivision. Two assumptions address subdivision efficiency: the efficiency on vacant parcels and that on developed parcels (or areas on the parcel in the case of split parcels). The default values, calculated empirically from recent developments in the town, are 15 percent on vacant parcels and 50 percent on developed parcels.[2]*

PRACTICAL CONSTRAINT ASSUMPTIONS

CONFORMING NONRESIDENTIAL BUILDINGS ON RESIDENTIALLY ZONED LAND *This assumption determines if conforming nonresidential buildings (e.g., churches, schools, cultural buildings,* *fire department buildings, hospitals, police, governmental buildings) will stay or can be replaced with new residential units. The default value is yes, which indicates that they can be replaced with new residential development. If only some of these can be replaced, others can be taken out through the local knowledge data layer.*

HIGH WATER TABLE *This assumption determines if areas that have a high water table are buildable or are impaired by their physical constraints. The default value was 50 percent, which indicated that the development capacity of this land will be reduced by 50 percent.*

LAND WITHIN 200 FEET OF THE COAST *While this practical constraint was eventually dropped from the final model, it is detailed here for the lesson learned. Development within 200 feet of the Atlantic coastline is difficult and uncommon in South Kingstown. Building codes require that any such development be built on pilings to protect it from flooding, and while development is not prohibited, this requirement creates considerable added cost and makes this land difficult to develop. The build-out model was developed with all land within 200 feet of the coast having a user-modifiable practical constraint, like high water table, but this ultimately proved to be an example of the cost of implementation not being equal to the added benefit.*

This practical constraint made a tiny impact on the overall capacity of the town, yet made the entire model much more complicated. The model required that proximity to the coast as well as zoning class and status of wetland, open space, and high water be known for each land parcel. The South Kingstown model operated on each unique combination of all these conditions, with capacity by parcel ultimately summed from each piece of land within each parcel that fit each unique condition. While the model's formulas were mathematically simple, they were very long, which made them look complicated and difficult to edit. Overlays such as the 200-foot buffer from the coast also added much to data processing and model maintenance. The benefit of this added component to results was minimal and too costly for inclusion in the final model.

CALCULATING VACANT HOLDING CAPACITY   After the nonconstrained area per parcel is calculated (separately for multifamily and single-family land use), the next step is to calculate holding capacity. Minimum lot size is calculated based on zoning density. In case of parcels split by a zoning district, the weighted minimum lot size on the parcel is calculated. The nonconstrained area divided by the minimum lot size shows the holding capacity of the parcel. The final step for calculating the vacant holding capacity is to subtract existing units from total holding capacity.

ALTERING ASSUMPTIONS   Scenario 360 possesses an excellent interface for altering assumptions and a built-in infrastructure that allows policy or sensitivity testing. The assumption interface for the South Kingstown model is reproduced as figure 8.4. The slider bars allow users to vary assumptions easily and then run the model to see how results change.

The scenario-construction functionality of Scenario 360 provides infrastructure that allows side-by-side comparisons between two or more scenarios.

Impacts of altered assumptions can be compared and evaluated. For example, the user can experiment with allowable densities in particular zoning districts. The result of each experiment can be saved as a scenario and the output for each can be compared showing the consequences of such a decision.

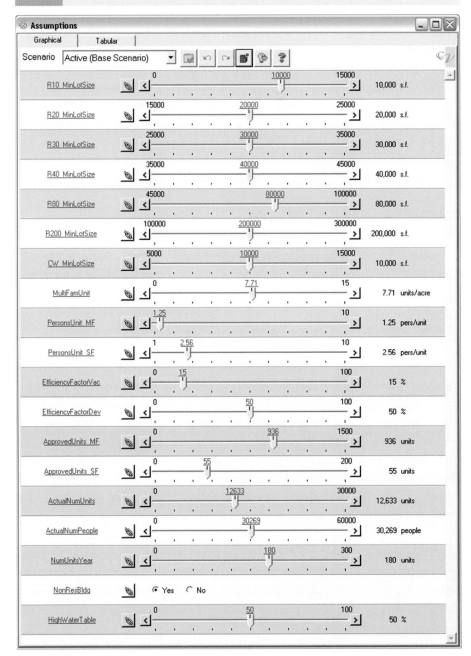

FIGURE 8.4 **Assumptions Interface, South Kingstown Model**
Source: Environmental Simulation Center, Ltd.

Task 3: Installation and Training

The build-out model was designed to be run and maintained by Town staff without the assistance of the ESC or outside consultants. This required that all elements of the model be documented thoroughly and that training materials be developed. These materials were used in a hands-on training with the Town's GIS administrator, who took responsibility for managing the model, updating the data, and producing outputs.

The Town has very competent staff and the GIS administrator picked up the functionality of the tool immediately, demonstrating it to planning staff and a joint meeting of the Town Council and Planning Board in 2006. There are two maintenance challenges, tasks that are only performed yearly—updating the data and installing updates to ArcGIS or Scenario 360. The ESC will field occasional questions, but Town staff have been able to perform operations and maintenance largely on their own.

"Final" Output

The 2005 build-out model was designed to test assumptions and to change as South Kingstown develops and changes. Therefore, no results are truly final. Nevertheless, using all default values as assumptions, the build-out model showed that the town had vacant capacity for an additional 5,696 units and 12,943 people.

Figures 8.5 and 8.6 show vacant holding capacity by parcel using default values. To be shown as having any holding capacity, a parcel must have room for at least one unit. If there is room for 0.99 units, capacity is shown as zero.[3] The parcel with the largest holding capacity has room for 181 units. The detail of the "core" of the town in figure 8.6 shows that infill development on many already developed parcels is still possible under current zoning densities.

During recent communication with South Kingstown, it was learned that several of the larger parcels shown as developable on these maps were removed for a variety of reasons during the 2006 update. The ability to analyze the results at this level allows staff to question the results of the model, investigate its output and, if necessary, make changes (usually through the local knowledge layer).

Challenges and Lessons Learned

The South Kingstown model was implemented by an ESC staff person who, while skilled with GIS analysis, had never before implemented such a model. The interfaces and wizards that are built into Scenario 360 allow individuals familiar with ArcGIS to pick up the functionality of Scenario 360 fairly quickly with no programming skills required. This low "cost of entry" remains a major empowering aspect of a model developed in Scenario 360. Planners and technicians with common skill sets can develop and maintain their own models. The Town engaged the ESC to develop this system for them. Had they had staff resources to commit to the development of the system, they probably could have developed the system themselves. The required skills were not overly specialized.

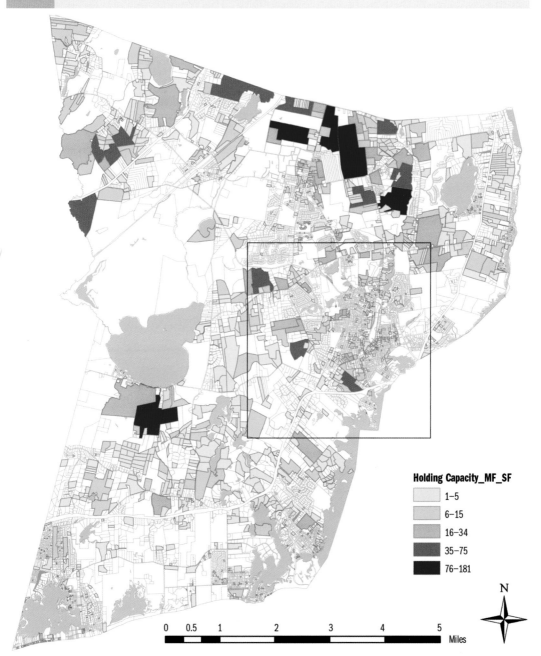

FIGURE
8.5
Result of the 2005 Build-out Model
Source: Environmental Simulation Center, Ltd.

Holding Capacity_MF_SF

	1–5
	6–15
	16–34
	35–75
	76–181

N

0   0.5   1   2   3   4   5
Miles

Nevertheless, the development of the model took considerable time. This had more to do with its iterative design than any other single aspect. Iterative model design allows for optimum results. It permits refinement during design in response to preliminary results. This kind of design approach also makes it difficult to develop and keep to a schedule since it was not predetermined how many iterations the model would require.

Result of the 2005 Build-out Model, Core Area
Source: Environmental Simulation Center, Ltd.

FIGURE 8.6

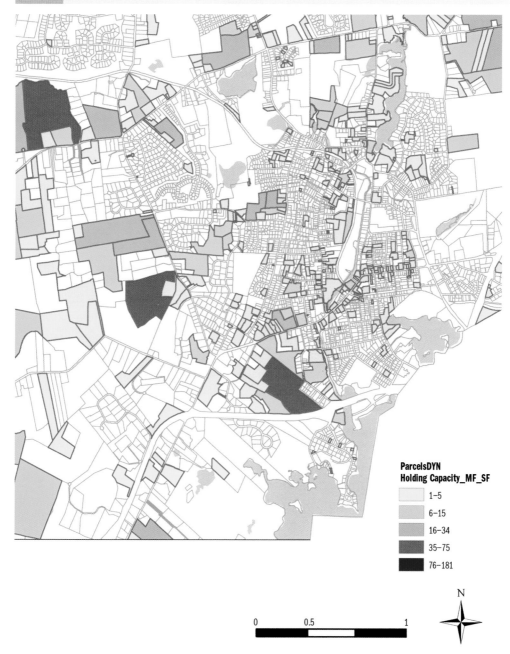

ParcelsDYN
Holding Capacity_MF_SF

- 1–5
- 6–15
- 16–34
- 35–75
- 76–181

N

0   0.5   1

The South Kingstown model is a custom-designed application. As such, the model has quirks and conditions that need to be managed. Software with wider applications should be designed to handle usual exceptions out of the box, whereas custom-designed applications are suitable only for their particular environment. As a result, when the environment changes, it can cause issues with operations. For example, when the model was updated for 2006, the Town updated the records in one field in one table with values that were null. Previously, this field had been defined as a real number and was never null. The model was not designed to handle the null exception and stopped with an error. The fix was simple, but diagnosing the problem took some time.

Conclusions

In the United States most land use decisions are made at the local level. Local development regulations interact with each other, with state and federal regulations, and with the decisions of local landowners and institutions, creating an array of overlapping and interacting requirements, rules, and intentions. It is impossible for the professional or citizen planner to understand fully how changes in a single regulation will impact the entire system without a way to track and measure interactions among all elements that affect development in the community. The South Kingstown build-out model attempts to be the system that tracks all these elements.

But unlike many larger-scale urban models, the South Kingstown model does not attempt to forecast what may happen in the future. Rather, it attempts to take what is known about the land and the laws that govern the land and tries to inform planners and decision makers about the consequences of those conditions. If those consequences are considered unacceptable, the build-out model is also designed to show how changing those conditions will impact development. It does this with comprehensive and up-to-date data, straightforward, and changeable assumptions, and understandable formulas. The South Kingstown model approach is made practical because of Scenario 360.

The use of simple formulas, transparent assumptions, and accepted data sources is extremely valuable for people who make local planning decisions. Citizen planners benefit from the opportunity to drill down into assumptions, formulas, and data so that if questions arise the issue can be investigated and explained. Furthermore, it is also useful when formulating policy to be able to analyze each component and to be able to state: Assuming there are no changes to any other regulations, if this regulation is changed it will alter our capacity by x. This kind of design also means that common steps found in other large-scale urban models are missing. Calibration, for instance, is not a part of the South Kingstown model. It is both unnecessary and undesirable, adding parameters and creating complexity.

The current movement in planning toward tools that are designed to support practical decision making is a major step forward for professionals, citizens, and elected officials. These straightforward tools are providing timely customized information to decision makers so that they can better plan for the future of their communities. The South Kingstown model is a single application of an entire system (Scenario 360) that has countless applications, including the 3D component that allows future conditions to be visualized. Likewise, other systems are being applied in other communities that address additional issues. But the common thread in most of these applications is that they are driven by the needs of the local planners and decision makers. Indeed, local planners and decision makers are beginning to take more control and drive the applications as they write requests for proposals (RFPs) and describe the tools they need. Eventually, as the tools become even simpler and easier to use, we may start seeing the widespread application of homegrown tools. Instead of issuing RFPs, communities will take complete control of the design and implementation of their decision-making tools.

Endnotes

1. For UrbanSim, see Waddell (2002) and this book, chapter 6. DRAM/EMPAL and METROPILUS are presented in Putman and Chan (2001).

2. Tear downs of existing buildings on underbuilt lots do not happen often in South Kingstown. The large efficiency factor for lots that are already developed takes into account that most development on these lots is as a subdivision that preserves the existing home, which often was built in the center of the lot. To maintain required setbacks, this kind of lot subdivision often requires inefficient lot splits. If tear downs become more common in the town, this number can be altered to reflect a more efficient use of land during subdivision.

3. Assemblages of multiple parcels, which would allow for more efficient subdivision, does not happen often in this town and was deliberately not included in the build-out model.

Development Control Planning Support Systems

9

Anthony G. O. Yeh

PLANNING SUPPORT SYSTEMS (PSS) CAN BE USED IN DIFFERENT STAGES AND functions of urban planning. General administration, development control, and plan making are the three major applications of information technology in urban planning (Yeh 1999). Most of the PSS that have been developed support the plan-making process. However, a significant amount of the work of a planner is in general administration and development control.

Planning is futile if a plan prepared cannot be implemented. There are many ways to implement a plan—through legislation, capital projects, and development control. Development control is the most commonly used method in making sure that any proposed project will take place according to the spirit of the plan. In the United Kingdom all material change of use has to go through an application process and obtain permission from the planning authority ensuring that the project will comply with the development plan (Bruton and Nicholson 1987). In governments using a zoning system, development cannot take place if it contravenes the zoning plan. Processing planning applications is a continuing responsibility of government agencies, and there is a statutory regulation about the length of time permitted to deal with an application.

Many applications of PSS focus on the preparation of a plan or project and the testing of planning scenarios. These systems are used to determine whether the land is suitable for the proposed development and whether there are any impacts on the natural, social, traffic, and visual environment. A geographic information system (GIS) often supports these PSS through such tools as buffers, overlay techniques, and network analysis. Three-dimensional visualization techniques also support these efforts. Rather than discussing these commonly used planning support systems, however, this chapter will discuss two new developments in PSS for facilitating administrative decision-making processes in development control.

Similar to the planning process, there are different stages in development control. Most planning applications in development control have a statutory time period for making a decision. In most cities, decisions on development control are made by a planning commission, town planning board, or similar entity, often with representation from the community. The role of the planning staff is to make certain that the statutory time period of the planning application is followed and that relevant government departments and the community have been consulted. They will compile all the inputs and decisions of similar past cases for members of the reviewing group to consider. A GIS-based Computer-Supported Collaborative Work Flow (CSCWF) system can help to keep track of different stages of the planning applications (Chen, Jiang, and Yeh 2004) and a case-based reasoning (CBR) system can help to store and retrieve past cases, thus aiding the decision making on the proposed development (Shi and Yeh 1999; Yeh and Shi 1999; 2003).

GIS-based Computer-supported Collaborative Work Flow (CSCWF) Systems

Development control is a collaborative decision-making process that involves urban planners and related government officials who are often spatially separated. They have to review and process planning applications submitted by a developer or citizen according to predefined regulations and workflow. The output of planning applications is either a legal permit describing both the geometric and thematic states of the land parcel, or a notice explaining to the applicant why the application has been rejected. In the past, the review process was done mainly by circulating the hard copies among different actors in the planning application process. This process can be automated and made more efficient through information technology. The application files and related plans, maps, and photos can be processed electronically through the local area network or intranet.

From the point of view of behavioral modeling, the three major components in the collaborative process of development control are agents, events, and states, as illustrated in figure 9.1. The staff in different departments (or levels) can be viewed as agents who have the responsibility to make decisions in the development control process. Each decision made by an agent triggers one or more reviewing events such as site location, land use permission, and title registration. The results of these reviewing events are states, such as planned land lots, delineated land use boundaries, and registered cadastral property. The state of a parcel consists of its geometry, thematic attributes, and topological relations with other parcels.

The relations among these agents, events, and states include the sequential order and hierarchical relations between any two agents, relations between agents and events, relations between events, causal relations between events and states, and relations between states (Jiang 2000; Jiang et al. 2000). For example, site location event E1 occurs before land use permission event E2, and title registration event E3 cannot begin until E2 is finished. The entire development control process can be represented by a composite event, such as E1, E2, and E3

The Collaborative Development Control Process

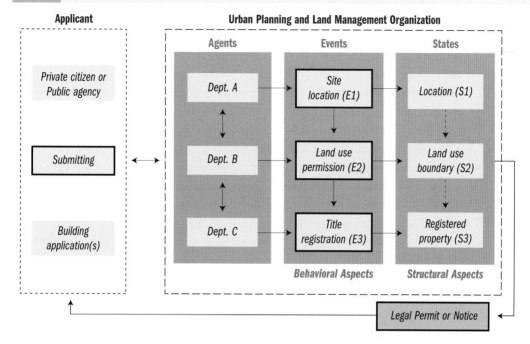

in figure 9.1. Each of these three events can be divided further into subevents. The causal relations between events and states of land parcels reflect the geometrical and thematic changes in the land parcels.

In general, any change of state would be driven or caused by a specific event. Let S0 be the initial state of a land parcel. After the execution of the event site locating E1, the location of parcel S1 is created. S1 was modified after executing E2 and land use boundary S2 was generated. The boundary of registered property S3 is further demarcated by the following event E3. There are relations between different states of the same land parcel. In fact, S1 is created on the basis of S0, and S1 was modified and transformed into S2. The one-to-one relationship between sequential states of the same parcel is considered in the entity-relation modeling of development control.

In earlier applications of urban GIS, the emphasis was placed on the representation of the states of spatial objects. The attributes of the states of the spatial system were modeled with the cartographic layers, features attribute tables, lookup tables, annotation, and a map library. Often an ESRI ArcInfo® database was used. Modeling both the structural and behavioral aspects is not new in computer science (Pernici 1990; Quer and Olive 1993). For example, Teisseire, Poncelet, and Cicchetti (1994) extended the IFO[1] model to integrate both the structural and behavioral representation of applications in a consistent and uniform manner in terms of both the formalization and the associated graphic representation. Snoeck and Dedene (1998) tried to express the semantic integrity of structural and behavioral schema with an existence-dependency graph.

However, the task was not easy, even in designing event-based nonspatial databases (Scheer 1992).

Some initial attempts have been made to represent both structural aspects and behavioral aspects in GIS applications. Peuquet and Duan (1995) proposed an event-based spatio-temporal data model, where the sequence of events through time was organized in increasing order along a time line. Claramunt and Theriault (1995; 1996) presented another event-oriented approach modeling changes among a set of entities. Spatial entities and their temporal versions were associated through intermediary logical tables (past events, present events, and future events) that permit the description of complex succession, production, reproduction, and transmission processes. Time, however, was treated as a complementary facet of spatial and thematic domains that are separated into distinct structures and unified by domain links. Allen, Edwards, and Bedard (1995) tried to develop a generic model for explicitly representing causal links within a spatio-temporal GIS. A small number of elements were presented in that model using an extended entity-relationship formalism, including objects and their states, events, agents, and conditions, as well as the relations (produces, is part of, conditions). However, these initial efforts gave priority to some local or partial behaviors of the applications rather than to an overview of the system's behavior. In the case of the development control reviewing system, both the structural and behavioral aspects of the overall system require modeling. The agents, events, and states, as well as the relations among them, should be taken into consideration in designing and developing a GIS-based CSCWF system for development control.

Hierarchical Representation of the Relations Among Agents, Events, and States

A hierarchical representation of agents, events, and states as well as their relations was proposed instead of using one large diagram. A first-level diagram of the development control process is shown on the left-hand side of figure 9.2, and each of its blocks can be detailed out on the second-level diagram. For instance, the block Department B was detailed out on the right-hand side of figure 9.2, with the subagents, subevents, and substates at the next level. The whole process is represented by a hierarchical set of diagrams.

Among the relations represented in the hierarchical set of diagrams, there exist the collaborative relations between agents, sequential relations between events, transitional relations between states, and executive relations between an agent and an event, triggering relations between an event and a state, etc. (Jiang 2000). The collaborative relation between agents is a dynamic process with actions such as require, reject, accept, and inform. The transitional relation between states reflects the transition from an intermediate result (such as a sketch map) to a final result (legal map). It is quite possible that several events in conjunction initiate an event, or that a state is the result of several events. Moreover, one agent might execute more than one event.

FIGURE 9.2

Hierarchies of Integrated Representation of Agents, Events, and States

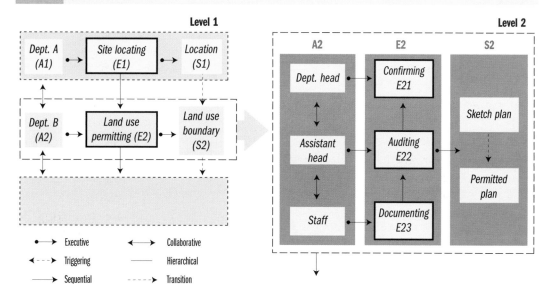

Formal representation of events and their relations with states can be modeled with the Event Pattern Language (EPL) (Gehani, Jagadish, and Shmueli 1992a; 1992b). An event can be described with a tuple (Eid, Ea, Epro, Es), where Eid is an identifier of the event, Ea represents the attributes of the event, Epro is the precondition of the event occurrence, and Es is the subsequential effects of the event occurrence. The id is a character string representing hierarchy and generalization. For instance, E2 in figure 9.2 is a composite event with E21, E22, and E23 as its subevents. A state of a spatial object can also be described by a tuple (Sid, Sec, See, Spro, Spost), where Sid is the identifier of the state, Sec is the event that creates the state, See is the event that ends the state, Spro is the previous state, and Spost is the poststate. With these expressions, the land use boundary in figure 9.1 can be represented as (S2, E2, E3, S1, S3). This tuple describes not only the relation between spatial objects and the related events, but also the corresponding relations between different states (Chen and Jiang 2000).

Integration of Heterogeneous and Disparate Spatial and Nonspatial Data

It is essential to have easy access to existing or newly created spatial and non-spatial data during the process of development control, which generally includes various plans, topographic maps, facility maps, administrative boundaries, cadastral maps, decision-related documents, various permits, laws and regulations, etc. These heterogeneous and disparate sources of data within an urban planning and land management bureau need to be assembled into an integrated database (Jiang, Chen, and Yeh 2002). To integrate these multiscale, multitype data, a unique identification code—the Feature ID (FID)—is assigned to each spatial object. The

FIGURE
9.3
Links Between Spatial Objects, Attribute Tables, and Multimedia Data

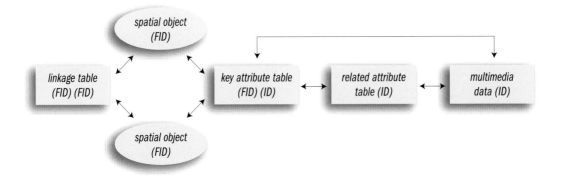

linkage between different spatial objects and between a spatial object and related attribute tables can be executed using the FID as shown in figure 9.3.

The successive spatial states in the development control process are defined as composite spatial objects, such as planned site location, delineated land use boundary, permitted building area, and registered property. The causal linkages between these states are represented explicitly with an entity-relation diagram as shown in figure 9.4. Each state might be composed of a set of primitive spatial objects, which are represented in the federated database.

A node-link structure was also used for the associative linking of a variety of multimedia information (Shiffer 1995). The aerial images, ground photos, 3D landscape, narrative descriptions, and digital video and sound can

FIGURE
9.4
An Entity-relation Diagram of States in Development Control

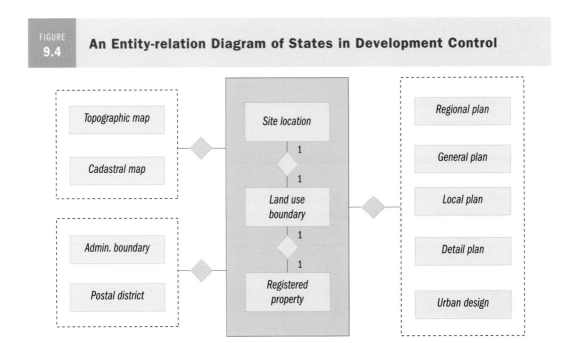

be encapsulated by nodes and associated with one or more spatial objects on digital maps. The maps are used as the spatial reference attached by other document nodes. Users can navigate in or through geographic space to retrieve the multimedia information about the past and existing conditions of a particular location. With the support of this hypermedia information, planners are able to show people explicit photo information of what their city will look like after a proposed change, instead of presenting citizens with abstract maps and descriptive text to explain, analyze, and debate design ideas and urban processes.

Specific Functions for Day-to-Day Routine Work

Once an application is submitted, a sequence of legally defined events will be executed by planning staffs and land managers according to the nature of the applied case, such as registering applications, delineating boundaries of land use and building construction, offering opinions, printing permits, and filing documents. In order to automate such manual processes with networked communication and spatial data–handling capabilities, three kinds of functionalities were developed for urban planners and land managers, i.e., office automation for paperwork, desktop boundaries mapping, and network-based generic queries.

OFFICE AUTOMATION FUNCTIONALITIES   Each planning application is considered as a case and assigned a unique code as its identifier. A series of office automation functions were developed within the Oracle environment, including application registering, document checking, staff memos, legal permits, and associated graphic documents. As these functions are executed, the results are processed and transferred immediately to the next stage.

DESKTOP SPATIAL DATA–HANDLING TOOLS   Delineating new land parcels and locating new buildings on large-scale digital maps is one of the key desktop spatial data–handling tasks. A specific toolkit was developed. Some of the toolbars are shown in figure 9.5, such as road-arc generating, coordinate and area measuring, legend labeling, official stamp mapping, etc.

NETWORK-BASED GENERIC QUERIES   Process query, facts query, map query, and laws query are four major generic queries developed on the basis of the classification of data and the integrated structure. For a given development application, it is possible to access its current, previous, and subsequent reviewing steps with the integrated structure of agent, event, and state. It is possible to know how many steps the development application has gone through and what the current and other remaining reviewing stages include. An example is given in figure 9.6. In order to provide easy and understandable access, visual interfaces are designed that integrate the workflow charts with icons and a help wizard. Differences in technical languages of different application areas are also taken into consideration. The end users do not always know the terms adopted by "experts" in

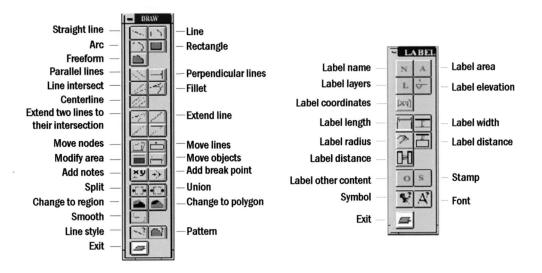

FIGURE 9.5 **Some Toolbars for Producing Development Control Maps**

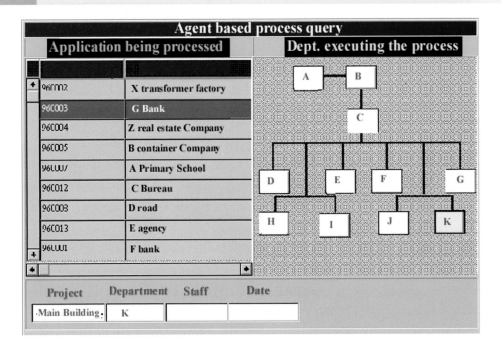

FIGURE 9.6 **Agent-based Process Query About a Development Application**

charge of development application. One example is that the term *project* is used in the interface instead of *record*, which is used by the system developers.

It is also possible to know for a given step how many application cases have been reviewed in a given period of time and what applications are under review.

The administrators, planning staff, and land managers at different levels can use this query to find out the progress of different stages of the development control process and speed them up if there are delays. The relevant states and other documents can also be retrieved with the help of the linkages between events and states. For instance, tracking issued permits is routine work in development control. Based on the records related to the parcels approved or building occupancy permitted, all the changes that have taken place since a specific time can be retrieved from the federated database. Maps, remote-sensing images, aerial photographs, and pictures related to the site can be retrieved and displayed through the system (Chen et al. 1998).

Case-based Reasoning (CBR) System

The GIS-based Computer-Supported Collaborative Work Flow system is a PSS for facilitating collaboration in processing planning applications in development control. It helps to control the sequence and monitor the status of the decision-making process of development control. It does not give any advice on whether a planning application should be approved. A case-based reasoning (CBR) approach can be used as a PSS by retaining corporate memory and providing more consistent decisions in development control.

Knowledge-based systems (KBS) and expert systems (ES) have aroused the interest of planners for many years. Researchers have explored many potential applications, and a few prototypes and even operational systems have been built (Kim, Wiggins, and Wright 1990). However, there are many limitations in using KBS in urban planning (Barbanente et al. 1995; Borri et al. 1994; Han and Kim 1990; Marchand 1993; Ortolano and Perman 1990). The two main obstacles in successfully applying KBS to urban planning are difficulties in building a practical system and the problems encountered in "inspiring confidence in the use of it" (Marchand 1993). Some of these problems can be overcome by the use of CBR, where previous similar cases suggest solutions to new cases (Yeh and Shi 1999). In contrast to rule-based reasoning or model-based reasoning, CBR directly uses concrete knowledge, where inference is basically the process of retrieval and adaptation. These features permit CBR to avoid some of the problems in building KBS, such as knowledge-elicitation bottlenecks, thereby gaining the confidence of users (Yeh and Shi 1999).

CBR Overview

Originating from the work of Schank and Abelson (1977), CBR has developed into a mature and important field of artificial intelligence (Aamodt and Plaza 1994; Kolodner 1993; Schank and Leake 1989; Watson 1997). Increasingly, many domains are using CBR, such as architectural design, law, medicine, and customer services (Watson 1997).

The basic philosophy of CBR is to use previous similar cases to help solve, evaluate, or interpret a current new problem (Kolodner 1993). It simulates human behavior in solving such new problems. When confronted with a new and difficult problem, it is natural for a human problem-solver to recall any previous similar instances from memory. In simulating the human brain in problem solving, a computerized case-based system (CBS) using CBR sees knowledge as encapsulated memories; its knowledge base is a case library storing these memories in the form of concrete stories. The user inputs the descriptions of a new problem into the system, and the computer looks for similar cases in its case library according to the predefined matching algorithms. Cases that meet certain criteria will be retrieved. Their solutions, or any other parts of the stories required, will be either directly proposed to the user or, if necessary, adapted to meet the new situation before being proposed. The user can evaluate or test whether the proposed solutions work well. When a satisfactory solution is obtained, the newly solved problem can be stored in the library as a new case and the knowledge of the system is expanded. The CBR process typically can be represented by a schematic cycle comprising the four *REs* as shown in figure 9.7: (1) *retrieve* the most similar case(s); (2) *reuse* the case(s) to attempt to solve the problem; (3) *revise* the proposed solution if necessary; and (4) *retain* the new solution as a part of a new case.[2]

A new problem is matched against cases in the case-base library and one or more similar cases are retrieved. The solution (transformational reuse) and the past method that constructed the solution (derivational reuse) of the retrieved cases is then reused and tested for success in application. Unless the retrieved case is a close match to the new problem, most likely the solution has to be revised in producing a new case that can be retained.

Advantages of CBR over Rule-based Reasoning

From the perspective of a KBS builder, since CBS tend to store knowledge in the form of concrete instances rather than abstract and general rules or models, the system builder can largely avoid meeting the knowledge-elicitation bottleneck. First, extracting knowledge "becomes a simple task of acquiring past cases" but not grasping the underlying reasoning in solving the problems (Watson 1995). Second, the knowledge-storing scheme of CBS provides a good way to record the informal information. This information can easily be recorded in the narration of a "story." Because this narration is on the level of a concrete case and has no effect on other cases, the system builder does not need to worry about the problems related to generalization. Third, different solutions to different cases representing a similar problem, quite common in planning, can be explicitly and conveniently represented. Finally, when the new problem is solved and the effects of the solution in the real world are known, the user can conveniently save this new case in the case base and increase the knowledge of the system. This learning method is very simple and can be performed by the users themselves in their daily work without the help of knowledge engineers. Even when conflicting cases are found, the experts can check what caused this conflict at case level, while in a conventional KBS the conflicts may cause a large modification to the whole knowledge base.

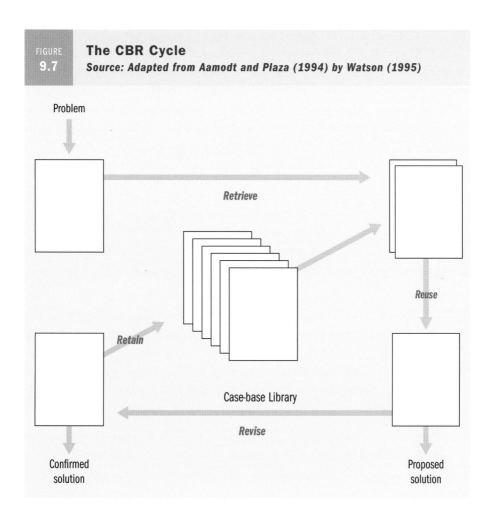

FIGURE 9.7

The CBR Cycle

Source: Adapted from Aamodt and Plaza (1994) by Watson (1995)

From the perspective of the users, the enlightening style of CBR may be more welcome to planners. There are five main reasons for this.

1. The reasoning process is more visible to the users. The user can directly obtain solutions to previous similar problems from the retrieved cases. More importantly, these results are based on actual past cases that can be presented to the user, providing more concrete support for the system's conclusions and recommendations (Leake 1996).

2. The user can take part in the inference process. Rule-based reasoning tries to abstract the experts' problem-solving methods into some fixed routines, and its inference is largely a closed iterative process that will usually reach a final result. The reasoning procedure of CBR is open and the user can take part in or even control the problem-solving process. For example, when a planner has retrieved several similar cases for a new problem, it is easy to understand how the solution was generated, why it was successful or failed, and what the consequence of a solution might be.

3. The way CBR provides help is compelling. CBR will not just tell the planner what to do. Instead, it presents cases related to previously handled similar problems and suggests what has been done under similar situations, what are the consequences of the applied solutions, and what advice the precedents can provide for dealing with the current problem. This process is analogical to what often happens in our brains and is the way in which experts teach novices about how to handle a difficult problem.

4. The cases can provide knowledge about exceptions. As discussed before, knowledge for handling exceptions is often what the user mostly requires, particularly in a domain such as urban planning that is characterized by uncertainty and subjectivity. While many conventional methods of knowledge representation try to omit the exceptions, a case record is all the knowledge about each concrete instance, including the exceptions (Kolodner 1993).

5. A real case is more inspiring than abstract knowledge. In their practical work, planners often refer to previous real examples but not abstract guidelines or regulations to inspire their creativity. A computerized system that facilitates the retrieval of relevant cases and provides required information and tools for visualization, analysis, evaluation, and adaptation would relieve the burden of the planner in trying to remember everything.

In summary, CBR leaves much room for the intelligence of planners to recognize, understand, and generate creative solutions to a new problem, while providing raw but comprehensive and original information and tools to facilitate the decision-making process. By studying previous cases, a new planner gains experience in handling similar problems, while an experienced planner may even generate new insights.

Use of CBR in Development Control

Development control is a relatively well-structured function of urban planning and, as a result, many attempts have been made to apply KBS to it (Leary and Rodriguez-Bachiller 1989; Borri et al. 1994). However, a rule-based KBS may still encounter difficulties similar to those in other fields of urban planning. One of the problems is knowledge acquisition. Some developers of KBS for development control found that "it is extremely difficult to find an expert who is able to formalize his/her decision processes and to communicate his/her knowledge in a satisfactory way, as a domain experience is often based on automatic physical and mental processes, and the expert is frequently led to mix facts and factors and to judge by his/her intuition and imagination" (Barbanente et al. 1995, 573).

Another issue is how to represent case-specific knowledge. Although the problems in development control and their solutions are largely well structured compared with problems in other fields of urban planning, special considerations and characteristics of a planning application case are often also important in making a decision. Borri et al. (1994, 36) found that "different context stimuli or pragmatic suggestions arising from the analysis of relevant context elements may produce microchanges in the problem-solving scheme."

Finally, although development control is relatively well defined, it is far from being without uncertainty. Leary and Rodriguez-Bachiller (1989, 20) pointed out that "officers and committees have discretion to interpret plans and policies"; also "aesthetic and political judgments introduce an element of arbitrariness in the decision-making process," thus "layers of complexity and uncertainty" are added to "what at first glance is a rigid rule-based system." There are always gray areas in development control and often these are the areas where the expertise and experience of the experts are most required. When dealing with such problems, the experts usually draw upon "previous experiences" or "the memory of how similar cases had been solved in the past" (Borri et al. 1994, 37). This is the type of problem that is most suitable for CBR. The advantages of using CBR in development control are summarized below.

- It is a retrieving tool that can help planners find relevant cases quickly.

- It is an intelligent library that can relieve the burden of experts' memory and also increase novices' memory. It is a corporate memory system that will retain knowledge of experienced experts even when they are absent or retired.

- It will provide knowledge directly at case level. The actions of the experts regarding a specific problem and their results as well as the comments from the experts are just descriptive records. There is no need to extract and generalize knowledge.

- It will use concrete cases instead of control branching to demonstrate the templates of different routines or methods.

- For problems with uncertainty, it will help planners explore further. From similar cases, the planner can get tips, hints, instructions, templates, or precedents, depending on what is needed.

- From the old cases the user can learn *how* to respond to a problem, not just what to do or what not to do.

System Design and Architecture

A CBR planning support system integrating a shell, ESTEEM®, and a GIS package, ArcView®, has been developed to support planners in the Planning Department of Hong Kong (Shi and Yeh 1999). In Hong Kong, outline zoning plans (OZP) are mainly used to control land development. These plans indicate areas that are zoned for various uses, for example residential, commercial, and industrial. Attached to each plan is a schedule of notes that shows two columns of land use categories that are permitted in different land use zones. Column 1 contains land uses that are always permitted without the need to seek planning permission. Column 2 shows land uses that may be permitted with or without conditions on application to the Town Planning Board, the statutory body for making decisions on a planning application. The board may either refuse the application or grant permission, with or without any conditions. If the proposed development is neither a Column 1 nor a Column 2 use, then it is not a permissible use within the zone.

Before a planning application is submitted to the Town Planning Board, the planners in the Planning Department will first inspect it. They will examine the new application according to the planning ordinances, regulations, and plans; collect opinions from relevant government departments; and prepare the evaluating documents. The application, together with the evaluating documents, will be submitted to the Town Planning Board which is primarily made up of nongovernment members. The aim of the CBS is to help the planners prepare reasonable, comprehensive, and consistent recommendations to the Town Planning Board for making decisions on applications.

SYSTEM ARCHITECTURE CBS is a promising methodology for building and applying more practical KBS for planners (Yeh and Shi 1999). The integration of CBS with GIS will further enhance its usefulness as a planning support system for development control. In the integrated system, CBS will provide the decision support. The GIS will provide the functions of storing, retrieving, and displaying spatial data. In the handling of spatial data, GIS can be a data generator, a database management system, and a visualization tool. It can store, display, and generate spatial information related to a planning case. It can also retrieve an old case that has a similar spatial relationship with the new problem.

Figure 9.8 shows the framework of the integrated system. From the functional perspective, the system has four basic parts: the user interface, the GIS module (ArcView), the CBS module (ESTEEM), and the case library. With relatively high flexibility in building the input/output interface, ArcView was chosen to be the platform for the integration. Except for some special operations such as creating a new template of retrieval method, all the user inputs will enter the system through the GIS, and all the retrieval or adaptation results will be displayed by the GIS.

The system provides two kinds of retrieval methods—spatial and nonspatial. For spatial retrieval, the system will let the user click within the outline of a specific case on an index map to retrieve that case. When the user clicks on that case, an identifying code is passed to the system and the GIS directly retrieves all the components of that case according to identification code from the case library and then displays them to the user. As for nonspatial retrieval, the GIS first receives from the user the formatted text or numeric descriptions of a new problem and then passes these descriptions to ESTEEM. The program looks for the similar cases through matching the descriptions of the new problem and the index values of the old cases. Then, ESTEEM returns to the GIS the identifying codes of those matched cases.

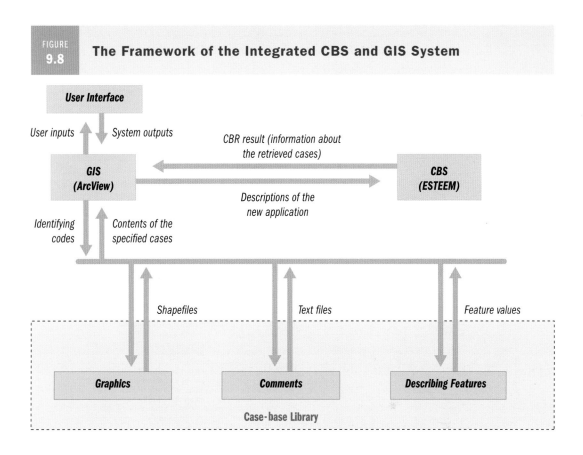

FIGURE 9.8 The Framework of the Integrated CBS and GIS System

BUILDING THE CBS   The building of a CBS includes building the case library, defining an index for the cases, and building retrieval and adaptation methods (Kolodner 1993). For our system, we also developed a simple method for the user to do quantitative evaluation with the retrieved cases.

CASE LIBRARY   The case library is the knowledge base, the fundamental core, of a CBS, and its construction is the first and most important step in building a CBS. Two questions must be answered before building a case library: What is a case in this domain? What should be used to describe a case or what is the content of a case? In the domain of handling planning applications, it is natural to think that each submitted application is a case. But if a planning application had been rejected, its applicant might submit modified versions, each with some improvements in the original design. Treating each application as a single case will not reveal the entire history of the application. Furthermore, the system could not correctly evaluate the new problem. For example, say the application had been rejected several times but finally got the permission. When evaluating a new similar application, the system would draw the conclusion that the new application would tend to be rejected because the rejected "cases" are more numerous than the approved "cases." Therefore, in our project a case contains the entire history of all applications. If an application is a modified version of an old one, both the old and the new one will

FIGURE
9.9

Representation of a Planning Application Case

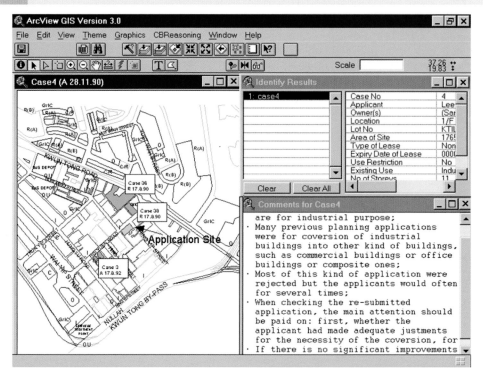

be included in a single case. In our system, a planning application case contains three parts: graphics, tabular features, and comments, as shown in figure 9.9.

GRAPHICS   The application stored in the Planning Department usually includes a map that shows the position and coverage of the land use referred to by the application. The nearby previous cases are also located on this map and outlined with their results and dates labeled beside their sites. This electronic map in figure 9.9 can provide or link to much more information than the original paper map. The user can also click on a specific old case outlined on the map to retrieve the materials of that case. Besides this basic map, the documents of a planning application case sometimes also contain charts, photos, or other graphics.

TABULAR FEATURES   Besides graphics, inevitably the case should include features (attributes) represented with numeric values or texts in tabular format. These features are listed in table 9.1. In our system, a planning application case includes four kinds of tabular features, although sometimes the boundaries between them are not very clear.

1. Features for organizing information: These features are used to manage the case library by organizing the materials, identifying cases, and retrieving related documents.

2. Features containing information about the problem itself: These features describe the application itself. Most of the items in table 9.1 are this kind of feature; for example, the classes of land use.

3. Features containing solution information: This is one of the objectives of the user. The main solution of the problem is shown in the Planning Department's view, the recommendations submitted to the Town Planning Board.

4. Features containing outcome information: This is another objective of the user. The final result of the application—that is, whether it was approved or rejected by the Town Planning Board—can be regarded as part of the outcome of the solution. Although the decision of the Town Planning Board does not totally depend on the opinions of the Planning Department, it is largely affected by these opinions.

TABLE 9.1 Example of the Representation of the Tabular Features of a Planning Application Case

Feature Name	Feature Value
General Information:	
Applications included	A/XYZ/01, A/XYZ/02, and A/XYZ/03
Beginning date	6/12/1989
End date	18/1/1991
Applicant(s)	ABC Investment Company Ltd.
Location	1/F DDD Building, 64 EEE Rd, FFF Area, KL
Use applied for	Office/Industrial composite use
Zoning on statutory plan	Industrial
Existing use	Industrial and associated offices
Result of the application	C
Approval score	0.8
Details of the Existing Use:	
Lot no.	YYYY nn
Area of site	1,765 sq m
Expiry date of lease	30 June 2047
Type of lease	Nonrenewable
Use restriction (if any)	No
Lease clause (design, disposition, height)	No
Other restrictions (traffic implications)	Rate of space for parking, loading/unloading: >=1 vehicle/1,000 sq ft of GFA or >=1 vehicle/5,000 sq ft of the area of the lot
Storey no.	11
Building type	Industrial
Approx. total floor area	15,500 sq m
No. of occupants (residential)	N/A

TABLE 9.1	Example of the Representation of the Tabular Features of a Planning Application Case *continued*

Feature Name	Feature Value
Details of the Proposed Development:	
Zoning plan no.	*X/XXX/X*
New building storey no. (if applicable)	*N/A*
Total site coverage (if applicable)	*N/A*
Proposed use of floors: Basement	*N/A*
Proposed use of floors: Ground floor	*Car parking, Loading/Unloading, Lobby*
Proposed use of floors: First floor	*Industrial/Office*
Proposed use of floors: Second floor	*Industrial/Office*
Proposed use of floors: Third floor and above	*Industrial/Office*
Number of houses	*N/A*
Total domestic ground floor area	*15,500 sq m*
Number of car parking spaces	*N/I*
Vehicular access	*Yes*
Justifications from the Applicant:	*1. Hong Kong's industry was undergoing a structural change that had resulted in demand for such building to accommodate industrial back-up services.* *2. The site, being in close proximity to the FFF MTR Station and FFF Town Centre, was suitable for a composite industrial-office building.* *3. The proposed conversion is technically feasible (a set of building plans was attached).*
The Site and Its Surroundings:	*The site is in close proximity to the FFF MTR Station and FFF Town Centre.*
Planning Intention:	*Industrial development, but the offices that need to be colocated with industrial operations tend to be permitted.*
Traffic Aspect:	*1. The site is close to the FFF MTR Station. This is a commuting convenience for the people working in the building.* *2. The site is at the junction of YYY Road and XXX Street, thus the provision of parking and loading/unloading space is required.*
Lands Aspect:	*The site is suitable for a composite industrial-office building.*
Design Aspect:	*The initial building plan was not up to the design requirements of the Board:* *1. Separate entrances and lift lobbies for goods and passengers should be provided.* *2. The prescribed window area and light angles were insufficient, on some floors by more than 65%.* *The applicant changed the building design:* *1. The use of ground floor was changed from "storage, car parking, loading/unloading" to "car parking, loading/unloading, lobby."* *2. The design of window area and light angle is modified.*
Drainage Aspect:	*N/A*

Feature Name	Feature Value
Consultation:	N/I
Processing:	Two fresh applications were submitted in which building design was modified according to the suggestions of the Board.
Planning Department's View:	1. The application was in line with the Board's guidelines to permit offices that need to be colocated with industrial operations to be established in industrial buildings.
	2. The site is suitable for such a composite industrial/office building because of its good commuting situation.
	3. Every unit within a composite industrial/office building must be designed, constructed, and made suitable for both industrial and office uses. Where building design requirements for industrial and office buildings differ, the more stringent requirements under the Buildings Ordinance should apply. Board should pay attention on:
	• the window area and light angle design;
	• the provision and layout of parking and loading/unloading facilities.

C: approved with conditions
N/A: not applicable
N/I: no information

Each feature must be recorded in a computer-based case library and involve the use of symbols. The symbolization of a problem is important in building AI systems (including CBS) because the reasoning performed by the computer has to be based on symbols (Stefik 1995). However, our system is primarily an aiding and advisory system. The main objective is to retrieve useful cases for the user and not do much inference work such as automatic adaptation (see Kolodner 1993; Leake 1996). We do not want the representation of our cases to be overly symbolic. The descriptions of the cases should be understandable to the user, as much as possible, without requiring much interpretation of the symbols. In addition, the cases should involve details—especially case-specific details—as much as possible. Details are very important for distinguishing one case from another and will directly affect the final decision.

COMMENTS   The content of the comments area is the advice on a case. It has two parts. One contains any valuable tips about the case, including anything special to this application that cannot be processed in a routine way or if the case has an unusual history. The other part of the comments is a list of cases relevant to this case, which the user may wish to examine.

CASE INDEXING   As discussed above, the case is not described symbolically so that users can easily learn lessons from it. Such a nonsymbolic description is not suitable for computational matching and retrieving. Furthermore, using the whole description to do matching and retrieving is usually not efficient or practical. Thus, we need to develop an index for each case. The index of a case is the symbolized and simplified or partial description of the case. With the index, cases can be more efficiently and appropriately retrieved (Kolodner 1993). Two types of indexes are used in our system. The first is a spatial index built with the GIS, ArcView. The second index is a conventional index of the CBS compiled by using ESTEEM. The vocabulary for indexing cases includes two parts: the dimensions describing the retrieving situation and the symbols describing each dimension (Kolodner 1993). The dimensions of the index for retrieving the cases with similar land uses to a new application and the data types of these dimensions are listed in table 9.2.

These dimensions can be classified into two categories. The first-level dimensions determine what can be called partial matching, finding all the cases that are potentially applicable to the new application (Kolodner 1993; Leake 1996). These cases are at least similar in some aspects to the new problem, but not necessarily all of them will make real contributions to handling the new problem. The most useful ones, if they exist, should be among these partial matching cases and will be picked up by further retrieving. In our system, the first-level dimensions include the existing, planned, and applied uses and their relationships.

When all the potential applicable cases are found by using first-level dimensions, the user may want to determine the most useful ones. Second-level dimensions then come into play. They include four kinds of features: (1) the justifications for the project; (2) the history of the project—number and nature of reviews, applications, and appeals; (3) the final decision made; and (4) the evaluation of the application, including the reasons for rejection and the approval score, the probability of approval ranging from 0 (absolute rejection) to 1 (absolute approval). These second-level dimensions will be able to help the user find the most useful cases from the partial matching set. In our system, we have the computer (ESTEEM) make retrievals based on first-level dimensions to find all the potential cases, while the most useful cases for planners are based on second-level dimensions. The most similar case is not necessarily the most useful one (Leake 1996).

RETRIEVAL METHODS   In performing the retrieval, the system should know how to match each feature (dimension) of a new application with an old case, and how to evaluate the similarity between the new application and the old case. Figure 9.10 shows a similarity-assessment template built with the Similarity Definition Editor of ESTEEM. In this template the similarity-assessment methods are defined and the value of each parameter of the algorithms is set.[3] The user can modify this template as needed, with different templates for different situations or tasks.

TABLE 9.2	The Dimensions of Index for Retrieving Cases with Similar Land Use

Dimension	Data Type	Value Range
Time of the End:	Number	1980–2000
Planned Use:	One of a list (an element from a defined list)	− I (industrial) − C (commercial) − Ra (residential group A) − Rb (residential group B) − Rc (residential group C) − G/I/C (government/institution/community) − CDA (comprehensive development areas) − V (village-type development) − OS (open space) − GB (greenbelt) − OST (open storage) − SSSI (site of special scientific interest) − UU (unspecified use)
Existing Use:	Text	(Simple words describing the existing land use such as industrial, office, oil depot, residential, natural protection, vacant, warehouse, agriculture, and so on. If the information is not available, N/I will be assigned to this dimension.)
Applied Use:	Text	(Simple words describing the proposed development such as industrial, warehouse, office, low-density residential, recreational, kindergarten, comprehensive development, PFS (petrol filling station), oyster cultivation, and so on.)
Relationship (applied–existing):	One of a list	− Regularize − Conversion − New − Redevelop − Relaxation of Restriction
Relationship (applied–planned):	Number	1 (the applied use is very relevant or conformable to the planned use) 2 (the applied use is somewhat relevant to the planned use) 3 (the applied use is not relevant or conformable to the planned use)
Justification:	Yes or No	Yes, No
Review:	Number	0, 1, 2, 3 . . .
Fresh Application:	Number	0, 1, 2, 3 . . .
Petition:	Number	0, 1, 2, 3 . . .
Result:	One of a list	− R (rejected) − C (approved with conditions) − A (approved without conditions)
Reason for Rejection:	One of a list	− U (because of concern on land use) − T (because of concern on traffic situation) − D (because of concern on design of the proposed development)
Tip:	Text	(Simple words describing the handling, especially why the application was approved or why the Board's decision changed. The words may include: change design, compatible with planning intention, more justification, temporarily permitted, compatible with environment, and so on.)
Approval Score:	Number	0–1

A Similarity-assessment Template for Retrieving Cases with Similar Land Uses

Similarity Definition Editor			_□×
Current Case-Base: hkplnapp	Current Similarity Definition: Simhkapp		Threshold 61 %
Automatic Weight Generation	Type of Similarity: Weighted Feature Computation		

Selected	Feature Name	Type of Feature Matching	Weight/Rule Base Name
✔	TimeEnd	Absolute Fuzzy Range : 20	0.05
✔	PlanUse	Exact	0.3
✔	ExistUse	Partial Word (case indifferent)	0.05
✔	ApplicationUse	Partial Word (case indifferent)	0.3
✔	RelAE	Exact	0.05
✔	RelAP	Absolute Fuzzy Range : 2	0.25

ADAPTATION METHODS   New planning applications are not totally the same as older cases. Although the planners can learn from similar older cases, they have to adapt this knowledge according to the particular context of the new problem. Automatic adaptation is one of the most challenging topics in CBR research (Leake 1996). In our system, the Planning Department's view of older, similar cases can be modified to some extent to fit the new situation. Usually the Planning Department's view is composed of several opinions on a new planning application. Thus, the results of adaptation could be suggestions for modifying old opinions.

LEARNING PROCESS OF THE SYSTEM   There is no special learning scheme in the system. The planner can add or delete cases at any time, thus modifying system knowledge. A new planning application can be stored as a new case when the planners in the Planning Department finish handling it, or when the result (approved or rejected) has been obtained from the Town Planning Board, or when any further processing has been performed. The planner makes a judgment on the approval score (ranging from 0 to 1) as input to the new case before it is stored in the case library. This decision is a judgment based on the decision by the Town Planning Board, and any problems occurring before approval or rejection are taken into account. If it is unanimously approved or rejected, the approval score of the new case can be 1 or 0, respectively. An application that was approved quickly should have a higher score than one approved after reviews and appeals. If an applicant applied more than once for a development, the planner can combine these applications to form a single case after the final decision is made. After the case is stored in the case library, the planners can still modify it later based on new knowledge. The planners can also delete obsolete cases when the situation changes. Because the cases are independent from each other, adding or deleting a particular one has no effect on the other cases. The CBS can be improved daily by the planners themselves without the assistance of knowledge engineers.

IMPLEMENTATION OF THE SYSTEM   The operation of the system conforms with a typical case based reasoning approach. When the descriptions of a new application are entered, the system will retrieve similar cases from the case library and adapt them according to the defined algorithms. Detailed information of similar cases and the suggested solutions from adaptation will be displayed to the user as shown in figure 9.11. When retrieving cases the system calculates the similarities of the old cases in the case library. Only those cases whose similarity values are larger than or equal to a threshold set by the user in the similarity definition editor will be retrieved. If more than one similar case is found, general information about each will be listed in a table and the user can choose particularly relevant cases.

FIGURE 9.11   **Retrieval of Old Cases and Evaluation of the New Application**

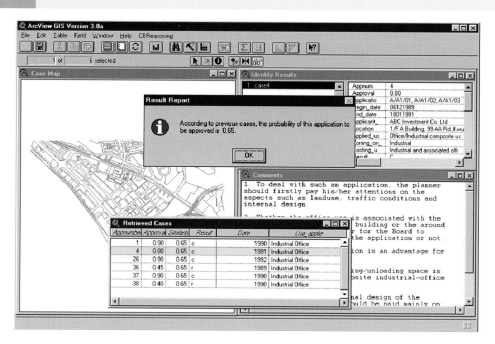

Evaluation of the CBR System

The CBR system simulates the way that applications are normally handled in a planning department. In deciding on a new application the planner has to recall and make reference to similar cases. Instead of doing it manually, relying on experience, the CBR system can help the planner to reuse previous similar cases in making decisions about new applications. The relevant past cases are revealed to the planners using a scoring system, overcoming the black-box approach of a rule-based system. The planner can still be creative in making the final decision. Justification would have to be made for any recommended decision that deviates from past cases.

The system can be an effective and efficient PSS in helping planners to make consistent recommendations. It is a corporate memory system (Smith et al. 2000; Stein 1995) that frees the planners from retaining a mental record of all past decisions. In using past cases to give guidance to new applications, the system helps to make consistent decisions for similar applications. This is especially useful in developing countries in which development control is mainly done by planners. A planner has to justify why the decision on the application is different from previous similar cases retrieved by the system. This can avoid inconsistency and corruption in making decisions. Because it is case-based and not rule-based, once the system is developed it can be applied to other cities. In addition to providing planning decision support to planners, CBR can also be used as an office-automation system for easy retrieval of relevant past cases. It can be used to enhance the present database system, which stores and retrieves past cases. It can easily retrieve the required relevant cases spatially or nonspatially. By integrating with GIS, it is also a visualization tool that brings the relevant graphics, data, and texts to the planner.

The capability of automatically adapting cases needs further exploration and development. For example, the system should automatically recognize the differences in the critical aspects between the new application and its precedent cases and perform an evaluation based on these differences, proposing modifications to the earlier solution. The capability of matching and adapting cases based on spatial similarities and relationship is another important topic that needs further research. For example, a pollution source has the spatial relationship of distance and direction to a residential building. The pollution source and residential building constitute a kind of spatial relationship. How to use GIS to automatically recognize this relationship and automatically retrieve cases with a similar pattern requires further research.

The use of case-based reasoning is not without limitations. Among the obvious issues are the lack of cases for new problems and changes in the planning environment. To overcome these limitations, there is a possibility that case-based reasoning can be integrated with rule-based reasoning. Different reasoning engines can be complementary to each other (Bartsch-Sport 1995; Smith et al. 2000; Kolodner 1993; Koton 1993). The integration of case-based reasoning with other KBS may make a more powerful and efficient system (Medsker 1995). Rule-based systems can be used when there are no cases in the CBS similar to the new application, or when new regulations are introduced that make old cases in the case library irrelevant. The integration of theses two reasoning engines may lead to a more powerful system for development control.

Conclusion

Event-based office automation with full integration with GIS can help to keep track of the decisions and the comments of different actors in the development control process. It can save the time of the staff in retrieving maps and information from a paper file. The system has been used in many planning departments in China since 1997, including Guangzhou, Changzhou, and Liuzhou. These systems have largely improved the efficiency of the collaborative decision making of development control by reducing duplication of effort, minimizing redundant data collection and analysis, maximizing the sharing of information, and coordinating and keeping track of the development control process. Planning staff and land managers as well as other government officials can perform the development control steps in a logical order instead of some ad hoc sequences. Apart from those in China, other cities in Asia, such as Kuala Lumpur (Yaakup et al. 2004), are also using such computer-supported collaborative workflow systems in development control. The Planning Department in Hong Kong is also implementing a similar system to facilitate better monitoring and tracking of the status and progress of planning applications. Workflow software such as Ultimas, Hummingbird, and Windows Workflow Foundation (WWF) can be used in developing the system and can be integrated with GIS.

PSS has great potential not only in the area of plan making but also in the processing of development control. A PSS that integrates GIS with an event-based, computer-supported collaborative workflow system and a case-based reasoning system can: (1) save time in obtaining the necessary documents, maps, and plans for decision making; (2) ensure and facilitate a sequence of consultation and decision making among different actors that takes place within a statutory time period; and (3) provide corporate memory for planning-application cases to avoid inconsistency and corruption in making decisions.

Endnotes

1. IFO (Is-a relationships, Functional relationships, complex Objects) is an object-oriented data model for spatial databases.

2. For details of the techniques of CBR, see Aamodt and Plaza (1994); Kolodner (1993); and Watson (1995; 1997).

3. The Nearest Neighbor algorithm is used by the system to find the similarity between a new problem and an old case. It is one of the most popular algorithms for comparing cases in CBS (Kolodner 1993; Watson 1995). The Nearest Neighbor algorithm is defined using the following score:

$$s = \frac{\sum_{i=1}^{n} w_i \times sim\,(f_i^I, f_i^R)}{\sum_{i}^{n} w_i}$$

where s (similarity score) is the sum of weighted similarities of each feature, and only those cases whose s is larger than a predefined threshold (for example, 60 percent) will be retrieved as the similar cases; w_i is the importance of feature i, sim is the similarity-assessing function for comparing feature f_i; and f_i^I and f_i^R are the values for feature f_i in the input new case and the retrieved old case respectively (Kolodner 1993). The weights (w_i) used in the study are assigned by the authors on the advice from the planners in the Planning Department. They can be adjusted, modified, and refined as the system develops.

Planning Support Systems in Practice   SECTION 4

Planning Support Systems

A Planner's Perspective

Stan Geertman

10

Stating the Problem

URBAN AND REGIONAL PLANNING CONCERNS THE DESIGN AND ORGANIZATION of urban physical and socioeconomic space and its encompassing activities to solve existing problems and/or to anticipate future problems. Alexander (1987, 454) defines planning as "the deliberate social or organizational activity of developing an optimal strategy of future action to achieve a desired set of goals, for solving novel problems in complex contexts, and attended by the power and intention to commit resources and to act as necessary to implement the chosen strategy." Although very general, this gives a rough idea of what planning is all about: developing a strategy for future actions to achieve desired goals and/or resolve indicated problems.

In this respect, a distinction should be made between the day-to-day, so-called operational decision making on the one hand, and planning as strategic choice on the other. Although this last term is used differently in different contexts (e.g., some consider strategic planning or decision making to be business-oriented planning), we base this distinction on the work of Friend and Jessop (1969, 97–110), who consider planning to be "a process of strategic choice" that can be distinguished from operational decision making. They go on to say that "any process of choice will become a process of planning (or strategic choice) if the selection of current actions is made only after a formulation and comparison of possible solutions over a wider field of decision relating to certain anticipated as well as current situations." So, operational decision making concerns the day-to-day activities and decisions of planners "that entail commitments and use resources and affect the lives of people" (Faludi 1986, 20). To add to that, planning also encompasses those activities that are focused on strategic choices and that provide these day-to-day decisions with a more thoroughly thought-out framework. This is parallel to the work of many others (e.g., see Harris 1989a).

In general, it can be argued that present-day planning is a complex activity. At least two factors contribute substantially to this complexity. First, the multi-dimensionality of numerous present-day spatial planning issues plays a complicating role. Attention in spatial planning is no longer solely focused on physical factors, but also on social, economic, and environmental factors, among others. The background of this is the increasing recognition of the fact that many problems are becoming interwoven and require integrated policies. A concrete example of this multidimensionality is the concept of sustainability and its spatial operationalization in planning concepts like smart growth and multiple land use. Second, the increase in involvement of a variety of interests in planning processes contributes to the increase in complexity. Associated organizations, stakeholders, the wider public, and so forth all have a say (or believe they do) in planning processes and will try to influence the foreseen decisions that are to be taken. To cope with this two-sided increase in complexity of the planning task, knowledge seems to be the appropriate solution.

Knowledge applied in planning situations is characterized by a variety of sources and a diversity of categories. It consists of scientific and experiential knowledge, implicit and explicit knowledge, technical knowledge, and social knowledge—and all by a range of societal actors (Dammers et al. 1999). Handling the various types of knowledge in the multiactor planning arena is challenging. Knowledge needs to be available to inform the participants, communicated among participants, and analyzed to make sure that underlying patterns in the knowledge that are relevant to the planning problem and its solution become available. Currently, planners find it difficult to deal with these different knowledge categories appropriately (Stillwell, Geertman, and Openshaw 1999). In particular, analysis and design processes could be passed on much better with knowledge, scenario evaluations could be much more effective by reflecting on the views vis-à-vis existing knowledge, and implementation could benefit substantially from using knowledge about the lessons learned. In fact, underemphasized knowledge has led to large planning failures with high cost spill-over effects (In't Veld 2000).

For a long time, geoinformation-technology developers have focused on supporting planners in knowledge handling. In particular, supports of information management and scenario analysis have received a great deal of attention (e.g., Hopkins and Zapata 2007b). Nonetheless, the large-scale urban models from the 1960s and 1970s failed to meet expectations and did not become widely accepted as planning support instruments (Batty 1979; Lee 1973; 1994; Openshaw 1979). Neither have the geographical information systems (GIS) from the 1980s and 1990s become widely used for the tasks that are so characteristic of planning, such as the generation of scenarios and the evaluation of alternatives (Croswell 1991; Innes and Simpson 1993; Stillwell, Geertman, and Openshaw 1999). Mainly, planners have used GIS for basic information functions like data management and cartographic visualization because they are a rather poor match for the specific demands and capabilities of planners.

This mainly negative picture is expressed in a number of statements made in the 1990s. Harris and Batty (1993), for example, conclude that the 1990s generation of GIS failed to incorporate the kinds of functions that planning in fact requires, like analytical and design functions. Klosterman (1998) suggested that instruments for planning support were no better developed than they had been ten years earlier. Moreover, he was equally pessimistic about the adoption of new instruments and computer applications in planning practice in the near future. And Britton Harris (1999) pointed to the fact that "planners and designers have remained at best distrustful, or at worst downright antagonistic, towards computer-based models of support." In fact, it can be stated that the number of planners who consider planning support instruments to be intrinsic to and indispensable for performing their job properly (as financial experts consider their use of spreadsheet software and medical specialists their ECG technology) remains remarkably low (Geertman and Stillwell 2003b). In general, the reasons expressed for the limited usage of planning support instruments in planning practice had to do with the fact that they do not readily fit the changing needs of the planning profession. They are far too generic, complex, inflexible, and incompatible with the "wicked" nature of most planning tasks. They are geared toward technology rather than problems, incompatible with the less formal and unstructured information needs, and too focused on strict rationality.[1]

More specifically, at least two more fundamental obstacles obstruct the path to more efficient performance of the support function of geoinformation technology. One barrier is the restricted policy support role of scientific information. Another is the discrepancy between geoinformation technology and the planning activity. First, despite the recognition of its indispensable and highly valued contribution to the policy process, the role of scientific information in policy support is not without problems. One problem is that the role of scientific information is context-bound. For instance, it may prove to be less evident within strategic decision making than at the level of operational decision making.

In addition to this contextuality, the role of scientific information in the policy process is relative in that the policy process is influenced by many other factors such as traditions and power relations (see Lindblom and Cohen 1979; Forester 1989). Its role is further problematic in that information based on scientific research is surrounded by problems related to factors such as the availability, accessibility, and/or utility of the underlying data and of the methods to process them (e.g., see Chorley 1988). As a consequence, scientific information does not constitute a neutral entity because it is loaded with inherent choices and biases (e.g., see Forester 1989). It follows that scientific research and its outcomes undoubtedly contribute to the policy process, though in a more or less contextual, relative, and problematic way. As a consequence, one of the primary conditions for more efficient performance of the support function of geoinformation technology in the framework of spatial planning seems to be to treat information and knowledge in an explicit way within a policy context.

A second category of obstacles to more efficient performance of the support function of geoinformation technology concerns some fundamental discrepancies between geoinformation technology and spatial planning activity (e.g., see Ottens 1990; Nijkamp and Scholten 1993). One such discrepancy lies in the concepts of space. According to Couclelis (1989b), the concept of space as employed by geoinformation technology is general, absolute, and tangible, while within the activities of spatial planning it is mostly abstract, subjective, personal, or relative. Another discrepancy exists between the nature of the spatial planning activity and that of geoinformation technology. Spatial planning is a highly dynamic, inherently contextual, and problem-oriented activity in which irrational, dynamic elements as well as political, juridical, economic, and other more or less nonspatial elements all play important roles. However, uncertainty, dynamics, and nonspatial elements are very hard to handle within geoinformation technology (Klosterman 1994a; Worrall 1994). Thus, the potential role of geoinformation technology in the framework of spatial planning support is always restricted to certain aspects of the planning problem at hand. As a consequence, the outcomes of scientific research, with or without the help of geoinformation technology, can rarely provide a complete answer to a spatial policy question.

Despite these obstacles, more recent evidence is mounting for developments that may have a positive impact on the adoption of the support role of geoinformation technology. Within the field of geoinformation technology itself, systems are rapidly becoming more user friendly, interoperable, cost effective, standardized, and platform independent. At the same time, geodata are becoming more abundant, cheaper, easier to obtain, and of a higher resolution and quality. Ongoing changes within planning practice are also increasing the needs and potential for planning-support instruments. The aforementioned growing involvement of participants in planning processes is one example, and the increasing sophistication of planning due to the growing complexity of real-world dynamics is another (Geertman and Stillwell 2000; Geertman 2002b). Moreover, the dissemination of data and plans is changing radically; for example, plans are put on the Internet making them easily accessible to a wide audience.

A new generation of planning support systems (PSS) is in fact entering the planning scene. It is safe to say that the current problematic situation of adopting planning support instruments in planning practice will improve substantially thanks to recent push (dataware, hardware, software, etc.) and pull (sophistication of planning, complexity of planning practice, etc.) factors. Nonetheless, it is likely that the pace of improvement will lag far behind what the potentials suggest. This is due to the previously mentioned fundamental obstacles that prevent or at least delay full adoption.

The PSS mentioned above entered the planning scene in about the mid-1990s. These geoinformation technology–based instruments are fully dedicated to supporting those involved in planning in the performance of their specific planning tasks (Batty 1995; Klosterman 1997). In a sense they are related to GIS, but while GIS are general-purpose tools, applicable for many different spatially related problems, PSS distinguish themselves by being specifically focused on supporting specific planning tasks. Although they are also related to spatial decision support systems (SDSS), they differ in that PSS generally pay particular attention to long-range problems and strategic issues, while SDSS are generally designed to support shorter-term policy making by isolated individuals or by business organizations (Clarke 1990). Moreover, the prime dedication of SDSS is toward supporting operational decision making rather than strategic planning activities. For that, PSS consist of a combination of planning-related theory, data, information, knowledge, methods, and instruments that take the form of an integrated framework with a shared interface (Geertman and Stillwell 2003b).

Many see PSS as good support tools that will enable planners to better handle the complexity of planning processes, leading to plans of better quality and saving much planning time and money. In that, it seems that a new, much more positive attitude concerning PSS has emerged with the turn of the century. At present much more attention is focused on planning support and its instruments than was the case for quite a long time. This seems to be supported by the amount of studies that are being performed, the dedicated conferences held, and the diversity of articles and books that continue to appear on the market.

Before continuing, a more precise definition of what is considered here as PSS must be provided. Harris and Batty (1993) associate the concept of PSS with combining a range of computer-based methods and models into an integrated system that is used to support a particular planning function. More precisely, in their opinion, a single PSS forms the framework in which three sets of components are combined: (1) the specification of the planning tasks and problems at hand, including the assembly of data; (2) the system models and methods that inform the planning process through analysis, prediction, and prescription; and (3) the transformation of basic data into information that, in turn, provides the driving force for modeling and design (through a cyclic process).

In a similar vein, Klosterman (1997; 1999a) and Brail and Klosterman (2001) have more recently described PSS as information technologies that are used specifically by planners to undertake their unique professional responsibilities. They suggest that PSS have matured into frameworks of integrated systems of information and software that synthesize the three components of traditional DSS—information, models, and visualization—and deliver them into the public realm. In the same vein, Batty (1995) defines PSS as a subset of geoinformation technologies dedicated to supporting those involved in planning to explore, represent, analyze, visualize, predict, prescribe, design, implement, monitor, and discuss issues associated with the need to plan. Finally Geertman and Stillwell (2003b) define PSS as geoinformation technology–based instruments that incorporate a suite of components (theories, data, information, knowledge, methods, tools, meta-information, etc.) that collectively support some specific parts of a unique professional planning task. This descriptive kaleidoscope invites the conclusion that for the time being, there is no strict definition of PSS, although all descriptions more or less coincide by touching upon the same category of support instruments.

In this chapter we present an overview of a range of studies conducted during the last couple of years regarding PSS and planning support. To this end, the planner's point of view has been adopted in looking at ongoing developments. Rather than taking only the supply side into account, as has often been done by others, this chapter takes the demand side as the dominant point of view. The aforementioned underutilization of PSS in planning practice has been taken as a starting point, considered in relation to PSS availability and their assumed potential. We therefore question why PSS are used in planning as infrequently as they are and how usage could be enhanced.

To achieve this aim, we have taken different approaches to the question. First, we performed an overview study to enlarge the insight into the availability and potentials and restrictions of the present generation of PSS. Subsequently some studies were conducted to enlarge insight into the bottlenecks blocking the application of these PSS into planning practice. This resulted in a range of recommendations and lessons that will contribute to their enhancement. To devise a more solid explanation of the underutilization of PSS in practice, a conceptual framework based on previous studies has been set up, which can help to account for the identified obstacles and the ways in which they appear and can be removed. Moreover, a PSS research agenda has been proposed to direct future PSS research in a more coherent direction. Finally, some conclusions and recommendations will be presented from a planner's perspective of PSS.

PSS Overview

This section provides an outlined overview of the state of the art in PSS development based on a worldwide inventory of PSS that was held during the years 2000 to 2001.[2] The starting point of this inventory was a widely held belief that a comprehensive picture of the extent of the development of PSS at the beginning of the new millennium was missing (Harris 1999; Stillwell, Geertman, and Openshaw 1999; Brail and Klosterman 2001). As a consequence, the planning community was not adequately informed as to where to look in the academic or planning literature for good examples of the use of PSS in practice and details of new instruments or advice and support for PSS. This was considered problematic at a time when the increasing need for geoinformation-technology support was perceived.

To arrive at the overview a Web-based worldwide inventory of PSS was established during the period from 2000 to 2001. About 50 contributions were received from more than 20 countries including the Netherlands, the United Kingdom, the United States, Italy, Colombia, Australia, New Zealand, Russia, South Africa, Malaysia, Sweden, Finland, the Czech Republic, and Hong Kong. Several conclusions were drawn from this group of contributions. First, the numbers of PSS are increasing worldwide, although most of the presented PSS appear to have been developed quite recently (during the last five years). As a consequence, many of the PSS are not mature and are still in an experimental or prototype stage of development. In fact, the large majority of PSS are not available as proprietary, off-the-shelf systems. Second, it became clear that practical experience with PSS in actual planning practice is currently very limited. The real-world application of many systems seems to be confined to experimental case studies such as educational meetings with students or training sessions with professional planners. Only a very small number of the systems had actually matured to the stage at which they found professional application. Third, the systems presented show a very wide diversity, both in the aims, capabilities, content, structure, and technology of the PSS and in their appearance to users. In fact, this diversity reflects the inability to agree on a specific definition of what a PSS is or to agree to work with several broad descriptions.

The inventoried PSS differ in their aims. Some are dedicated to facilitate and/or enhance participation, while others are tools for the uniform handling of building permits, for example. They differ in capabilities in that some are dedicated to the support of modeling activities for future population distributions or land use patterns, while others provide tools to support the sketching of new spatial structures or for the visualization of potential spatial developments. The content of the PSS differs in that they possess selections from the range of components, including data sets, information, and meta-information, storage and query tools, analysis methods, modeling capabilities, conceptual theories, indicator systems, and so forth. They also differ greatly in structure, in that some can be considered fully integrated systems in which all components are closely interconnected while others possess a range of components that are only loosely connected within a toolbox of loosely coupled components. Moreover, the inventoried PSS differ greatly in the technology applied: Some are stand-alone programs while others are developed solely for an intranet or for the Internet environment. Furthermore, the functionality of the PSS differs greatly. In line with the intended aims of the systems, some are mainly dedicated to sketching, others to modeling, and still others to supporting information and/or communication processes.

Based on the outcomes of this inventory, a range of recommendations can be made.[3] A first recommendation is that PSS should be integral parts of the planning process and its context. These PSS should be attuned to the specific characteristics of the planning process and the given context. For instance, each phase within a planning process is subject to certain time constraints and involves a certain amount of publicity, and these factors should be taken into account. Likewise, the characteristics of the policy context (e.g., the degree of participation) influence the preferred PSS technology (e.g., the need for transparency or black box) and the way in which it is used.

The second recommendation is related to the first: PSS should meet user and context requirements, too. For example, PSS should be developed that reflect the knowledge and skills of their direct applicants. Moreover, their functionalities should be attuned to the professional tasks required at specific phases in the planning process—such as sketching, modeling, impact assessment, and evaluation—and to the capabilities of the audience with whom communication is required, that is the knowledge and skill levels of laypersons and stakeholders as well as more technical users.

Third, PSS should address issues at an interdisciplinary level. In contrast to science, in which the study of reality has been categorized into separated disciplines, in the real world neither the problems nor their solutions are confined to these artificial disciplinary boundaries. As a consequence, PSS should address issues in an interdisciplinary manner, linking the spatial to the social, the environmental to the economic, and so forth.

Fourth, PSS should take its users seriously and leave them with the feeling that they have been taken seriously. Although this may seem obvious, a number of practical experiences had the opposite result. For example, the population of a local community in one of the American states participated actively in planning sessions in which environmentally sensitive futures were designed for their region. At the same time, the governor of the state, who claimed to be a strong supporter of participative sessions, was making secret deals with the federal government for the construction of a large nuclear waste disposal site in that region.

A fifth recommendation is that PSS should focus in particular on the strategic planning issues at stake. For some strategically oriented planning tasks, this means the incorporation of tools for sketching, modeling, and impact analysis. The activities of detecting the most likely future, exploring potential scenarios, and designing desirable futures belong to the core of strategic planning tasks. In this respect, a particularly interesting question arises regarding the acceptance of the inputs (such as reliable, up-to-date data) and outputs (such as meaningful modeling results) of a PSS application. In general, transparency in the way in which they are handled is one of the most important prerequisites for supportive instruments in general and for PSS in particular.

To conclude, with the help of a Web-based worldwide inventory of existing PSS and their experiences, an extensive overview has been generated detailing the rich diversity of PSS and their various characteristics and of their most common experimental application. This last point supports the conclusion that a great number of steps must still be taken before these potentially supportive instruments can be applied in real-world planning practices in a more regular fashion.

PSS Bottlenecks

As a result of the overview study described above, a range of additional studies have been performed to generate a more in-depth picture of the potentials for and bottlenecks blocking the adoption and application of PSS in current planning practice.[4] Three complementary studies have been executed to generate a more in-depth picture in which the viewpoints of three different groups have been examined: PSS developers, scientific PSS experts, and the group of potential PSS users.

First of all, user views of PSS have been gathered on the basis of a series of interviews held with 43 employees of 12 highly comparable Dutch regional spatial planning organizations. In particular we interviewed three archetypes of users that currently fulfill an important role in potentially using and evaluating PSS: the geoinformation specialist, the planner, and the manager.

Second, the views of PSS developers concerning potentials and bottlenecks are well recorded in scientific literature. About 58 PSS and their developers were examined on the basis of a literature review. These constitute a relatively accurate overview of system developers' perspectives.

Third, the expert views of PSS have been gathered by means of conducting two additional worldwide Web surveys. Via several PSS-related listserv e-mail networks 800 PSS-interested persons were asked to participate. The first survey had 96 respondents and the second had 40 respondents. Of these two surveys, 86 respondents in the first and 30 in the second were considered experts, since they recognized at least two PSS from a list. The majority of the expert respondents appeared to be university researchers and employees of public planning research or advisory bureaus dealing with planning support in their work. In the end, the findings of the literature survey, the interviews, and the Web surveys were combined in order to learn lessons on the usage of PSS, their potentials, and bottlenecks.

To be able to interpret the results of these studies, three different viewpoints and their associated conceptual underpinnings have been applied: the "instrument approach," the "user approach," and the "transfer approach" (figure 10.1). The instrument approach explains usage mainly in view of the instrumental quality of the information technologies, in this case PSS, focusing particularly on fitness for use and user friendliness. The user approach explains usage in relation to the extent of user acceptance of PSS, focusing on a broader set of factors related to the accepting environment. The transfer approach explains usage with regard to the extent of diffusion, focusing particularly on the flow of information concerning PSS from system developer to user and among users. In fact, the three approaches overlap in that they all look at the same issue of usage, but each emphasizes slightly different aspects.

Each of these approaches highlights different bottlenecks and in doing so also highlights the different components of the solution space to overcome these bottlenecks.

The first is the instrument approach, which focuses on those characteristics of the instrument that determine their instrumental quality. Instrumental quality is defined here as consisting of a judgment of: (1) how well the instruments are capable of carrying out the tasks for which they were made; and (2) how well they fit to the capabilities and demands of intended users. Goodhue and Thompson (1995) showed the importance of these characteristics as determinants of usage of information technologies in their model of task-technology-user fit (Dishaw and Strong 1999; Dishaw, Strong, and Bandy 2002; Goodhue 1995). In terms of this model, underusage of PSS is explained by insufficient fit of PSS technology to user characteristics on the one hand and to the planning task characteristics on the other.

Based on this model it follows that PSS technology—which is still in an early stage of development and has a large variety of systems and very few standards associated with this development stage—is characterized by large differences in

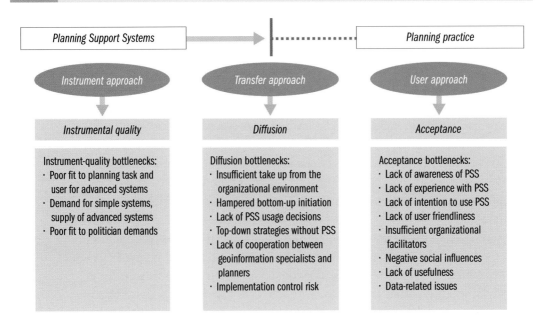

FIGURE
10.1

Factors Explaining Underusage of PSS from Three Different Approaches
Source: Vonk (2006)

instrumental quality. Another finding shows that a large dichotomy exists between PSS demanded in practice by potential users and PSS supplied by system developers. In short, while practice demands rather simple PSS for exploratory tasks such as making an inventory of conditions, the majority of PSS focus on more analytical tasks, especially modeling. These, in turn, are seen as a poor match for the demands of planning practice. The instrumental quality of simple instruments is considered acceptable while that of advanced instruments is generally considered to be poor. Results suggest that simple instruments have a relative advantage over doing it all by hand, while for many currently existing advanced instruments the advantage is doubtful, at the least.

The user approach focuses in particular on characteristics of users that determine the acceptance of PSS. This approach emphasizes how users should change in order to enhance usage of PSS. In this case "acceptance" is defined as "the process through which an individual or other decision-making unit passes from first knowledge of an innovation, to forming an attitude toward the innovation, to a decision to adopt or reject, to implementation of the new idea, and to confirmation of his decision" (Rogers 1995). This process is influenced by user characteristics, instrument characteristics, organizational characteristics, characteristics of the social environment, characteristics of the external environment, and facilitating conditions. These factors that influence acceptance have been framed in the so-called technology acceptance model (e.g., Davies 1986; Frambach and Schillewaert 2002; Rogers 1995).

Studies with the PSS technology acceptance model show a large variety of bottlenecks blocking widespread acceptance of PSS in planning practice. The main bottlenecks are: the lack of awareness of the existence of PSS and the purposes for which they can be used; the lack of experience with PSS, which leaves users unaware of the benefits of PSS and the conditions under which they can be used; and the lack of interest in starting to use PSS. Other high-scoring bottlenecks are insufficient user friendliness and usefulness, the absence of the required organizational facilitators and social influences, and data quality and accessibility problems (Vonk, Geertman, and Schot 2005).

The transfer approach explains usage of PSS in planning practice based on characteristics of the diffusion of PSS toward planning practice. Innovation diffusion has been defined as "the process by which an innovation is communicated through certain channels over time among members of a social system" (Rogers 1995). It is concerned with the process of moving from an innovation context to a practical context through acceptance by individuals, groups, and organizations. Diffusion is envisioned as a process that takes the innovation from the system developers toward widespread usage in practice over the various levels of aggregation. In diffusion, the aggregation of individuals within groups, groups within planning organizations, and planning organizations that have adopted the innovation follows a path such as described by the innovation adoption curve (Rogers 1995). The curve shows that a group of "innovators" are the first individuals, groups, or organizations to see opportunities and are most likely to perceive the complexity of adoption as a challenge, or to perceive themselves as capable of handling the complexity. This group is followed by "early adopters," "early majority," "late majority," and finally the "laggards," who have little choice but to accept the innovation after having been confronted with it everywhere by individuals, groups, and organizations who adopted the innovation before they did.

Studies show that diffusion of PSS in planning organizations is more likely to start bottom-up than top-down since geoinformation specialists are more likely to spot and take up developments concerning PSS emerging from the environment. Nonetheless, lack of opportunity for innovation and personal characteristics often cause geoinformation specialists at the bottom of the organization to be unable to take the technology from the external environment and bring it to the attention of management at the top. In addition, they are not able to bring PSS to the attention of planners since geoinformation specialists themselves are often unable to reach spatial planners and set up cooperation. Innovative ideas are also poorly diffused due to differences in appreciation of PSS between individual geoinformation specialists and others within the organization. For example, geoinformation specialists often encounter a discrepancy between planners' questions and their ability to respond. In practice, regional planning organizations often exploit management-supported strategies on geoinformation technology diffusion.

The above information enables us to make several recommendations. As far as instruments are concerned, there is a desire and an intention to improve the instrumental quality. Those in practice willing to use PSS are often unable to improve the instrument quality of PSS on their own. Nonetheless, if they coop-erate with researchers and system developers, they can contribute to PSS quality improvement. This requires that the demands expressed by potential users be taken much more seriously than has been the case thus far.

With regard to the users, much more awareness of and subsequent expe-rience with PSS are needed. We recommend that those willing to start using PSS in planning practice actively spread the news of the existence of PSS and their potential through the appropriate communications channels. Furthermore, they should make the PSS message better suited to the receivers. Subsequently, positive experiences with PSS applications should be encouraged and broadcast. Good examples of applications and best practices will help to overcome some of the bottlenecks having to do with lack of awareness and experience.

Regarding the transfer approach, a distinction can be made between diffu-sion toward planning organizations and diffusion within planning organizations. Some intermediate actors in particular can fulfill a role in the diffusion toward planning organizations. Of these actors, government research agencies and con-sultant organizations usually have greater knowledge of and accessibility to plan-ning practice than scientists working within universities. They are expected to be capable of getting the actors of the PSS-innovation network working together to engage in cooperative development due to their already intermediate position between policy and research.

It is therefore recommended that they play a major role in PSS quality improvement. This can start a process of interactive learning concerning PSS among the relevant actors within the innovation network: scientists, system developers, government research institutes, consultants, planners, geoinforma-tion specialists, managers, and executives. Close cooperation in experimental settings can lead to learning useful lessons regarding the alignment of PSS and application environments as well as lessons pertaining to the improvement of the instrumental quality of PSS. Much remains to be learned, particularly about the more advanced PSS. The resulting lessons may be used to develop very dedicated systems and increase the overall compatibility of systems to the application environment. This will enhance instrumental quality, acceptance, and diffusion of PSS.

For the diffusion within planning organizations, managers are advised to adopt the paradigm of the "learning organization" (Senge 1990) and to adopt knowledge management (Nonaka and Takeuchi 1995). Managing information technology adoption and implementation in complex environments is challeng-ing. One reason is that demands and opportunities differ over multiple workflow processes and change over different development phases. Another reason is that individuals and organizations in different departments must quickly learn how to work together as a unified team.

Managing innovation, adoption, and implementation of PSS in practice is even more challenging because there appears to be little cooperation and learning among the actors involved in PSS adoption and implementation. The empirical results indicate that adopting the managerial paradigm of the learning organization can change this because it stimulates flow of knowledge toward and within organizations, thereby stimulating innovation, acceptance, and diffusion of PSS. This allows geoinformation specialists to function as gatekeepers, matching innovations in the organizational environment with internal demands, and subsequently innovation managers can then function as champions. This last role entails bringing the PSS innovation farther into the organization toward utilization of the opportunities PSS offer. To achieve this innovation, these champions need to convince planners of the use of PSS in their daily practices and other managers to decide on adoption or give room for experiments.

In conclusion, the instrumental quality, the awareness and experiences of potential users, and the diffusion across groups all need improvement to overcome the identified bottlenecks and fulfill the potentials of PSS. Spreading the news about useful applications and best practices and improving cooperation (e.g., between geoinformation specialists and planners) can be considered the key variables in enhancing PSS use in practice.

Conceptual Reflection

Based upon previous overviews and in-depth studies into planning support by way of PSS, a conceptual framework can be constructed that provides a range of utilization lessons (figure 10.2). These lessons can be presented as influential factors on the adoption of planning support–dedicated information, knowledge, and instruments in planning practice.[5]

The first factor concerns the *content of the planning issue* at stake. Many strategic, nonroutine planning issues can be said to be ill-structured or semistructured. It is not so much the answer to the planning question that is of prime importance, but more the adequate interpretation of the question itself. As a consequence, the potential role of planning support is very much dependent on

FIGURE 10.2

Factors Influencing Potential Planning Support Role of Dedicated Information, Knowledge, and Instruments in Planning Practice
Source: Geertman (2006)

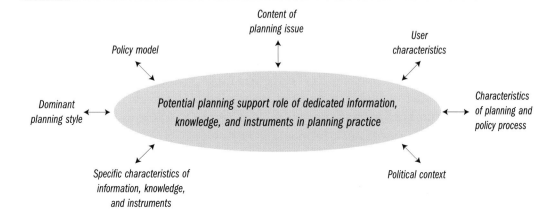

the clarification of the problem at hand. This requires the input of a variety of knowledge categories: formal and informal knowledge, scientific and ordinary knowledge, proven knowledge and intuitive ideas, etc. It is a great challenge for planning-support instruments to handle this large variety of information and knowledge categories, but it is inevitable nonetheless.

The second factor comprises the *characteristics of the users,* including their profession, working habits, and so on. Each category of user possesses certain qualities and restrictions and has specific demands and wishes concerning the content of information needed and the form of the technology to be handled.

The third factor covers the *characteristics of the planning and policy process.* Each planning and policy process possesses distinctive characteristics that influence the support role of information, knowledge, and instruments. These characteristics include time span (the time pressure), the participation rate (e.g., early bird participation or consultation of final version), publicity, the degree of political sensitivity, and so forth.

The fourth factor forms the so-called *political context,* or the factual political environment in which the planning and policy process is embedded. This context has specific characteristics and these can range from a dictatorial regime to a democratic system. Each of these political contexts exerts influence on the technology choice (for instance, the desired degree of transparency) and on the way in which this technology is implemented and handled in associated policy processes.

The fifth factor concerns the *specific characteristics of information, knowledge, and instruments themselves* that also influence the appropriateness of their planning-support role. The characteristics of information and knowledge are contextual, relative, and problematic. For instance, even scientific knowledge is not a neutral entity, but is influenced by presumptions, choices, and biases that are also inherent to scientific research.

The last factors in the figure comprise the *dominant planning style and policy model.* A planning style can be described as the dominant form of planning during a certain period of time (e.g., blueprint planning, communicative planning). They represent time-bound normative opinions concerning the way in which the planning job should be performed. Policy models represent the specific policy context of planning styles and therefore the time-bound normative insights into policy making (e.g., comprehensive rationalism, participatory). It can be described as the way in which a policy agency, such as a planning institution, transforms an identified problem, placed on the political agenda, into a politically sanctioned policy. These planning styles and policy models can be envisioned as abstract and general, more or less time-bound, normative notions concerning the "what"—the role and function within society—and the "how"— the working methods—of planning and policy making.

In conclusion, these factors must explicitly be accounted for to attain an appropriate state of planning support by dedicated information, knowledge, and instruments. Taking them seriously and unequivocally into account can be considered a preliminary step for their appropriate handling in factual planning practice. In my opinion, more clarity and, in particular, transparency regarding these factors and the way in which they are handled within a specific planning situation will enhance their potential for performing a more effective planning supportive role. Given all these factors, it is best to remain realistic about the potentials of actual planning support that can be provided by dedicated information, knowledge, and instruments. The input of dedicated information, knowledge, and instruments is contextual, relative, restricted, etc., and should be considered but one among many potentially valuable inputs to factual planning practice.[6]

PSS Research Perspective

The preceding observations raise the question of what steps and actions should be taken to enhance the role of PSS in practice. In fact, this calls for a coherent research program that will help to prevent overlaps or gaps in research. In PSS history several attempts have been undertaken to set up such an agenda. For example, Harris (1989b) put forward a research agenda for URISA (Urban and Regional Information Systems Association), in which he called for special attention to social process models and continual field testing and user review. Remarkably, these recommendations are still quite valid given their appearance in present-day approaches (e.g., see Voss et al. 2004).

Another example of PSS-related research agendas can be found in Nedovic-Budic (2000), wherein a group of United States scientists under the auspices of the UCGIS (University Consortium of Geographic Information Science) identified four PSS-related research areas within the context of urban and regional planning. They state that the analytical, design, administrative, communicative, and decision-making support functions of PSS should be developed and more fully customized to the specific needs of urban and regional planning. Moreover, tool development should be more intensively linked with organizational contexts, processes, theories (e.g., collaborative decision making), and methods in planning, so as to become more useful in urban and regional planning practice. In addition, a better understanding is required of the relationship between planning theory (e.g., rational, social, postmodernism) on the one hand, and the methods and geoinformation technologies that are factually suitable to planning practice on the other hand. Finally, the visualization of spatial processes and phenomena and the simulation of the outcomes of proposed plans and policies should be substantially enhanced—through 3D modeling and virtual reality, for example. In retrospect, these propositions still seem very relevant to the present PSS situation.

Based on these research agendas and with the help of a method appropriate for that—the so-called Validity Network Schema (VNS) (Brinberg and McGrath 1985)—an updated research agenda for PSS has been set up.[7] The outcome of this research agenda for PSS can be summarized in some action points. First of all, the prime focus in present PSS research is mainly attuned to the development of PSS tools (= means) and not to the planning support role

(= goals) of these tools. In this respect, the intentional support role of the technology is presupposed to equal the factual support role of the PSS technology. Although this is quite logical in an emerging field of technological innovation, at the present stage of development it should not prevent us from moving on to pay much more attention to the factual support role of the technology.

Second, there is still a need for improving the technology itself given the prototypical state of most instruments. In particular, there is a need for PSS tool development in close cooperation with practice from relatively early stages of development on to their subsequent application. This demands "Integrated Communities of PSS Research and Practice" (Wenger 1998), in which the parallel instrumental development and planning application of PSS by developers and potential users will take place as a means to arrive at mutually adjusted directives for future PSS development and application.

Third, research in the field of PSS should be expanded to include explicitly the context in which planning support takes place. This context sensitivity is important because the context will influence the way in which and to what degree planning support will be attained. For example, case studies show that some specific categories of research-oriented planners are much more willing to adopt analytical PSS instruments (e.g., land use modeling tools) and their outcomes within a planning process than design-oriented planners.

Fourth, much more attention needs to be paid to the manner in which research into planning support is conducted; in other words, the methodology. This is important, because the methodology handled will influence the process, the support function, and the appropriateness of the outcomes. Two questions that could be asked are: What kinds of research strategies will be needed (e.g., case studies, laboratory experiments, gaming) to be able to support certain forms of planning best? Which research methods and techniques and methodologies should we use for that purpose (e.g., comparative analysis of case studies)? If we do not develop a more systematic research design into these methodological facets of the research into planning support, we will not be able to prove the ultimate worth or added value of all our efforts.

Fifth, much more attention is needed for the theoretical/conceptual part of research into planning support, which also appears to be highly underrepresented in international literature at the moment. This could be aided by answering such relevant questions as whether the newly emerging "complexity" planning theoretical approach will demand users, activities, or instruments possessing characteristics that deviate substantially from those that fit the earlier "communicative" planning theoretical approach. Insight into these more conceptual questions is needed to be able to provide sufficiently underscored guidelines for practice to attain planning support.

And finally, on a more general note, we currently have very little directly usable knowledge concerning the notion of planning support—what it is, how to initiate or monitor it, under which conditions it should or would take a certain form, how we can make sure that we are proceeding in the right direction, and so on. One example of a question that remains to be answered is how governance influences tool development or adjustment. Also, what kind of characteristics should these PSS tools possess assuming their dedication to the factual situation and context at hand? Another question concerns how to use PSS tools developed in and attuned to first-world contextual settings in less developed countries. How can PSS tools based on complex modeling principles, such as cellular automata or multiagent-based principles, fulfill factual planning support roles within a participatory planning context given the fact that these tools should be attuned to the abilities of users to fulfill a factual planning support role? Additional research into these kinds of cross-sectional questions into planning support is urgently needed. There is a demand for PSS applications in real-world planning situations instead of the present-day settings, which are mainly case study oriented, and in which many context-related factors are controlled in a quasireality.

Much more dedicated research into planning support is needed to provide planning practice with directives and recommendations on how to make the best of PSS instruments entering the market. The conceptual framework variables discussed above play an important directional role here: Fit PSS explicitly to the application-specific characteristics of the content of the planning issue, the users' abilities, the planning and policy process, its political context, the specific planning tasks, specific characteristics of information, knowledge, instruments, and the dominant planning style and policy model. It is to be hoped that more scientists, planners, and technicians will take these recommendations seriously and start finding out how to enhance their planning-support role to be able to cope with the increasing complexity of present-day planning tasks.

Conclusions and Recommendations

It is clear from the above that we have come a long way. As early as 50 years ago, Britton Harris (1965) requested more dedicated attention for planning support, given the noted discrepancy between the instruments then entering the market and the associated demands within planning practice at that moment in time. Looking back, we have to conclude that history shows a sequence of discrepancies between the time-bound demands of planners in practice and the instruments offered to them for planning support. Sometimes these instruments were technically far more advanced than what was needed by the planners; at other times the planners demanded much more advanced support than could be provided by that generation of support instruments. Not surprisingly, these subsequent generations of support instruments have hardly reached the planning practice, while quests for support actions have not abated.

However, it seems that, at present, we are ready, or at least trying to make a breakthrough in bringing together demand and supply of support and support instruments, respectively. The upcoming generation of PSS plays an important role in this. Some of these instruments support the provision of information and knowledge to those involved in or affected by planning actions. Some instruments support the communication of information and knowledge in planning processes and some other categories of instruments support the design, modeling, and analysis of information and knowledge, all for the sake of supporting planning decisions. Of course it is far too early to evaluate the application of these instruments in planning practice. However, the first signs are promising, at least for the information-provision and communication-support instruments. In my perspective, the design/modeling/analytical instruments are lagging behind, although the enormous amount of attention devoted to these kinds of instruments in present-day international literature points to a positive attitude.

Despite the positive outlook, we have to recognize the fact that we still have a long way to go. If all goes well, the recommendations made in the last paragraph will be taken into account seriously. However, I believe that the use/user-oriented factors mentioned require much more attention if a more sustainable relationship between the demand and supply side of PSS is to be realized. A short-lived hype resulting from fancy instruments should be prevented, however, because the complexity of present-day planning demands long-term support. Therefore, more research into these use/user-oriented factors should be executed and its results should likewise be widely communicated. Best practices and appropriate methodologies will and can be of great help in this.

Endnotes

1. See Couclelis (1989a); Ottens (1990); Scholten and Stillwell (1990); Klosterman (1994a; 2001a); Worrall (1994); Bishop (1998); Nedovic-Budic (1998); and Geertman (1999).

2. For an extended overview of this inventory, please refer to Geertman and Stillwell (2003b).

3. For an extended overview of these recommendations, please see Geertman and Stillwell (2004).

4. For a more elaborated explanation of these studies, please refer to Vonk (2006) and Vonk, Geertman, and Schot (2005; 2007a; 2007b).

5. For a more elaborated explanation of these factors, see Geertman (2006).

6. For a further elaboration of their role in planning support, see Geertman (2006).

7. For an extensive elaboration of the process of set up and the outcomes of the research agenda, see Geertman (2008).

Planning Support Systems

What Are Practicing Planners Looking For?

Terry Moore

Who's the Tool: The Model or Me?

The Parable

BONANZA IS A WESTERN METROPOLITAN AREA IN THE STATE OF PANIC. The population of the metropolitan area has grown at an average annual rate of 4 percent for 10 years; some areas have grown at annual rates of over 12 percent. That growth has been possible only by letting private development grow faster than public infrastructure: Little by little, the excess capacity of the highway, water treatment, school, and other systems has been drawn down.

Growth under those conditions is possible temporarily, but it is not sustainable. Funding systems have to change to allow the state, county, municipalities, and service districts to provide adequate public facilities and services. As with most growing areas, a big reason Bonanza is not farther behind on new facilities is that its service providers have deferred maintenance on existing facilities. Moreover, the facilities that do eventually get built may not be the right ones. Should the mix shift, for example, to better environmental systems, or more emphasis on transit? Land use arrangements (location and mix of uses) and densities might need to change. If nothing changes, either quality of life will deteriorate, growth will slow down, or both.

The Bonanza region has a metropolitan planning organization (MPO) with federal authority to facilitate regional transportation planning and to consider the effects of transportation on land development and vice versa. Like many MPOs, it is leveraging that authority to back into a regional plan. The plan's focus, for both federal and local reasons, must be transportation, but transportation issues cannot be resolved without reference to land use, other public infrastructure, and services that facilitate and shape land development, environmental quality, and economic development. In short, a federal mandate for and local acceptance of regional transportation planning cracks the door open to regional land use planning. The MPO is peering through that crack and considering the safest way to steal through.

At one level, the MPO is already in the land use planning business: It creates and adopts the long-run population and employment forecasts that drive the transportation model that informs the decisions the regional transportation plan comprises. The transportation model requires an allocation of population and employment to relatively small subareas (transportation analysis zones, or TAZs). Such allocations, through a different lens, look a lot like a regional land use plan, though parties to the coup are careful not to call it that.

How "good" are those allocations, and how is *good* defined? The MPO has not paid much attention to the rigor of the allocation process because it was always just an intermediate step buried in the model that delivered the real output: link assignments and level of service on the regional transportation system. But lots of people and groups are now asking questions about future locations and patterns of growth: What is likely, desirable, and possible? They are looking to the MPO to provide and defend the answers.

The MPO considers its options. It has a competent staff, good GIS capabilities, and a relatively sophisticated transportation-demand model. It has previously used in-house, relatively simple, ad hoc, but quantitative techniques (spreadsheets) for its allocations of future population and employment growth to TAZs. It generalizes its options as:

1. Upgrade the in-house allocation model (more sophisticated and transparent spreadsheets with better documentation).

2. Create a new in-house allocation model (shift to a GIS platform and use spatial tools in the GIS software to help with the allocation).

3. Buy an off-the-shelf allocation model and calibrate it to Bonanza.

4. Purchase or create with consultants a new megamodel that integrates land use and transportation modeling.

Bonnie and Biff, the MPO's senior land use and transportation planners, get the job of evaluating the options. They have a good basis for assessing options 1 and 2 and are experienced enough to know that any estimate they make of time and cost is much more likely to be an underestimate than an overestimate. They eliminate option 4 as beyond the scope, budget, and schedule of the MPO.

But what about option 3? What off-the-shelf models are out there? Where is the *Consumer Reports* rating, reliable blog, or journal article that even clearly describes their different characteristics, much less their relative advantages for different applications and overall ratings? They do what you would expect: check the American Planning Association's Planning Advisory Service reports; scan the tables of contents for the last three years of the *Journal of the American Planning Association*; call friends; surf the Internet. They assemble a list. They go to the Web sites for the software on the list.[1]

It is not a dead end, but it is a maze, with little direction on how long it takes to come out the other end and what is likely to be there when they do. The Web sites are suggestive, but not definitive. Are they supposed to call every vendor? They start, but uniformly find that the vendors need a lot of specifics to give specific answers—about data, uses, users, desired outcomes, model interfaces, and so on—all of which require a lot more work by the MPO. Bonnie and Biff start to think they may need to issue a request for proposals (RFP) to find consultants to help them make a decision. But, at least initially, that is more work for them. And is the RFP addressed to software vendors or to consultants that actually do the work of allocation analysis and use vendor software (or not)? That process, even if successful, might not get work going on this allocation issue for up to six months.

Their conclusion: option 1. We know what we are getting into; we will have a model that we can understand and explain; it is faster and cheaper in the short run; we will think about something better next time after somebody else has spent the money to make standard software reliable, transparent, effective, and cheap.[2]

The Point

The MPO wants to be able to predict what is highly uncertain. Its constituents want certainty; the MPO wants to deliver that certainty or, where it is not possible, a compelling illusion of it.

The uncertainty about the future is compounded by uncertainty about the tools that might be available to tame it. Bonnie and Biff understand and accept tools for supporting planning decisions that are common and generic. Word-processing, spreadsheet, database, and graphics software are obvious examples in use at all planning jurisdictions. GIS is another example. It has been around for more than 20 years; all MPOs use it; and, importantly, it is a generic tool like spreadsheet software itself (e.g., Microsoft® Excel), not a specific and sometimes opaque tool like a 30-worksheet allocation model built on an Excel platform.

But Bonnie and Biff have budget constraints and time constraints; they have a demand for a tool that allows a relatively quick, engaging, transparent, and theoretically sound simulation of possible futures. An expensive megamodel with a black box forecast is not what they want. If planning support systems (PSS) as defined in this book are going to be attractive to Bonnie and Biff, they have to move from single-design, academic experiments to clear, simple, flexible work tools like a spreadsheet and GIS—tools that allow local planners to model their own regions.

There is ample evidence in the literature and in this book that PSS forecasting tools are not yet mainstream, and that an important reason is that they have yet to cross some technical and political thresholds that would make them so. That explains Bonnie and Biff's choice—work with our existing models—which I think is the likely one now—in 2008—for most planning agencies. But I also think that things could change rapidly for PSS over the next few years. Later parts of this chapter discuss some of the things that could speed the change.

Putting Planning Support Systems in Context

In the context of this book, I am in the enviable position of being an outsider, of whom little is expected. I am not a modeler and am not expected to speak specs or talk tech. I am relatively well suited to this task. Though the editor was too polite to describe it to me this way, my role allowed me to view my weaknesses in all things modeled and mathy as a virtue and to provide the writers of other chapters some ideas about what I and the other practitioners with whom I consort naïvely believe to be practical directions for improvements to their models.

During my career as a practicing planner I have compensated for my quantitative quaintness not by learning more math, but by selectively collecting information that suggests that long-run forecasting in social systems—with economic activity and land development being the subset of such systems that I care about—is a very uncertain business, and that sophisticated forecasting models may be inherently incapable of providing anything better than one could get from a straight line and straight thinking. Maybe I cannot develop or completely understand all the equations in a general equilibrium model, but if the results of the model are really no better than predispositions and guesses dressed up, why bother?

Before giving some support to that bias, I note an important assumption: Planning cannot exist without forecasting. Planning implies that some actions taken now will lead to "better" futures than alternative actions. If planners do not believe that, they are in the wrong line of work. That assumption implies another: We can know something about the future effects (impacts) of those different actions. In other words, it implies that we can forecast with, if not a feeling of certainty, at least a modicum of empirically based hopefulness. No forecasting, no planning.

Thus, my position is not that uncertainty makes planning irrelevant, but that planning must explicitly acknowledge that uncertainty to be relevant. As I note later, legal requirements and political desires often treat a forecast as what *will* happen, rather than as what *might* happen. Moreover, futures presented as forecasts often have a normative component (sometimes without acknowledging it): This is what *should* happen.

Though planning support systems have other objectives as well (Klosterman and Pettit 2005, 477–478), I focus in this chapter on their forecasting aspects, which I consider to be the most fundamental.[3] I acknowledge that I am focusing on but one area of planning practice that PSS forecasting tools attempt to support: population, employment, and land development allocations and impact evaluations in metropolitan areas. There are certainly other applications. For example, CommunityViz® helps planners with site design issues that are not subject to the kind or level of economic and social uncertainty that I focus on below.

Most of the literature in planning about forecasting is about how to do it and do it better. In 1994 the *Journal of the American Planning Association* (vol. 60, no. 1) contained several articles summarizing the state of the practice on large-scale urban models. Though old, that collection of articles is still a good place for any planner to get oriented to the issues. Klosterman's introductory article (1994c) gives a good synopsis of the events—30 years of them since the pioneering work of, among others, Britton Harris (1968), who also has an article in that collection—leading to the state of the practice at that time.

In that issue of the *Journal of the American Planning Association*, Lee (1994) defended and reinterpreted his article from 21 years earlier, "Requiem for Large-Scale Models" (Lee 1973). I find a lot to agree with in Lee's article (and in Harris's rebuttal), but especially with his footnote clarifying his critique: "It was never my intention to attack the use of quantitative methods, or rationality in planning. I was and am a committed believer in society's ability to improve itself, to make use of relevant information, and to distinguish between better and worse actions on the basis of logic and empirical data and analysis" (Lee 1994, 40).

Amen, and me, too. Quantification helps in many places, but it hurts when it allows planners, citizens, and their decision makers to pretend that model output is destiny, that the future is knowable and singular, and that plans will inevitably work.

Since 1994 efforts to create and improve large-scale land use models have continued, funded largely by transportation money. Some of those models are well known to regional planners at MPOs because they are linked (usually exogenously) to transportation-demand models. Those models are, in essence, doing or assisting with the allocation of population and employment to TAZs, based in part on land use characteristics and development theory (e.g., DRAM/EMPAL[4]). TRANSIM is a newer brand of transportation-demand model (based on tracking individual trips rather than zone-to-zone averages) that, by definition, must allocate households and businesses (activities) to specific places. One of the biggest efforts in the United States to develop these types of models is occurring in Oregon with support of federal transportation money. Its goal is to be a state-of-the-art, statewide, integrated, microsimulation model of transportation, land use, and economic systems. The project began over 10 years ago. Big models take big time.

Other chapters in this book reference those bigger models, but they are not the central topic of this book. Klosterman (1999a) and Klosterman and Pettit (2005) define the bulk of PSS tools as something less grand and more applicable and accessible for day-to-day planning. They make the point that approximate definitions are good enough, that in general PSS are about helping analysis or communication, and that describing PSS tools based on their intentions and performance on multiple characteristics is better than an *ex ante* taxonomy. But, relevant to my point in this chapter, they list analysis and forecasting as one of two key objectives of PSS, and Brail (2006, 308) defines the purpose of PSS as "either projection to some point in the future or estimation of impacts from some form of development."

In other words, forecasting—predicting the future—is at the core of PSS.

Can Anyone Predict? Uncertainty and the Limits of Knowledge

My skepticism about forecasting in social systems has both logical and empirical support. Yes, classical mechanics in physics can forecast with consistent accuracy: We landed people on the moon just where we predicted we would. Closer to home, engineers make other practical forecasts based on empirical relationships that stand the test of time: Tall buildings and bridges function as predicted. Science and technology have demonstrated that even the fickle weather operates mainly within knowable bounds established by global variables that can be measured and used to predict temperature and precipitation in the short run with better success than guesses based on current local weather.

But social systems? Their prediction of overall population and employment growth in 20 years in Bonanza (forget about the allocation of that growth to subareas of Bonanza for a moment) depends on factors that span the globe: international competition, climate change, national policies on immigration and homeland security, state polices and ballot measures on transportation and school funding, the stock market and the future incomes of retirees, and on, and on.

It is commonplace to observe that our predictions vary increasingly from eventual reality the farther out we try to forecast. Most planners that do forecasting know that in big metropolitan areas one can often be wrong about many things in particular but make it up on averages. For most mature metropolitan areas (not Bonanza, as I described it), history suggests that planners have a good shot at getting future population approximately right by using an average annual growth rate of, say, 1.3 percent. At a regional scale, forecasts can prove to be approximately right about the amount of population and employment.

But as the forecasts try to get more specific spatially, temporally, or topically their abilities to correctly predict will decrease rapidly. As business cycles come and go, the average regional growth might be way off of its long-run average for any particular year. What might be true for the region on average is not true for all of its subareas, some of which will be growing rapidly while others are losing population. The distributional issues matter a lot for all kinds of reasons, not the least of which is that there are hundreds of different units of government providing services in the region, some to relatively small subareas.[5] These problems with small-area forecasts (which are often done as allocations for forecasts for larger areas) have been recognized for a long time (Isserman 1977), but they are still problems.

Flyvbjerg, Holm, and Buhl (2002) document a different example of uncertainty, finding that estimates of the costs of large transportation projects are not random but consistently low. After considering various explanations, they conclude that the problem "is best explained by strategic misinterpretation, that is, lying." They note, however, that while one cannot predict exactly which problems will cause cost overruns, a long history of experience suggests that something will and that the overruns are thus predictable in a statistical sense.

In a related study, the same authors (Flyvbjerg, Holm, and Buhl 2005) find that rail forecasts overestimate ridership (forecast versus later actual counts) by an average of over 100 percent. Also, 50 percent of road projects were off on forecasts of traffic volumes by 20 percent in either direction. Relevant to my arguments about uncertainty and the need to deal with it better, they suggest that if planners really want to do a better job of forecasting they should not try to forecast specific, uncertain events, but should place the issue of interest (in their case, the use or cost of a transportation project) in the context of a statistical distribution of "reference projects." They note that the check against a reference class is an "outside" view, while much forecasting is based on an "inside" view. Local knowledge and interest nudge evaluation toward considerations of why the local area is special, will do well, and will (without knowing that they are saying so) be an outlier in the reference class.

Planners are well aware of the problems with doing long-run forecasting in metropolitan areas, but they are sometimes constrained to proceed as if they do not matter that much. Moore (2007) notes situations in which regulations presume certainty: In Oregon, state regulations require that each county accept a 20-year forecast of population growth done by the state and that it conduct a process that ends with all cities in its boundaries agreeing on the specific share of the county total for which they will plan.

Even where not required by law, uncertainty and variation may be beaten back by the actual or presumed political realities planners must accommodate. The common rule of keeping the analysis to a page lest decision makers not read it does not give much space to a discussion of alternative futures, the reasons they might occur, and the best way to prepare for changes that can only be predicted if one accepts that large shocks to the status quo will not occur.

But Taleb (2007) points out that large shocks are exactly what we should expect, and that they will be unknowable.[6] The following are among his many relevant points.

- Business as usual is ultimately a bad assumption: There is nothing usual about the future.

- We substantially overestimate the accuracy of our predictions about things we think we understand.

- More information is sometimes not better; it just contributes to confirmation bias (making us believe more strongly what we already believe).

- Forecasters, like all people, make attribution errors that protect their status as experts. If I got it right, it is because I am a good forecaster; if I got it wrong, it is because of external factors that no one could have predicted.

- The effects of the unexpected are not random: They are more likely to push in the direction of higher costs and a longer time to completion.

- Policies should depend more on the range of final outcomes than on an expected final number.

- We cannot know what we cannot know. If we did, we would already be acting on that knowledge.

In short, much of what really affects the economic system that drives development (that planners are compelled by their practice and predispositions to predict) are unknowable events that have very big effects. Planners need to understand that point and propose policies that expose their jurisdictions to opportunities for positive events where the costs of failure would be small and reduce their exposure to potential negative events of consequence.

Examples abound. Two recent ones for Oregon support the argument. All forecasting of the amount and location of growth in Oregon for the last 30 years has relied fundamentally on the assumption that urban growth boundaries strongly limited the conversion of farm and forest land to residential uses. That assumption worked for a long time. But plans did not plan for the backlash of Oregon's property-rights referendum, Measure 37. Depending on how it plays out, it could, in some areas, substantially change the look of the landscape, if not farming practices.

Another example from Oregon concerns the downtowns of the cities of Eugene and Springfield, which are just over two miles apart. For 30 years they have had a single urban-growth boundary. But the two councils represent constituencies with different views about growth. Springfield's council has pursued economic development opportunities more aggressively and has felt constrained by both the amount of buildable land in the boundary and the institutional relationship with Eugene that makes it difficult to expand the boundary in ways that state law would allow. Planning did not foresee that Springfield would go to the state legislature and win authority to have its own boundary: Future growth will almost certainly be allocated differently.

Events like these seem predictable when looking backwards, but so would any other of dozens of possible futures that might have occurred given the same foundational conditions.

Among the conclusions I draw from these examples is that predicting policy variables is very difficult. Political support for different policies waxes and wanes over short periods—terms of office are two to four years in length—and long periods (during which attitudes about the proper scope of government regulation and property rights can change). No model can handle that kind of uncertainty in a definitive way with unassailable mathematics. Though agent-based models conceptually can include the public sector as an agent, they are dealing with politics at a much grosser level than what I have described. Klosterman and Pettit (2005) note a PSS that goes farther (Saarloos et al. 2005) by simulating the land use planning *process*. (Other models would make assumptions about the regulatory outcomes of that process and use them as rules for the model.) One reason that small-area forecasts are so uncertain is that local policy variables play a bigger role relative to broad economic and demographic forces.

Klosterman (1994b, 42) comments on a comprehensive review of large-scale urban models that found that variability in model results "result more from problems in setting up the models, such as poor data quality, inadequate model calibration and validation and insufficient documentation, than from deficiencies in model structure or computational procedures." But those problems may be inherent characteristics of any model that attempts to predict urban spatial structure in the context of uncertainty and the demands of policy makers for relatively quick answers to shifting policy questions.

I sound pessimistic and academic, which was neither my charge nor intent. I am not saying no to planning and forecasting. To do so would be contrary to my belief, shared by most planners, that society has real choices that make a difference, ways to simulate how they might affect what we collectively choose to care about, and processes for debating the simulations and their results. Though it may seem like semantic caviling, I see the conceptual distinction between a forecast (which is often interpreted as "this is what the future *will* be") and a simulation ("this is what the future *might* be") as hugely important in planning practice. One gets different (and better) plans if one prepares reasonably well for a range of changes than if one prepares very well for a single change.[7] Though practicing planners understand this point, they are often constrained by schedule, budget, and politics to proceed as if they do not.

My comments to this point have been about the ability of PSS tools to predict future facts. Even if they could do that with some reliability, they face another problem if they are really going to support decision making: placing values (relative weights) on their predicted (simulated) impacts. At this point, only a few of the physically based PSS tools address this issue at all, and not rigorously.[8]

There is a place in planning for PSS. The issue—at least, my issue—is less with the details of the tools themselves than with how they are used. Most model developers are well aware of the limitations of their models and are happy to discuss them with anyone who shows an interest. But the public planning process has a low tolerance for ambiguity and uncertainty. Common and political sense say that if there are two extremes, the correct answer is between them. There is pressure to define a most likely future and plan for it as if "most likely" meant 100 percent rather than the 5 percent that is probably a better estimate.[9]

There are many more and different extremes than just two. PSS models are useful if they prepare us to respond to change, which they can. They are potentially harmful if they are tuned to a comforting mode—tomorrow will be just like today, but a little bigger—that justifies business as usual and inhibits our ability to take advantage of and mitigate the unknowable and inevitable changes ahead.

Cost of Reducing Uncertainty

Planners and their constituents dislike uncertainty. But urban and regional planners cannot ignore it: They *must* forecast urban and regional growth and development patterns. They *should* have a strong interest in PSS tools that make such forecasts quick and credible, and assist with their evaluation and visualization.

But even if one is optimistic that reducing the uncertainty of long-run, disaggregated forecasts of urban growth and development patterns beyond some minimum level is not logically impossible, one has to acknowledge that it can be very costly. It is the assessment that planners make of costs that explain why many of the PSS tools described in this book have yet to be accepted into common planning practice.

Set aside the theoretical issues about the limits of knowledge and assume that PSS models really can predict something useful. I think most planners are willing to make that assumption, or at least a softer version of it: PSS tools can help planners simulate and describe alternative futures. They can describe the uncertainty so that we can plan for it, even if they cannot eliminate it.

Then the question for planners is a cost-benefit one: Are the systems worth the effort? Importantly, that question gets answered in a world of alternatives: Many ways to forecast (to confront uncertainty) are much easier and cheaper than a fully calibrated PSS.

Moreover, 20 years of scenario analysis leads consistently to the same results: (1) the choices for urban form in metropolitan areas usually get reduced to dispersion (a.k.a. suburbanization, sprawl, trends, business as usual); concentration (a.k.a. density, compactness, centers, smart growth); or concentrated dispersion (a.k.a. dispersed concentration, satellite cities); and (2) concentration performs best, sometimes not by much, on the factors we choose to value and evaluate, and the alternatives do not usually lead to Armageddon. The models do not produce a range of choices sufficiently different in their implications so as to overcome the political obstacles necessary to achieve the marginally better results.

The capacity and cost of computers and the cost of software are not the obstacle. Cheap, ubiquitous desktop computers can run the PSS tools described in this book. Software cost is trivial: some of the PSS tools described in this book are free; all are cheap relative to what gets spent on regional planning processes.

The real obstacles are the costs of start up and of the uncertainty about whether start up will ever end and lead to something useful—evidence sufficient for politically compelling policy change. Both the professional literature and the tales of practitioners are replete with warnings about start-up costs. There are three main costs.

■ Data. Some of the PSS tools require large amounts of data that are not readily available or useable from standard sources. Data collection and cleaning have taken, literally, years for some models.

■ Calibration. Some models take some work to get them to settle down, even when they have the data.

■ Training. Learning the software can run up potentially big costs—not just learning the basic mouse clicks, but fundamentally understanding the structure of the model, its quirks and weaknesses, and how to interpret its results. The greater these costs, the more problematic it will be to keep the model operational if the model master takes a new job.

As PSS tools develop, all of these problems are being addressed. Some off-the-shelf software is not quite plug-and-play, but close. It works with the data you have, requires no calibration, is relatively simple and intuitive (for people with a planning and GIS background), and has good documentation. Nonetheless, the essential tradeoff is never going to disappear: Powerful and flexible software cannot also be really simple.

Geertman (2002a) notes that most planners that use software such as spreadsheets and GIS employ only a very small percentage of their database management and analytical capabilities. They use spreadsheets to make simple tables and GIS to make thematic maps. I agree and think the reasons are that most do not have time given pressing demands, and local government officials will not allocate the budget that any realistic estimate of the full costs to realize a useful product would suggest. A possible implication for the kind of PSS tools discussed in this book is that maybe they are trying to do too much. Instead of complex forecasting and analysis tools, planners may only have time for simple accounting tools—a transparent platform for testing intuitions, with default intuitions available and well documented.

Timmermans (2003) says that complex phenomena require complex models. Said a different way, in forecasting development for subareas of metropolitan regions, simplicity runs dangerously close to simplemindedness. Spreadsheet or GIS software packages have obvious and multiple applications, and there is little worry about what is under the hood—users justifiably assume that the spreadsheets do all the basic arithmetic correctly. PSS models, in contrast, have more specific purposes and have planning assumptions built into them in order to operate. A choice between two spreadsheet packages is based on operating system, price, some benchmark standards, and personal preferences. There is no concern that a spreadsheet will fail to perform basic calculations. PSS models are not standardized; they do not have tens of thousands of users communicating in blogs, nor trade journals doing benchmark comparisons and evaluations. There is a lot of uncertainty about performance and effective costs, and that uncertainty tends to get resolved, as noted above, disproportionately toward less benefit and more cost.

The reasons that I suggest for the limited use of PSS are ones I inferred from my experience, but a review of the literature shows that they are not original. Geertman's (2002a) and Brail's (2006) assessments seem right to me. Among other things they note that a low price of software does not necessarily mean a low cost of development. Thus, the gap between what a small group of relatively impecunious public-sector users might pay for PSS, and what it costs developers to create it, is a problem that cannot get solved without regulation (e.g., federal requirements for MPO transportation plans) and monetary subsidies (ultimately from federal or NGO sources, funneled to academic, state, MPO, or private PSS developers) or time (by private model developers). Vonk, Geertman, and Schot (2005) cite lack of awareness and a low assessment of the value of PSS.

These points are not inconsistent with my characterization: Uncertainty about the costs (will they be high?) and benefits (will they be low?) means that planners are slow to commit. In such a situation, the prescription of Vonk, Geertman, and Schot (2005) makes sense: Get more and better information out about the existence of PSS and their potential benefits.

These elements of uncertainty are simultaneously evaluation criteria: What planners want is what PSS developers will have to deliver if they want their PSS to become mainstream. Developers need look no farther than the history of the acceptance of transportation-demand models and GIS to get a feel for the process and the criteria. My list is a relatively obvious one.

- Make learning and operation simpler by tying the PSS to standard software (spreadsheet and GIS).

- Make the PSS flexible—that is, customizable to local circumstances and useful at different levels of sophistication. That suggests a rule-based structure, which I think has the best chance of being adopted by midsized planning organizations. If rule-based, provide a complete but simple set of default rules, with good documentation on their sources. Users have to be able to get under the hood to understand and adjust the rules. (CommunityViz®, INDEX, and PLACE^{3}S seem to do this to greater or lesser degrees.)

- Develop standard, accepted benchmarks, and conduct peer review.

- Along the lines of standardization, develop more thorough promotional literature that addresses in a consistent and common way the kinds of issues raised throughout this book. For example, does the model allocate growth, or just compute impacts of growth based on an exogenous allocation? What does the model do well, and what does it do not so well? Are short case study descriptions of applications included?

- Focus on reliability. Accuracy may not be possible given the inherent uncertainty, but reliability should be. Similar inputs should lead to similar results, and users should be able to understand and explain why those results occurred. Do a decent job at what you know how to do, and do not aim for precision about things beyond specification or understanding.

- Reduce data needs by simplification and standardization. That could mean, for example, tying more of the model operation to standard federal and third-party data sources and providing advice on how to get local data (e.g., buildable lands) specified in a simple way that the model can accept (e.g., a nested hierarchy of land use types so that users can specify at whatever level they have the data).

- Produce output that local governments want. They will certainly want what they are required to have (e.g., by state or federal requirements), or what has clear relevance to short-run investment decisions. This is a lesson learned from transportation-demand modeling and from GIS.

■ Get federal support through regulatory requirements or subsidies. Such support was an important contributor to the acceptance of transportation-demand models.

It is possible that PSS cannot be mainstreamed until it is mainstream. Less cryptically, there may be a tipping point. One fax machine is not very useful; 1,000 fax machines that cannot reliably talk to each other are not much better. But when the interfaces have been standardized and costs reduced, every new fax machine makes all its surviving ancestors more valuable. PSS is not there yet.

I want to take a short detour to talk about the accuracy of PSS models. I think there is more to the definition of *accuracy* than "the retrospective comparison showing that old forecasts resemble what actually occurred." If some model could be shown to consistently describe the future development of urban areas, that would be pretty amazing, and there are many investors and developers who would pay good money for that tool. But I cannot imagine that happening. The more likely situation is that the PSS will always be looking forward and will rarely be evaluated for what they *have* done because by then the model will be different.

What is important for any model of land use and transportation in use for urban areas is its ability to differentiate reliably among policy options and to display fully the costs and benefits of each. The tools should highlight unforeseen consequences of well-intended decisions. The advantage of a good PSS is less its predictive "accuracy" than its ability to treat an entire urban area consistently and completely over time and space and to produce politically compelling results.

If I am right, even roughly, that planners really cannot predict the economic and social future with much certainty, then our long-run forecasting models for public policy (and land use is clearly a long-run issue, not just a short-run one) may be being evaluated against the wrong standard. First, PSS have not been around long enough to test how they are performing. Second, any testing that is occurring is probably backcasting (predicting the present from the past) and does not address the kind of big and uncertain change that I have discussed above. Third, the empirical record is that few people compare the old forecasts of models (e.g., ones done in 1992) to current conditions for many reasons, including the fact that the model used 15 years ago almost certainly does not exist in any recognizable form today. Fourth, even if such evaluations were done, it is quite possible that a model got it right for the wrong reasons. In that context, what does it mean when evaluating a current model to say that it is more accurate than another?

A different measure of a model's usefulness is consistency. A model that was right about the relevant policy issues to consider, but wrong in its guesses about how future decision makers would resolve those issues (such as, for example, Measure 37 in Oregon) may have proved more useful in evaluating policy options than the model that got the future development pattern right for the wrong reasons. What is important is that your model identifies key exogenous assumptions and policy variables and treats them consistently in developing forecasts. As economists might say, one can still make good choices, even if the absolute forecasts are uncertain, provided that the model deals with different alternatives consistently and clearly: Then decision makers can have a little more confidence about the likely *differences* among the choices. They do not have to know the exact distance to start, but they do need the right direction.

Examples That Give Support to the Argument

In this section I illustrate some of my points with two examples of specific PSS tools not addressed in other chapters of this book.

Portland Metro and MetroScope

Metro is the regional planning agency in Portland, Oregon. Its enjoys celebrity status among MPOs because it is in a state with a strong commitment to land use planning, has planning and enforcement authority for regional land use, has an elected regional government with real authority, and has a reputation for high-quality technical work. Some characteristics of importance to its choice of PSS are listed here.

- Metro is a big agency with a relatively big budget.

- Metro has a mandate for planning and public decisions about regional development, which creates a need for showing the impacts of all proposed actions and policies on its adopted plan for the pattern of urban development. The description of those impacts must be understandable and must withstand public comment and technical scrutiny.

- At the time Metro started looking for planning tools that could meet those requirements (more than 10 years ago), no off-the-shelf software was available that could meet all Metro's requirements. It had a good GIS platform from which to build and a staff capable of doing the building.

- Metro decided to build its own model: MetroScope. It proceeded incrementally. Once it had started, the marginal choice was always to expand its own model rather than to buy an off-the-shelf package.

MetroScope was developed in spreadsheet form in 1996 as a one-zone, residential real estate model.[10] It was developed and used by Metro technical staff for housing-needs analysis. In 1998 staff added a 20-zone location module that interacted with the transportation model and later developed a linked 20-zone nonresidential real estate model. From 2001 to 2004 Metro converted the spreadsheet-based real estate models to Visual Basic operation and increased the number of residential and nonresidential zones to 425 and 72, respectively. Metro built in travel demand and network assignment models and by 2006 had a fully "code-integrated" land use and transportation model.

In 2002 MetroScope model runs for one five-year forecasting period took as long as a week of computer time. In 2007 runs for thirty-five years (seven five-year forecast periods) take about two to six staff hours to input policy assumptions (e.g., zoning capacity, urban growth boundary expansion areas, and transportation network) and run in thirty-six hours.[11]

At all points in its incremental development MetroScope provided useful information to Metro's decision-making process. It rarely absorbed more than about 25 percent of a full-time staff position. It was 100 percent locally funded. It was not developed as a commercial endeavor, so staff could focus exclusively on Metro's specific needs. They were free to make use of proven research and theory[12] because there was no pressure to be on the cutting edge of publishable urban research.

For any given set of exogenous and policy assumptions (e.g., about regional population and employment growth, or transportation and land use supply), MetroScope presents a conditional forecast that consistently implements the logic of its assumed relationships. The model calculates and displays the results in sufficient detail to illustrate the impacts of different policies on variables of interest. Figure 11.1 shows the model's structure.

The Metro conditions and decisions are consistent with ideas in this chapter. Metro staff had political support for stronger technical evaluation. Off-the-shelf PSS were limited when Metro was looking for applications software, and Metro already had strong in-house GIS and modeling capabilities (transportation, land use, and economics). Metro's Data Resources Center was relatively well funded. The logical step was also the easiest: Build a Metro-specific spreadsheet model that could interface with GIS. It started simple and grew incrementally as policy changed, technology improved, and staff skill grew.

Staff at Metro conceived of MetroScope and did most of its development. Asked to comment on MetroScope in the context of the themes presented here, the staff believes that MetroScope has been successful as a PSS because it has demonstrated three important points.

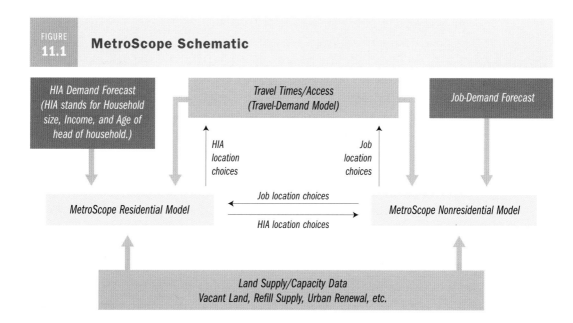

FIGURE 11.1   MetroScope Schematic

HIA Demand Forecast (HIA stands for Household size, Income, and Age of head of household.)

Travel Times/Access (Travel-Demand Model)

Job-Demand Forecast

HIA location choices

Job location choices

MetroScope Residential Model

Job location choices
HIA location choices

MetroScope Nonresidential Model

Land Supply/Capacity Data
Vacant Land, Refill Supply, Urban Renewal, etc.

NOT ALL GOOD IDEAS WORK.   Figures 11.2 and 11.3 display model output in response to increases in the amount of land for medium- to high-density housing in strategic centers, a result of a proposed Metro housing-subsidy policy. Figure 11.2 shows the increase in medium- and high-density housing that resulted from moving the investment level from a low level targeted to a few centers to a high level targeted to centers throughout the region. The high investment level was prompted by an intermediate result that indicated that choice of housing type and location could be significantly influenced by a 15 to 25 percent subsidy for high-density housing construction in urban renewal areas. If a moderate level of subsidy produced favorable results, should an even higher level not produce more? Figure 11.3 shows the model's result: Most of the increase in higher-density housing comes at the expense of diversion by diverting market-rate housing of the same type and density into the subsidized category.

EVERY BENEFIT HAS A COST.   Metro continually explores policies that aim to limit urban expansion and the growth of vehicle miles traveled (VMT): limiting urban growth boundary (UGB) expansion, increasing zoning capacity, limiting transportation investment, and subsidizing medium- to high-density development in urban centers. Figures 11.4 and 11.5 show some of the outcomes of a policy that combines widespread subsidies for dense housing in centers with a policy of not expanding the UGB after 2015. Figure 11.4 indicates that, compared to the baseline forecast (existing policies in effect), the policy changes do increase the number of high-density units built in center areas. Figure 11.5, however, shows that single-family construction has been displaced outward a few miles by the lack of competitive building sites with the Metro UGB. While the new occupants of high-density housing use less land, take shorter trips, and make a higher percentage of them by means other than auto, these advantages are offset by the larger number of single-family homeowners commuting very long distances from low-density developments in neighboring, non-Metro jurisdictions.

THERE ARE NO SILVER BULLETS.   Metro's plan to limit expansion and reduce the growth in per capita VMT is called the 2040 Plan. Years of discussion have led to a broad public awareness, at least among those who follow land use issues, that the Portland area has chosen "to build up, not out." But ten years after adopting the plan and two successive expansions of the UGB totaling almost 20,000 acres, Metro is evaluating what it really takes to achieve the aims of the original plan. Figure 11.6 shows that, through 2035, the region continues to consume substantial acreage for urban purposes, particularly outside Metro. Figure 11.7 likewise shows that tight policies to redirect demand and supply into existing urban areas result in higher prices within the central city areas. Land consumption drops to about one thousand acres per year from a historical average of two thousand. New residential densities are roughly 50

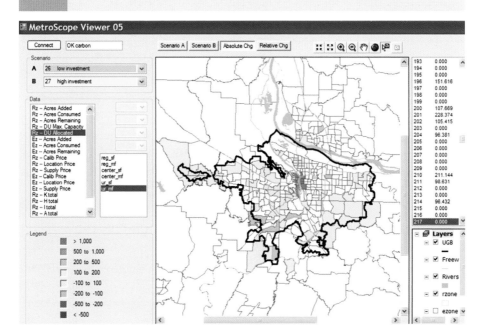

FIGURE 11.2 Moderate Increase in Housing Subsidy, Portland Metro

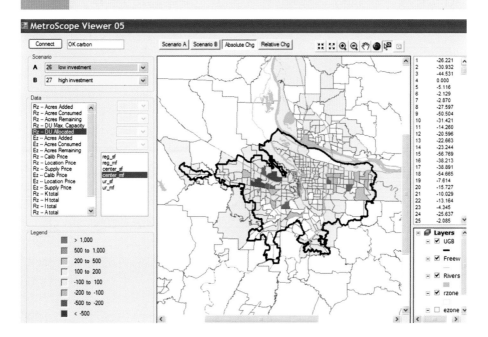

FIGURE 11.3 Higher Increase in Housing Subsidy, Portland Metro

Additional High-density Housing Units, Subsidy and Growth Boundary Policy, Portland Metro

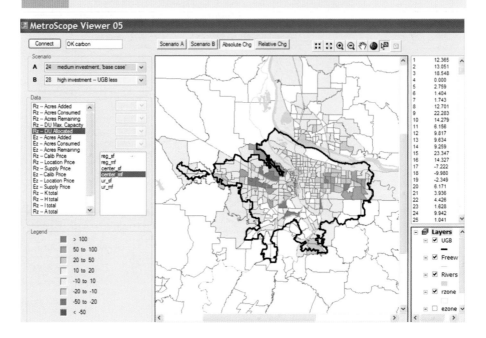

Additional Single-family Housing Units, Subsidy and Growth Boundary Policy, Portland Metro

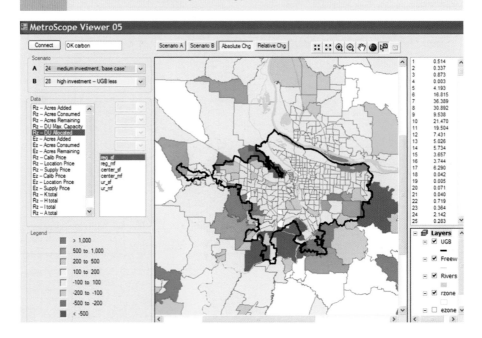

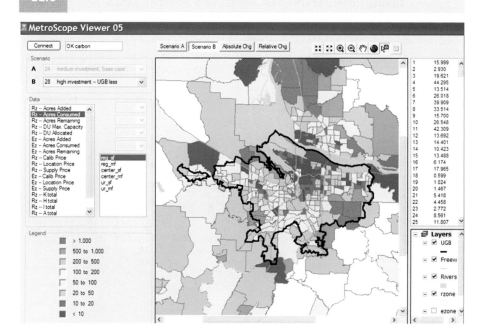

FIGURE 11.6 Projected Urban Acreage, Portland Metro, 2035

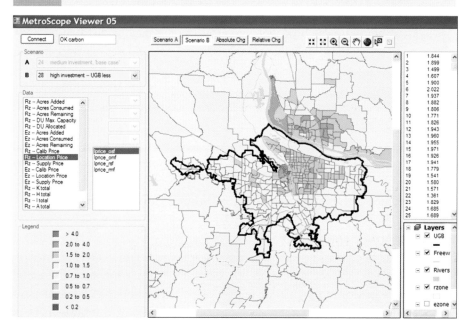

FIGURE 11.7 Projected Price Changes, Growth Boundary Policy, Portland Metro, 2035

FIGURE
11.8 **Projected One-person, Low-income, Elderly Households Living in Apartments, Portland Metro, 2035**

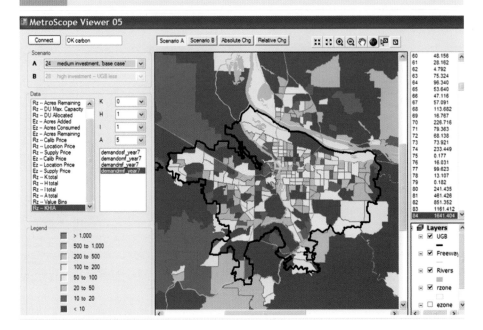

percent higher than the 1970 to 1990 averages, and per capita VMT drops at least 4 to 5 percent. No single policy initiative solves the problem. The Portland region cannot simply choose to "build up, not out." However, Metro 2040 Plan policy does make progress. Figure 11.8 depicts the concentrations of one-person, low-income, elderly households living in apartments in 2035. The largest concentrations of such vulnerable households are in high-access, high public–service areas.

These examples show how large amounts of data may be distilled to a few talking points relevant to policy decisions. The examples do not reinforce institutional bias, but inform policy about the difficulties and unintended consequences of pursuing any policy agenda. No one policy or plan adoption automatically reaches Metro's objectives. A number of policy initiatives may, but each has a cost associated with it.

MetroScope output is presented by staff and generally understood by decision makers as contingent simulations that are best interpreted relatively rather than absolutely. The focus is less on accuracy than on whether a policy moves performance measures in the desired direction, and whether it is worth the cost.[13]

The Maryland Scenario Project

The Maryland Scenario Project (MSP) is, at least superficially, a good contrast to MetroScope. The project is new, ad hoc, and run by a consortium of research and advocacy institutions, with the managing partner being the National Center for Smart Growth Research and Education (NCSG) at the University of

Maryland.[14] It grew out of an earlier project, Reality Check Plus, a statewide series of workshops at which hundreds of participants discussed growth issues and used maps to show how and where growth should occur. Reality Check Plus learned how participants around the state *desired* growth to occur. But it only conducted a cursory evaluation of how *likely* that pattern would be. What forces support and constrain the desired pattern? Which might public policy be able to influence? How, and how much? And if those patterns did occur, what would the impacts be on things people in Maryland care about? Those are the questions MSP addresses.

The project is more about technical evaluation than public process. It does not have the extensive outreach to the public that Reality Check Plus did. Instead, it relies on a group of about 30 experts with extensive experience in various aspects of growth issues in Maryland. The objective is to define plausible growth scenarios in a way that is useful for further evaluation, and then to do that evaluation.

The MSP expert participants identified combinations of driving forces and policies that led to different patterns of development. In other words, they created in words and maps a prototype of what a PSS allocation model would create in equations and output in tables and maps. That is the point of intersection with PSS: The experts' ideas cannot easily be operationalized and evaluated without some type of computational and mapping software.

NCSG staff had additional issues to consider. Most significantly, it had just negotiated a contract with the Maryland Department of Transportation to deliver, with extensive consultant participation, a statewide transportation model. That model would require as input a statewide model for allocating to counties control totals for growth of population and employment by sector; another consultant was to work on that model. Another longer-term contract with the U.S. Environmental Protection Agency was to deliver models for estimating stormwater run off (as a function of development and impervious surface) and energy consumption. Thus, the key pieces that NCSG staff felt lacking were a land use model and a platform for integrating the output of all the other models into an evaluation framework.

MSP project managers took steps similar to the ones taken by Bonnie and Biff. They had the same choice: Expand the GIS-based model that NCSG created to handle spatial input received during Reality Check Plus, shift to commercially available PSS software, or get consulting help to create something different. They went through the same search process. Some of the PSS tools investigated have been described in other chapters of this book.

As of late 2007, the NCSG staff have been doing the Bonnie and Biff ballet for six months and are likely to come to a similar conclusion: Build off of an ad hoc GIS model that NCSG developed earlier for Reality Check Plus.[15] NCSG will probably choose to extend the GIS model for the following reasons.

- *The incentive to build from a prior model developed on a tested and well-understood software platform was strong.*[16] NCSG staff members were competent with GIS software and urban spatial theory. They had graduate students as resources. They built rules into the GIS-based allocation algorithm that they understood, could justify, and were relevant to the issues and data in Maryland.

▪ *Evaluating commercially available models was difficult.* It was easy to get vendors to supply testimonials from satisfied customers; it was much more difficult to get a glance at the fundamental equations on which software was built. Also, in the opinion of the project team, much of the commercially available software offered little beyond what the team could in time create itself.

▪ *The decision not to use a commercial PSS was partially technical and partially personal.* NCSG did not need a transportation or economic component to the model; it was helping to build statewide models for both. At the other extreme, it never expected to do much site-specific work (e.g., neighborhood design). It needed a platform that would deal with large data sets and would allow relationships and rules to be incorporated easily and interact flawlessly.

☞ *PSS need to provide both disaggregation and integration.* NCSG wanted a platform that could take advantage of the economic, environmental, land use, and other models previously developed by researchers located in many different state agencies and academic departments. It wanted a platform that would facilitate communication among a variety of models, while allowing the users of any of those models to continue their work independently.

Concluding Thoughts

Forecasting is essential to planning and public policy. Though I have focused on the problems inherent in the uncertain nature of long-run economic, social, and technological change, there are reasons for optimism. The biggest is that one may be uncertain about many of the factors that affect land development and still be able to do a reasonable job of predicting the general pattern of future development.

Infrastructure and buildings last a long time: What you see is largely what you will get. There is a lot of inertia in the "vintage capital," programmed investment, and institutions in urban areas. It may take 10 to 20 years for a future development pattern (even at the margin, much less in the aggregate) to be very different from the present one. Certain natural and built features that are large and largely immutable give form to urban development. Urban development, unlike the stock market, does not change overnight. In the words of Flyvbjerg, Holm, and Buhl (2002) such PSS models might start with an "outside view," predicting future urban size and form broadly based on statistical evaluation of a large and relevant reference class of urban areas.

A dilemma for planners is that the decision makers make irreconcilable demands of PSS. On the one hand, they know metropolitan areas are complex, and that everything affects everything else. They want a model that deals with that complexity and especially with the myriad policy choices that they want investigated. The finer the grain of policy they want to test, the finer the grain of the model required. They want confidence, if not certainty: The model should be "accurate." They also want quick turnaround, proposing a policy and seeing its effects at the same meeting, or certainly the next one. All of those desires argue for a relatively complicated model that can produce output quickly.

On the other hand, they want transparency. They claim not to want a black box, implying that they want to understand all the relationships and be able to adjust on the fly. My experience is that such claims, while perhaps initially sincere, rarely are followed by compatible behavior. Few decision makers have the combination of expertise, inclination, and time to get into the workings of the models. Substitute for the term *black box* the less pejorative *specified empirical relationships*: Without such *ex ante* specification it is impossible to have a model that better reflects real complexity, or that runs quickly.

A possible solution to that dilemma is to make the *development* of the model open and transparent. If stakeholders help with the specification of the relationships, then it is *their* black box and they can accept the output because they trust what is inside.

Others have stated most of what I have said here. But I have not seen in the literature any reference to the importance of a model's master and interpreter. In public policy, the human factor is critical. It is my belief that (1) there are many possible futures for a metropolitan area that can be simulated but not definitively predicted; and (2) the competing desires of policy makers and the public for a thorough treatment of real-world complexity, but also for speed and simplicity, will resolve in favor of the latter. Given these beliefs, I conclude that the role of the model's interpreter is pivotal.

Decision makers will decide on whether to trust model output based on their confidence in the messenger. They are not going to open the black box. They will test the modeler with largely ad hoc questions, listening in part to the technical answers, but more to the logic and tone. Is the modeler on point, sensitive to our concerns, addressing those concerns clearly and directly, well-prepared, articulate, and so on? In short, is the modeler someone we can rely on to give us an honest, understandable, and defensible description of exogenous forces that suggest different possible futures and of how policy and investment variables over which we have some control might change those futures? If the answer is yes, then the black box can remain opaque and closed most of the time. They want to have confidence that their mechanic knows what is inside and can keep it running reliably. They do not want to read the manual, much less handle the greasy parts.

If this argument is correct, then the success of PSS depends in part on getting bright people well trained and committed to a place in the public sector. The MetroScope story is illustrative of this. A model was built and used incrementally. Decision makers participated by asking for and using the initial output and then by asking for additional capabilities that made the box bigger and blacker. Metro staff has very low turnover,[17] with the result that they know the theory, the models, the data, the issues, the policies, and the politics. Though

Metro councilors and other stakeholders have different ideas about policy direction, there is a small but growing tendency to push in those directions by asking for analysis (usually based on the transportation and MetroScope models) of those policies on the presumption that such analysis will show better performance as measured against council goals.

These anecdotes suggest a strategy for improving analysis through the introduction of PSS tools that simulate the amount and pattern of growth and development in the long run.

- Find MPOs ripe for introducing PSS. Some characteristics of the MPO that should be sought include a history of acceptance of transportation modeling, adequate funding for technical work, a concern about the interaction of transportation and land use (since transportation funding will have to leverage the land use modeling), and a capable and respected staff working in a stable political environment.

- Produce and introduce the model incrementally, and start during the development stage. The way to reduce the black box critique is to have an open and well-documented process concerning what is in the box. Participation will be variable, and that is fine. An advisory committee including some elected officials and stakeholder representatives can get informed about and help direct the development and specification of the model. That process could take a year or more. Again this is fine—you are in it for the long pull. If successful, at the end of that process you will have political allies that appreciate how hard it is to develop a model and how thoroughly you have tried to make a model that is honest, complete, and flexible. You will need good documentation of the process. If all goes well, you will build the foundation for personal credibility needed when future model results are presented.

- Groom the interpreters. You cannot stop turnover, but you can reduce it and you can train backup. It is not surprising that professional articles about PSS do not discuss personnel issues, but people and personalities are critical. Interpretation requires technical competence, political intuition, and the ability to tell an understandable and interesting story. If you cannot get all these skills in one person, create a team that has them.

In short, decision makers and the public want to vet the model, but a key part of that evaluation is the vetting of the modeler.

One last pitch related to uncertainty: Planners and policy makers often make the mistake of thinking that policy can do too much in a world of market forces, but modelers sometimes make the unintentional mistake of presuming public policy is a marginal redirection of an economic avalanche. Markets operate in the context of policy, and policy effects are small only to the extent that we are reluctant to make big changes to the status quo. But such changes are clearly possible: China's change in economic policy over the last 25 years has had a huge effect on the amount, distribution, and type of its urban development. These are changes of a magnitude that "last year plus a little" forecasts could never have predicted.

Policy, in setting the context for public and private investment, can make a big difference in what our future urban areas will look like. PSS tools, used properly, can help us think about, prepare for, and perhaps even help create one of the many futures that are possible.

Endnotes

1. For a recent summary of models, with references to both academic articles and Web sites, see Klosterman and Pettit (2005). They are more optimistic than I about the ability to use the Internet to get state-of-the-practice information that would allow Bonnie and Biff to make their decision quickly about a PSS platform, though every year that optimism becomes more warranted.

2. Richard Bolan, reviewing a draft of this chapter, noted an additional motivation for that decision: They may want to prove to themselves and their boss that they have the capacity to do the job themselves.

3. An important point in the evaluation of PSS, but not central to my focus here, is that PSS are not uniform sets of tools, and the sets differ in their successfulness. Included in a broad definition of PSS would be decision-support software (e.g., for benefit-cost analysis, multiattribute utility analysis, decision analysis, and even real estate financial analysis) and what I would call accounting tools (e.g., specialized software designed for tracking building permits, or all of the potential transportation improvements in a 20-year metropolitan transportation plan). Some of those tools are more like spreadsheets: tools that increase the efficiency of what are essentially counting and accounting jobs and are not subject to the kinds of uncertainty problems that I focus on in this chapter.

4. Now incorporated into the TELUS/TELUM modeling suite developed by Institute for Transportation of the New Jersey Institute of Technology and the Center for Urban Policy Research, Rutgers University.

5. Richard Bolan, commenting on a draft of this chapter, maintains that PSS tools need to go beyond gross allocations to address "the critical dynamic social/economic problems that underlie the emergent spatial form of urban areas."

6. His thesis should probably be required reading for quantitative methods classes at planning schools.

7. Sometime in high school I was required to read a biography of Winston Churchill. Little stuck but this anecdote (which may not be true as told, and may be mangled by memory): In his prep school years Churchill apparently had better things to do than study and found himself cramming the night before a critical geography exam, on which he would have to draw a map of one of the many British territories. Rather than studying them all he picked one at random—New Zealand, in my memory—and studied its map thoroughly. The exam question was "draw a map of New Zealand"—his good luck and ours, the book led me to believe, since he otherwise would have flunked out and Hitler would not have been defeated. In hindsight, and in the context of this chapter, I suspect Churchill's strategy for defeating Hitler was more diverse and nuanced.

8. For example, INDEX allows users to pull sliders to adjust relative weights, but does not have any rigorous system for developing mutually exclusive, nonoverlapping evaluation criteria that get weighted in a consistent way.

9. The percentages are only suggestive, and they clearly depend on what is being forecast. If one were trying to forecast average population in 20 years by TAZ in a developed metropolitan area, one might be likely to get within 20 percent in 80 percent, or even 90 percent, of the TAZs. But if one were trying to forecast the composition of employment by sector, the error would be higher and the percentage of outliers would be higher. And if one were trying to forecast the composition of employment (by type), households (by size, age of head, and income), and vehicle miles traveled, the large number of combinations make any single forecast very unlikely.

10. This history is based on Conder and Stabler (2007).

11. This does not address the issue of output visualization. Highly endogenous market models such as MetroScope output millions of data items. Data mining and converting output into a relevant "policy story" may take three to six person-weeks.

12. MetroScope's developer, Sonny Conder, describes it as a "130 year old Walrasian/Paretian, demand and supply, aggregate, static, partial equilibrium model" (Conder and Stabler 2007).

13. This does not suggest that MetroScope is not used for quantitative forecasting. It is used for the "official" RTP forecast as well as other numerical assessments. Unfortunately, some modeling approaches producing output at odds with present reality have been termed "policy instruments," with the implication that they are unfit for quantitative forecasting. MetroScope is used for both quantitative forecasting and policy analysis.

14. The project sponsor is PLAN (Partnership for Land Use Success), a coalition of the NCSG (managing the project), 1000 Friends of Maryland, the Home Builders Association of Maryland, the Maryland Municipal League, the Citizens Planning and Housing Association, and the Greater Baltimore Urban League.

15. NCSG considered many of the packages described in this chapter and elsewhere in this book and is still considering some (e.g., LEAM and What if?™).

16. ArcInfo® from ESRI.

17. The developer of MetroScope, the developer of Metro's economic model, all of its top GIS experts, and the head of the Data Resources Department have all been at Metro for more than 10 years, most for 15, and some for almost 30. The lead transportation modeler had been at Metro or its predecessor, CRAG, for about 30 years when he retired; the head of the transportation/land use section has been there almost that long.

References

Aamodt, A., and E. Plaza. 1994. Case-based reasoning: Foundational issues, methodological variations, and system approaches. *AI Communications* 7(1): 39–52.

Acevedo, W., and P. Masuoka. 1997. Time-series animation techniques for visualizing urban growth. *Computers and Geosciences* 23: 423–435.

Adler, T., and M. E. Ben-Akiva. 1979. A theoretical and empirical model of trip chaining behaviour. *Transportation Research B* 13: 243–257.

Aerts, J. C. J. H., K. C. Clarke, and A. D. Keuper. 2003. Testing popular visualization techniques for representing model uncertainty. *Cartography and Geographic Information Science* 30: 249–261.

Agarwal, C., G. M. Green, J. M. Grove, T. P. Evans, and C. M. Schweik. 2002. A review and assessment of land-use change models: Dynamics of space, time, and human choice. General Technical Report NE-297. Newton Square, PA: U.S. Department of Agriculture, Forest Service, Northeastern Research Station.

Alberti, M., and P. Waddell. 2000. An integrated urban development and ecological simulation model. *Integrated Assessment* 1: 215–227.

Alexander, E. R. 1987. Planning as development control: Is that all urban planning is for? *Town Planning Review* 58: 453–467.

Allen, A., G. Edwards, and Y. Bedard. 1995. Qualitative causal modeling in temporal GIS. In *Spatial information theory: A theoretical basis for GIS*, A. U. Frank and W. Kuhn, eds., 397–417. New York: Springer.

Allen, E. 1999. *Measuring the environmental footprint of new urbanism*, Volume IV, No. 6. Ithaca, New York: New Urban News.

———. 2000a. *Analysis of impacts from smart growth land-use planning*. Atlanta, GA: Georgia Regional Transportation Authority.

———. 2000b. *Transportation and environmental impacts of infill versus sprawl*. Washington, DC: U.S. Environmental Protection Agency.

Arentze, T. A., A. W. J. Borgers, and H. J. P. Timmermans. 2006. A heuristic method for land-use plan generation in planning support systems. In *Progress in Design & Decision Support Systems*, J. Van Leeuwen and H. J. P. Timmermans, eds., 135–152. Eindhoven: Eindhoven University of Technology.

Arentze, T. A., and H. J. P. Timmermans. 2003. Modelling agglomeration forces in urban dynamics: a multi-agent system approach. In *Proceedings of the Computers in Urban Planning and Urban Management Conference*. Sandai, Japan: CUPUM.

Arthur, S. T. 2001. A satellite based scheme for predicting the effects of land cover change on local microclimate and surface hydrology. PhD diss., Pennsylvania State University.

Asgary, A., R. Klosterman, and A. Razani. 2007. Sustainable urban growth management using What if? *International Journal of Environmental Research* 1: 218–230.

Aurambout, J. P., A. G. Endress, and B. Deal. 2005. A spatial model to estimate habitat fragmentation and its consequences on long-term persistence of animal populations. *Environmental Monitoring and Assessment* 109: 1–3.

Avin, U. 2007. Using scenarios to make urban plans. In *Engaging the future: Forecasts, scenarios, plans, and projects*, L. D. Hopkins and M. Zapata, eds. Cambridge, MA: Lincoln Institute of Land Policy.

Azaz, L. K. A. 2004. Monitoring and modelling urban growth in Alexandria, Egypt, using satellite images and geographic information systems. PhD diss., School of Architecture, Planning and Landscape, Newcastle University.

Barbanente, A., D. Borri, N. Maiellaro, and F. Selicato. 1995. Expert systems for development control: Generalizing and communicating knowledge and procedures. In *Proceedings of 4th International Conference on Computer in Urban Planning and Urban Management*, R. Wyatt and H. Hossain, eds., 571–586. Melbourne: Australia.

Bartsch-Sport, B. 1995. Towards the integration of case-based, schema-based and model-based reasoning for supporting complex design tasks. In *Case-based reasoning research and development*, M. Weloso and A. Aamodt, eds., 145–156. Berlin: Springer-Verlag.

Batey, P. W. J., and M. J. Breheny. 1978. Methods in planning. Part II: A prescriptive review. *Town Planning Review* 49: 502–517.

Batty, M. 1979. Progress, success, and failure in urban modelling. *Environment and Planning A* 2: 863–878.

———. 1994. A chronicle of scientific planning: The Anglo-American modeling experience. *Journal of American Planning Association* 60: 7–16.

———. 1995. Planning support systems and the new logic of computation. *Regional Development Dialogue* 16 (1): 1–17.

———. 1997a. Cellular automata and urban form: A primer. *Journal of the American Planning Association* 63: 264–274.

———. 1997b. The computable city. *International Planning Studies* 2: 155–173.

———. 2007. Model cities. *Town Planning Review* 78(2): 126–151.

———. 2008. Virtual reality in geographic information systems. In *Handbook of geographic information science*, S. Fotheringham and J. Wilson. eds., 317–334. Oxford, Eng.: Blackwell.

Batty, M., D. Chapman, S. Evans, M. Haklay, S. Kueppers, N. Shiode, S. Smith, and P. Torrens, 2001. Visualizing the city: Communicating urban design to planners and decision-makers. In *Planning support systems: Integrating geographic information systems, models, and visualization tools*, R. K. Brail and R. E. Klosterman, eds., 405–443. Redlands, CA: ESRI Press.

Batty, M., H. Couclelis, and M. Eichen. 1997. Urban systems as cellular automata. *Environment and Planning* 24: 159–164.

Batty, M., and Y. Xie 1994. From cells to cities. *Environment and Planning B: Planning and Design* 21: 31–48.

Bernard, R. N. 2001. Policy Simulator: A decision support system for local government. White paper of PricewaterhouseCoopers, LLP.

Bhat, C. R., and S. K. Singh. 2000. A comprehensive daily activity-travel generation model system for workers. *Transportation Research Part A* 34: 1–22.

Bierwagen, B. 2003. The effects of land use change on butterfly dispersal and community ecology. PhD diss., Bren School of Environmental Management and Science, University of California, Santa Barbara.

Bishop, I. D. 1998. Planning support: Hardware, software in search of a system. *Computers Environment and Urban Systems* 22(3): 189–202.

Borgers, A. W. J., and H. J. P. Timmermans. 1987. Choice model specification, substitution and spatial structure effects: A simulation experiment. *Regional Science and Urban Economics* 17: 29–47.

Borri, D., E. Conte, F. Pace, and F. Selicato. 1994. Norm: An expert system for development control in underdeveloped operational contexts. *Environment and Planning B: Planning and Design* 21: 35–52.

Bowman, J. L., and M. E. Ben-Akiva. 1999. The day activity schedule approach to travel demand analysis. *Proceedings of the 78th Annual Meeting of the Transportation Research Board*. Washington, D.C.

Bowman, J. L., M. Bradley, Y. Shiftan, T. K. Lawton, and M. E. Ben-Akiva. 1998. Demonstration of an activity-based model system for Portland. *Proceedings of the 8th World Conference on Transport Research*. Antwerp.

Box, G. E. P., and N. R. Draper. 1987. *Empirical model-building and response surfaces*. New York: Wiley.

Boyce, D. F., N. Day, and C. McDonald. 1970. *Metropolitan plan making*. Regional Science Research Institute. Philadelphia, PA: University of Pennsylvania.

Brail, R. K. 2001. Introduction. In *Planning support systems: Integrating geographic information systems, models and visualization tools*, R. K. Brail and R. E. Klosterman, eds., ix–xxi. Redlands, CA: ESRI Press.

———. 2006. Planning support systems evolving: When the rubber hits the road. In *Complex artificial environments*, J. Portugali, ed. New York: Springer.

Brail, R. K., and R. E. Klosterman, eds. 2001. *Planning support systems: Integrating geographic information systems, models and visualization tools*. Redlands, CA: ESRI Press.

Brewer, D. 1973. *Politicians, bureaucrats, and the consultant: A critique of urban problem solving*. New York: Basic Books.

Brinberg, D., and J. E. McGrath. 1985. *Validity and the research process*. Beverly Hills, CA: Sage Publications.

Brooks, M. P. 1988. Four critical junctures in the history of the urban planning profession: An exercise in hindsight. *Journal of the American Planning Association* 54: 241–248.

Bruton, M., and D. Nicholson. 1987. *Local planning in practice*. London: Hutchinson.

California Legislature. 2005. Assembly bill 1020, 2005–06, Regular Session. Sacramento, California.

Campbell, S. 1996. Green cities, growing cities, just cities? Urban planning and the contradictions of sustainable development. *Journal of the American Planning Association* 62: 296–312.

Candau, J. 2000. Visualizing modeled land cover change and related uncertainty. First International Conference on Geographic Information Science. Savannah, GA.

———. 2002. Temporal calibration sensitivity of the SLEUTH urban growth model. M.A. thesis. University of California, Santa Barbara.

Candau, J., and K. C. Clarke. 2000. Probabilistic land cover modeling using deltatrons. *Proceedings of the 38th Annual Conference of the Urban Regional Information Systems Association*. Orlando, FL.

Candau, J., S. Rasmussen, and K. C. Clarke. 2000. Structure and dynamics of a coupled cellular automaton for land use/land cover change. 4th International Conference on Integrating GIS and Environmental Modeling (GIS/EM4). Banff, Alberta, Canada, September.

Cecchini, A. 1996. A general automaton and some specialized automata for urban modeling. *Environment and Planning B* 23: 721–732.

Chen, J., and J. Jiang. 2000. An event-based approach to spatio-temporal data modeling in land subdivision system for spatio-temporal process of land subdivision. *Geoinformatica* 4(4): 387–402.

Chen, J., J. Jiang, S. P. Jin, and R. H. Yan. 1998. Developing an office GIS by integrating GIS with OA. *Journal of Remote Sensing* 2(3): 59–64. [In Chinese]

Chen, J., J. Jiang, and A. G. O. Yeh. 2004. Designing a GIS-based CSCW system for development control with an event-driven approach. *Photogrammetric Engineering & Remote Sensing* 70(2): 225–233.

Choi, W., and B. Deal. 2007. Assessing hydrological impact of potential land use change through hydrological and land use change modeling for the Kishwaukee River Basin. *The Journal of Environmental Management*. In publication. Ref. no. JEMA-D-06-00565.

Chorley, R. 1988. Some reflections on the handling of geographical information. *International Journal of Geographical Information Systems* 2: 3–9.

Chrislip, D. D., and C. E. Larson. 1994. *Collaborative leadership: How citizens and civic leaders can make a difference*. San Francisco: Jossey-Bass.

Claggett, P., C. A. Jantz, S. J. Goetz, and C. Bisland. 2004. Assessing development pressure in the Chesapeake Bay watershed: An evaluation of two land-use change models. *Environmental Monitoring and Assessment* 94: 129–146.

Claramunt, C., and M. Theriault. 1995. Management time in GIS: An event-oriented approach. In *Recent advances in temporal databases*, J. Clifford and A. Tuzhilin, eds., 23–42. Berlin: Springer.

———. 1996. Toward semantics for modeling spatio-temporal processes within GIS. In *Advances in GIS research II (Proceedings of the 7th International Symposium on Spatial Data Handling)*, M. J. Kraak and M. Molenaar, eds., 47–64. London: Taylor and Francis.

Clarke, K. C. 1997. Land use modeling with deltatrons. The Land Use Modeling Conference. Sioux Falls, SD. http://www.ncgia.ucsb.edu/conf/landuse97.

———. 2005. The limits of simplicity: Toward geocomputational honesty in urban modeling. In *Geo-Dynamics*, P. Atkinson, G. Foody, S. Darby, and F. Wu, eds., 215–232. Boca Raton, FL: CRC Press.

Clarke, K. C., and L. Gaydos. 1998. Loose-coupling a cellular automaton model and GIS: Long-term urban growth prediction for San Francisco and Washington/Baltimore. *International Journal of Geographic Information Science* 12: 699–714.

Clarke, K. C, N. Gazulis, C. K. Dietzel, and N. C. Goldstein. 2007. A decade of SLEUTHing: Lessons learned from applications of a cellular automaton land use change model. In *Classics from IJGIS: Twenty Years of the International Journal of Geographical Information Systems and Science*, P. Fisher, ed., 413–425. Boca Raton, FL: Taylor and Francis, CRC.

Clarke, K. C., S. Hoppen, and L. Gaydos. 1997. A self-modifying cellular automaton model of historical urbanization in the San Francisco Bay area. *Environment and Planning B* 24: 247–261.

Clarke, K. C., G. Olsen, and J. A. Brass. 1993. Refining a cellular automaton model of wildfire propagation and extinction. *Proceedings of the Second International Conference on the Integration of Geographic Information Systems and Environmental Modeling*. Breckenridge, CO.

Clarke, K. C., P. Riggan, and J. A. Brass. 1995. A cellular automaton model of wildfire propagation and extinction. *Photogrammetric Engineering and Remote Sensing* 60: 1355–1367.

Clarke, M. 1990. Geographical information systems and model-based analysis: Towards effective decision support systems. In *Geographical Information Systems for Urban and Regional Planning*, H. Scholten and J. Stillwell, eds., 165–175. Dordrecht: Kluwer.

Cogan, C. B., F. W. Davis, and K. C. Clarke. 2001. *Application of urban growth models and wildlife habitat models to assess biodiversity losses*. Santa Barbara, CA: University of California, Santa Barbara, Institute for Computational Earth System Science. U.S. Department of the Interior, U.S. Geological Survey, Biological Resources Division, Gap Analysis Program, Santa Barbara, CA.

Conder, S., and B. Stabler. 2007. Reimplementing MetroScope: Portland's land use model. TRB Planning Applications Conference, May 7, 2007, Daytona Beach, Florida.

Couclelis, H. 1985. Cellular worlds: A framework for modeling micro-macro dynamics. *Environment and Planning A* 17: 585–596.

———. 1988. Of mice and men: what rodent populations can teach us about complex spatial dynamics. *Environment and Planning A* 20: 99–109.

———. 1989a. Geographically informed planning: Requirements for planning relevant GIS. Paper presented to the 36th North American Meeting of Regional Science Association, Santa Barbara, CA.

———. 1989b. Macrostructure and microbehaviour in a metropolitan area. *Environment and Planning B: Planning and Design* 16: 141–154.

Craig, W. J., T. M. Harris, and D. Weiner, eds. 2002. *Community participation and geographical information systems*. Boca Raton, FL: CRC Press.

Crecine, J. P. 1964. TOMM (Time oriented metropolitan model). *CRP Technical Bulletin* 6. Pittsburgh: Department of City and Regional Planning.

———. 1968. *A dynamic model of urban structure*. Santa Monica, CA: Rand Corporation.

Criterion Planners. 2007. INDEX PlanBuilder user guide. Portland, OR. www.crit.com/documents/planuserguide.pdf.

Croswell, P. 1991. Obstacles to GIS implementation and guidelines to increase the opportunities for success. *URISA Journal* 3: 43–56.

Dammers, E., R. Kranendonk, P. Smeets, L. Adolfse, C. van Woerkum, M. Horrevoets, and L. Langerak. 1999. *Innovation and learning: Knowledge management and rural innovation*. The Hague, National Council for Agricultural Research (NLRO).

Davies, F. 1986. A technology acceptance model for empirically testing new end-user information systems: Theory and results. PhD thesis, MIT, Cambridge, MA.

Dawson, R. J., J. W. Hall, S. Barr, M. Batty, A. Bristow, S. Carney, S. Evans, A. Ford, J. Köhler, M. Tight, and C. Walsh. 2007. A blueprint for the integrated assessment of climate change in cities. Tyndall Centre working paper 104. Norwich, UK: University of East Anglia. Available at http://www.tyndall.ac.uk/publications/working_papers/twp104.pdf.

de la Barra, T. 1989. *Integrated land use and transport modelling*. Cambridge, Eng.: Cambridge University Press.

———. 2001. Integrated land use and transport modeling: The TRANUS experience. In *Planning support systems: Integrating geographic information systems, models, and visualization*, R. K. Brail and R. E. Klosterman, eds., 129–156. Redlands, CA: ESRI Press.

de la Barra, T., M. Echenique, M. Quintana, and J. Guendelman. 1975. An urban regional model for the central region of Chile. In *Urban development models*, R. S. Baxter and M. H. Echenique, eds., 137–174. Lancaster, Eng.: J. Owens Construction Press.

de Palma, A., N. Picard, P. Waddell. 2007. Discrete choice models with capacity constraints: An empirical analysis of the housing market of the greater Paris region. *Journal of Urban Economics* 62: 204–230.

Deal, B. 2001. Ecological urban dynamics: The convergence of spatial modeling and sustainability. *Journal of Building Research and Information* 29(5): 381–393.

———. 2003. Sustainable land-use planning: The integration of process and technology. PhD diss. University of Illinois at Urbana-Champaign.

Deal, B., C. Farrello, M. Lancaster, T. Kompare, and B. Hannon. 2000. A dynamic model of the spatial spread of an infectious disease. *Environmental Modeling and Assessment* 5(1): 47–62.

Deal, B., and V. Pallathucheril. 2003. The Land-use Evolution and impact Assessment Model (LEAM): Will it play in Peoria? *Proceedings of the 8th International Conference on Computers in Urban Planning and Urban Management*. Sendai, Japan. 27–29 May.

———. 2007. Developing and using scenarios. In *Engaging the future: Forecasts, scenarios, plans, and projects*. L. D. Hopkins, M. A. Zapata, eds., 221–242. Cambridge, MA: Lincoln Institute of Land Policy.

Deal, B., and D. Schunk. 2004. Spatial dynamic modeling and urban land use transformation: A simulation approach to assessing the costs of urban sprawl. *Journal of Ecological Economics* 51(1–2): 79–95.

Deal, B., and Z. Sun. 2006. A spatially explicit urban simulation model: Land-use Evolution and impact Assessment Model (LEAM). In *Smart growth and climate change: Regional development, infrastructure and adaptation*, M. Ruth, ed., 181–203. Northampton, MA: Edward Elgar.

Dietzel, C. K., and K. C. Clarke. 2004. Spatial differences in multi-resolution urban automata modeling. *Transactions in GIS* 8: 479–492.

———. 2007. Toward optimal calibration of the SLEUTH land use change model. *Transactions in GIS* 11(1): 29–45.

Dietzel, C., M. Herold, J. J. Hemphill, and K. C. Clarke. 2005. Spatio-temporal dynamics in California's Central Valley: Empirical links to urban theory. *International Journal of Geographical Information Science* 19(2): 175–195.

Dietzel, C., H. Oguz, J. J. Hemphill, K. C. Clarke, and N. Gazulis. 2005. Diffusion and coalescence of the Houston metropolitan area: Evidence supporting a new urban theory. *Environment and Planning B: Planning and Design* 32(2): 231–246.

Dipasquale, D., and W. C. Wheaton. 1996. *Urban economics and real estate markets.* Englewood Cliffs, NJ: Prentice Hall.

Dishaw, M., and D. Strong. 1999. Extending the technology acceptance model with task-technology fit constructs. *Information & Management* 36: 9–21.

Dishaw, M., D. Strong, and B. Bandy. 2002. Extending the task-technology fit model with self-efficacy constructs. Eight Americas Conference on Information Systems, AMCIS. Dallas, TX: Association for Information Systems.

Downs, A. 1992. *Stuck in traffic: Coping with peak-hour traffic congestion.* Washington, DC: Brookings Institution Press.

———. 2004. *Still stuck in traffic: Coping with peak-hour congestion.* Washington, DC: Brookings Institution Press.

Echenique, M. H. 1994. Urban and regional studies at the Martin Centre: Its origins, its present, its future. *Environment and Planning B* 21: 517–533.

Echenique, M. H., D. Crowther, and W. Lindsay. 1969. A spatial model of urban stock and activity. *Regional Studies* 3: 281–312.

Echenique, M. H., P. Moilanen, K. Lautso, and H. Lahelma. 1995. Testing integrated transport and land-use models in the Helsinki metropolitan areas. *Traffic Engineering and Control* 36: 20–23.

Engelen, G., R. White, and I. Uljee. 1995. Using cellular-automata for integrated modeling of socio-environmental systems. *Environmental Monitoring and Assessment* 34: 203–214.

Faludi, A. 1986. *Critical rationalism and planning methodology.* London: Pion.

Flowerdew, A. D. J. 1977. An evaluation package for a strategic land use/transportation plan. In *Urban transportation planning*, P. Bonsall, Q. Dalvi, and P. Halls, eds., 241–258. Turnbridge Wells, UK: Abacus Press.

Flyvbjerg, B., M. S. Holm, and S. Buhl. 2002. Underestimating costs in public works projects: Error or lie? *Journal of the American Planning Association* 68(3): 279–295.

———. 2005. How (in)accurate are demand forecasts in public works projects? *Journal of the American Planning Association* 71(2): 131–146.

Forester, J. 1983. The coming design challenge. *Journal of Planning Education and Research* 3: 57–60.

———. 1989. *Planning in the face of power.* Berkeley: University of California Press.

Fosgerau, M. 1998. PETRA: An activity based approach to travel demand analysis. *Proceedings of the 8th World Conference on Transport Research.* Antwerp.

Fotheringham, A. S., and D. C. Knudsen. 1984. Critical parameters in retail shopping models. *Modeling and Simulation* 15: 75–80.

Frambach, R., and N. Schillewaert. 2002. Organizational innovation adoption: A multilevel framework of determinants and opportunities for future research. *Journal of Business Research* 55: 163–176.

Friend, J., and N. Jessop. 1969. *Local government and strategic choice: An operational research approach to the processes of public planning.* London: Tavistock.

Fujii, S., R. Kitamura, and T. Monma. 1997. A study of commuters' activity patterns for the estimation of induced trips. *Journal of Infrastructure Planning and Management* 562: 109–120.

———. 1998. A utility-based micro-simulation model system of individuals' activity-travel patterns. *Proceedings of the 77th Annual Meeting of the Transportation Research Board.* Washington, DC.

Garin, R. A. 1966. A matrix formulation of the Lowry model for intra-metropolitan activity location. *Journal of the American Institute of Planners* 32: 361–364.

Garrett, M., and M. Wachs. 1996. *Transportation planning on trial: The clean air act and travel forecasting.* Thousand Oaks, CA: Sage.

Gaunt, C., and L. Jackson. 2003. Models for assessing the effects of community change on land use patterns. In *Planning Support Systems in Practice*, S. Geertman, and J. Stillwell, eds. Berlin: Springer.

Gautschi, D. A. 1981. Specification of patronage models for retail center choice. *Journal of Marketing Research* 18: 162–174.

Gazulis, N., and K. C. Clarke. 2006. Exploring the DNA of our regions: Classification of outputs from the SLEUTH model. In *Cellular Automata. 7th International Conference on Cellular Automata for Research and Industry, ACRI 2006. Perpignan, France, September 2006, Proceedings. Lecture Notes in Computer Science,* S. El Yacoubi, B. Chapard, and S. Bandini, eds. No. 4173. New York: Springer.

Geertman, S. 1999. Geographical information technology and physical planning. In *Geographical Information and Planning,* J. Stillwell, S. Geertman, and S. Openshaw, eds., 69–86. Heidelberg: Springer Verlag.

———. 2002a. Inventory of planning support systems in planning practice: Conclusions and reflections. 5th AGILE Conference on Geographic Information Science, Palma, Balearic Islands, Spain.

———. 2002b. Participatory planning and GIS: A PSS to bridge the gap. *Environment and Planning B: Planning and Design* 29: 21–35.

———. 2006. Potentials for planning support: A planning-conceptual approach. *Environment and Planning B: Planning and Design* 33(6): 863–881.

———. 2008. Kick-off for a PSS agenda. *Journal of the American Planning Association* (submitted).

Geertman, S., and J. Stillwell. 2000. Geoinformation, geotechnology and geoplanning in the 1990s. Working Paper 00/01. School of Geography, University of Leeds, Leeds.

———. 2003a. Interactive support systems for participatory planning, In *Planning support systems in practice*, S. Geertman and J. Stillwell, eds. Berlin: Springer.

———, eds. 2003b. *Planning support systems in practice.* Berlin: Springer Verlag.

———. 2004. Planning support systems: An inventory of current practice. *Computers, Environment and Urban Systems* 28: 291–310.

Gehani, N. H., H. V. Jagadish, and O. Shmueli. 1992a. Event specification in an active object-oriented database. *ACM SIGMOD Record* 21(2): 81–90.

———. 1992b. Composite event specification in active databases: Model and implementation. In *Proceedings of 18th International Conference on Very Large Databases*, Le-Yan Yuan, ed., 327–338. 23–27 August, Vancouver, British Columbia, Canada. San Francisco: Morgan Kaufmann.

Geraldes, P., M. H. Echenique, and I. N. Williams. 1978. A spatial economic model for Bilbao. *Proceedings PTRC.*

Gerend, T. 2005. Unpublished personal digital communication with Brian Deal. Peoria, IL: Tri-County Regional Planning Commission. 14 April.

Gibson, M., and M. Pullen. 1972. Retail turnover in the East-Midlands: A regional application of a gravity model. *Regional Studies* 6: 183–196.

Gilder, G. 1989. *Microcosm: The quantum revolution in economics and technology.* New York: Simon and Schuster.

Goldner, W. 1971. The Lowry model heritage. *Journal of the American Institute of Planners* 37: 100–110.

Goldstein, N. C. 2004a. Brains vs. brawn: Comparative strategies for the calibration of a cellular automata–based urban growth model. In *GeoDynamics*, P. Atkinson, G. Foody, S. Darby, and F. Wu, eds. Boca Raton, FL: CRC Press.

———. 2004b. A methodology for tapping into the spatiotemporal diversity of information in simulation models of spatial spread. *Proceedings of the Third International Conference on Geographic Information Science*. College Park, MD.

Goldstein, N. C., J. Candau, and K. C. Clarke. 2004. Approaches to simulating the "March of Bricks and Mortar." *Computers, Environment and Urban Systems* 28: 125–147.

Goldstein, N.C., J. Candau, and M. Moritz. 2000. Burning Santa Barbara at both ends: A study of fire history and urban growth predictions. *Proceedings of the 4th International Conference on Integrating GIS and Environmental Modeling (GIS/EM4)*. Banff, Alberta, Canada. http://www.colorado.edu/research/cires/banff/pubpapers/60.

Goldstein, N., C. Dietzel, and K. Clarke. 2005. "Don't stop 'til you get enough": Sensitivity testing of Monte Carlo iterations for model calibration. *Proceedings, 8th International Conference on GeoComputation*. In *GeoComputation* CD-ROM, Y. Xie and D. G. Brown, eds. http://www.geocomputation.org/2005/index.html.

Goodhue, D. L. 1995. Understanding user evaluations of information systems. *Management Science* 41: 1827–1844.

Goodhue, D. L., and R. L. Thompson. 1995. Task-technology fit and individual performance. *MIS Quarterly* 19: 213–235.

Guy, C. M. 1987. Recent advances in spatial interaction modelling: An application to the forecasting of shopping travel. *Environment and Planning A* 19: 173–186.

———. 2007. *Planning for retail development*. London: Routledge.

Han, S. Y., and T. J. Kim. 1990. Intelligent urban information systems: Review and prospects. In *Expert systems: Applications to urban planning*, T. J. Kim, L. L.Wiggins, and J. R. Wright, eds., 241–261. New York: Springer-Verlag.

Harris, B. 1965. Urban development models: New tools for planning. *Journal of the American Institute of Planners* 31: 90–183.

———. 1968. Quantitative models of urban development: Their role in metropolitan policy-making. In *Issues in urban economics*, H. S. Perloff and L.Wingo, Jr., eds. Baltimore: Johns Hopkins Press.

———. 1985. Urban simulation models in regional science. *Journal of Regional Science* 25: 45–568.

———. 1989a. Beyond geographic information systems: Computers and the planning professional. *Journal of the American Planning Association* 55(4): 85–90.

———. 1989b. Geographic information systems: Research issues for URISA. *Proceedings of the 1989 Annual Conference of the Urban and Regional Information Systems Association, Boston* 4: 1–14.

———. 1999. Computing in planning: Professional, institutional requirements. *Environment and Planning B: Planning and Design* 26: 321–333.

Harris, B., and M. Batty. 1993. Locational models, geographic information and planning support systems. *Journal of Planning Education and Research* 12: 184–198.

Harwood, S. A. 2007. Using scenarios to build planning capacity. In *Engaging the future: Forecasts, scenarios, plans, and projects*, L. D. Hopkins and M. Zapata, eds. Cambridge, MA: Lincoln Institute of Land Policy.

Hemmens, G., ed. 1971. Urban development models. Special Report 97. Washington, DC: Highway Research Board, National Research Council.

Herold, M., N. C. Goldstein, and K. C. Clarke. 2003. The spatio-temporal form of urban growth: Measurement, analysis and modeling. Remote Sensing of Environment 86: 286–302.

Herold, M., N. Goldstein, G. Menz, and K. C. Clarke. 2002. Remote sensing based analysis of urban dynamics in the Santa Barbara region using the SLEUTH urban growth model and spatial metrics. *Proceedings of the 3rd Symposium on Remote Sensing of Urban Areas*. Istanbul, Turkey.

Hirton, J. E., and M. H. Echenique. 1979. An operational land use and transport model for the Tehran region. *Iran Transport Research Circular* 199: 6–7.

Hoos, I. R. 1972. *Systems analysis in public policy: A critique*. Berkeley: University of California Press.

Hopkins, L. D. 1999. Structure of a planning support system for urban development. *Environment and Planning B: Planning and Design* 26: 333–343.

Hopkins, L. D., N. Kaza, V. G. Pallathucheril. 2005a. A data model to represent plans and regulations in urban simulation models. In *GIS, spatial analysis, and modeling*, D. J. Maguire, M. Batty, and M. F. Goodchild, eds., 173–201. Redlands, CA: ESRI Press.

———. 2005b. Representing urban development plans and regulations as data: A planning data model. *Environment and Planning B: Planning and Design* 32(4): 597–615.

Hopkins, L. D., and M. Zapata. 2007a. Engaging the future: Tools for effective planning practices. In *Engaging the future: Forecasts, scenarios, plans, and projects*, L. Hopkins and M. Zapata, eds. Cambridge, MA: Lincoln Institute of Land Policy.

———, eds. 2007b. *Engaging the future: Forecasts, scenarios, plans, and projects*. Cambridge, MA: Lincoln Institute of Land Policy.

Hunt, J. D. 1994. Calibrating the Naples land use and transport model. *Environment and Planning B* 21: 569–590.

———. 2005. Integrated land-use and transport models: An introduction. Washington, DC: Transportation Research Board, Workshop 162.

Hunt, J. D., J. E. Abraham, and T. Weidner. 2004a. The household application (HA) module of the Oregon2 model. Paper presented at the Annual Meetings of the Transportation Research Board. Washington, DC.

———. 2004b. The land development module of the Oregon2 modeling framework. Paper presented at the Annual Meetings of the Transportation Research Board. Washington.

Hunt, J. D., R. Donelly, J. E. Abraham, C. Batten, J. Freedman, J. Hicks, P. J. Costinett, and W. J. Upton. 2001. Design of a statewide land use transport interaction model for Oregon. Unpublished paper.

Hunt, J. D., E. J. Miller, and D. S. Kriger. 2005. Current operational urban land-use transport modeling frameworks. *Transport Reviews* 25(3): 329–376.

Innes, J. E. 1996. Planning through consensus building: A new view of the comprehensive planning ideal. *Journal of the American Planning Association* 62: 460–472.

Innes, J., and D. Simpson. 1993. Implementing GIS for planning. *Journal of the American Planning Association* 59: 230–236.

In't Veld, R., ed. 2000. *Willingly and knowingly: The roles of knowledge on nature and environment in policy processes*. Utrecht: Lemma.

Isserman, A. 1977. The accuracy of population projections for subcounty areas. *Journal of the American Institute of Planners* 43(3): 247–259.

———. 1985. Dare to plan: An essay on the role of the future in planning practice and education. *Town Planning Review* 56: 483–491.

Itami, R. M. 1994. Simulating spatial dynamics: cellular automata theory. *Landscape and Urban Planning* 30: 27–47.

James, R. 2004. Predicting the spatial pattern of urban growth in Honolulu County using the cellular automata SLEUTH urban growth model. Masters thesis, University of Hawaii at Manoa.

Jankovic, L., W. Hopwood, and Z. Alwan. 2005. CAST-city analysis simulation tool: An integrated model of land use, population, transport, and economics. *Proceedings CUPUM*. London.

Jantz, C. A., and S. J. Goetz. 2005. Analysis of scale dependencies in an urban land use change model. *International Journal of Geographic Information Science* 19(2): 217–241.

Jantz, C. A., S. J. Goetz, and M. K. Shelley. 2003. Using the SLEUTH urban growth model to simulate the impacts of future policy scenarios on urban land use in the Baltimore/Washington metropolitan area. *Environment and Planning B* 31: 251–271.

Jiang, J. 2000. Research on event based spatio-temporal database. PhD diss., Surveying and Land Science Department, China University of Mining and Technology, Beijing, China. [In Chinese]

Jiang, J., J. Chen, R. H. Yan, and L. L. Xu. 2000. A CSCW system for building reviewing by integrating GIS with OA. *Geo-Spatial Information Science* 3(1): 45–49.

Jiang, J., J. Chen, and A. G. O. Yeh. 2002. A GIS-based computer supported collaborative work (CSCW) system for urban planning and land management. *Photogrammetric Engineering & Remote Sensing* 68(4): 353–359.

Kim, T. L., L. L. Wiggins, and J. R. Wright, eds. 1990. *Expert systems: Applications to urban planning.* New York: Springer-Verlag.

Kingston, R., A. Evans, and S. Carver. 2003. Public participation via on-line democracy. In *Planning support systems in practice*, S. Geertman and J. Stillwell, eds., 46–64. Berlin: Springer.

Kirtland, D., L. Gaydos, K. C. Clarke, L. DeCola, W. Acevedo, and C. Bell. 1994. An analysis of human-induced land transformations in the San Francisco Bay/Sacramento area. *World Resources Review* 6: 206–217.

Kitamura, R., and S. Fujii. 1998. Two computational process models of activity-travel choice. In *Theoretical foundations of travel choice modelling*, T. Gärling, T. Laitila, and K. Westin, eds., 251–279. Oxford: Elsevier.

Klein, W. R. 2000. Building consensus. In *The practice of local government planning*, 3rd ed., C. J. Hoch, L. C. Dalton, and F. S. So, eds. Washington, DC: International City/County Management Association.

Klosterman, R. E. 1978. Foundations for normative planning. *Journal of the American Institute of Planners* 44: 37–46.

———. 1980. A public interest criterion. *Journal of the American Planning Association* 46: 323–333.

———. 1983. Fact and value in planning. *Journal of the American Planning Association*, 49: 216–225.

———. 1994a. International support for computers in planning. *Environment and Planning B: Planning and Design* 2: 387–391.

———. 1994b. An introduction to the literature on large-scale urban models. *Journal of the American Planning Association* 60: 41–44.

———. 1994c. Large-scale urban models: Retrospect and prospect. *Journal of the American Planning Association* 60(1): 3–6.

———. 1997. Planning support systems: A new perspective on computer-aided planning. *Journal of Planning Education and Research* 17(1): 45–54.

———. 1998. Computer applications in planning. *Environment and Planning B: Planning and Design*, Anniversary Issue: 32–36.

———. 1999a. New perspectives on planning support systems. *Environment and Planning B: Planning and Design* 26: 317–320.

———. 1999b. The What if? collaborative planning support system. *Environment and Planning B: Planning and Design* 26: 393–408.

———. 2001a. Planning support systems: A new perspective on computer-aided planning. In *Planning support systems: Integrating geographic information systems, models, and visualization tools*, R. K. Brail and R. E. Klosterman, eds., 1–23. Redlands, CA: ESRI Press.

———. 2001b. The What if? planning support system. In *Planning support systems: Integrating geographic information systems, models, and visualization tools*, R. K. Brail and R. E. Klosterman, eds. Redlands, CA: ESRI Press.

———. 2007. Deliberating about the future. In *Engaging the future: Forecasts, scenarios, plans, and projects*, L. D. Hopkins and M. A. Zapata, eds. Cambridge, MA: Lincoln Institute of Land Policy.

Klosterman, R. E., R. K. Brail, and E. G. Bossard. 1993. *Spreadsheet models for urban and regional analysis.* New Brunswick, NJ: Center for Urban Policy Research, Rutgers University Press.

Klosterman, R. E., and C. J. Pettit. 2005. Guest editorial: An update on planning support systems. *Environment and Planning B: Planning and Design* 32: 477–484.

Klosterman, R. E., L. Siebert, M. A. Hoque, J. Kim and A. Parveen. 2002. Using an operational planning support system to evaluate farmland preservation policies. In *Planning support systems in practice*, S. Geertman and J. Stillwell, eds. Heidelberg: Springer.

———. 2006. What if? evaluation of growth management strategies for a declining region. *International Journal of Environmental Technology and Management* 6(1/2): 79–95.

Kolodner, J. 1993. *Case-based reasoning*. San Mateo, CA: Morgan Kaufmann.

Koomen, E., J. Stillwell, A. Bakema, and H. J. Scholten, eds. 2007. *Modeling land-use change: Progress and applications*. Heidelberg: Springer-Verlag.

Koton, P. 1993. Combining causal models and case-based reasoning. In *Second generation expert systems*, J. M. David, J. P. Krivine, and R. Simmons, eds., 69–78. Berlin: Springer-Verlag.

Kramer, J. 1996. Integration of a GIS with a local scale self-modifying cellular automaton urban growth model in Southeastern Orange County, New York. MA thesis, Hunter College CUNY.

Kwartler, M., and R. Bernard. 2001. CommunityViz: An integrated planning support system. In *Planning support systems: Integrating geographic information systems, models, and visualization*, R. K. Brail and R. E. Klosterman, eds., 285–308. Redlands, CA: ESRI Press.

Kweon, I., and J. Kim. 2002. Urban land use planning with a PSS-based land use change model. *Journal of the Geographic Information System Association of Korea* 10(4): 512–532.

Kweon, I., J. Kim, and B. Choi. 2004. A simulation of the growth of the Seoul metropolitan's build-up area with a GIS-based PSS model. *Journal of the Korean Planners Association* 39(7): 69–84.

Landis, J. 1994. The California urban futures model: A new generation of metropolitan simulation models. *Environment and Planning B* 21: 399–420.

———. 1995. Imagining land use futures: Applying the California urban futures model. *Journal of the American Planning Association* 61: 438–457.

———. 2001. CUF, CUF II, and CURBA: A family of spatially explicit urban growth and land use policy simulation models. In *Planning support systems: Integrating geographic information systems, models, and visualization*, R. K. Brail and R. E. Klosterman, eds., 157–200. Redlands, CA: ESRI Press.

Landis, J., and M. Zhang. 1998a. The second generation of the California urban futures model. Part 1: Model logic and theory. *Environment and Planning B* 25: 657–666.

———. 1998b. The second generation of the California urban futures model. Part 2: Specification and calibration results of the land use change submodel. *Environment and Planning B* 25: 758–824.

Lautso, K. 2003. The SPARTACUS system for defining and analyzing sustainable land use and transport policies. In *Planning support systems in practice*, S. Geertman and J. Stillwell, eds., 453–463. Berlin: Springer. Also available at http://www1.wspgroup.fi/lt/propolis/index.htm.

Le Page, M. 2000. Expansion urbaine à la frontière du 1er monde: Analyse et modélisation de la croissance spatiale de Tijuana, Mexique. PhD diss., Université Paul Valéry.

Leake, D. B. 1996. CBR in context: The present and future. In *Case-based reasoning: Experiences, lessons, and future directions*, D. B. Leake, ed., 3–30. Menlo Park, CA: AAAI Press/MIT Press.

Leão, S., I. Bishop, and D. Evans. 2001. Assessing the demand of solid waste disposal in urban region by urban dynamics modelling in a GIS environment. *Resources Conservation and Recycling* 33: 289–313.

———. 2004. Spatial-temporal model for demand allocation of waste landfills in growing urban regions. *Computers Environment and Urban Systems* 28: 353–385.

Leary, M., and A. Rodriguez-Bachiller. 1989. Expertise, domain-structure and expert system design: A case study in development control. *Expert Systems* 6(1): 18–23.

Lee, D. B., Jr. 1973. Requiem for large-scale models. *Journal of the American Institute of Planners* 39(3): 163–178.

———. 1994. Retrospective on large-scale urban models. *Journal of the American Planning Association* 60 (1): 35–40.

Lindblom, C. E., and D. K. Cohen. 1979. *Usable knowledge: Social science and social problem solving*. New Haven: Yale University Press.

Liu, Y., and S. R. Phinn. 2004. Mapping the urban development of Sydney (1971–1996) with cellular automata in a GIS environment. *Applied GIS* 49.

Lowry, I. S. 1964. *A model of metropolis*. Santa Monica, CA: Rand Corporation.

Ma, L., T. A. Arentze, A. W. J. Borgers and H. J. P. Timmermans. 2006. A multi-agent model for generating local land-use plans in the context of an urban planning support systems. In *Progress in design and decision support systems*, J. Van Leeuwen and H. J. P. Timmermans, eds., 153–168. Eindhoven: Eindhoven University of Technology.

Mackett, R. L. 1983. The Leeds integrated land use transport model (LILT). Supplementary Report 805. Crowthorne, UK: Transport and Road Research Laboratory.

———. 1990. The systematic application of the LILT model to Dortmund, Leeds and Tokyo. *Transportation Reviews* 10: 323–338.

———. 1991. LILT and MEPLAN: A comparative analysis of land-use and transport policies for Leeds. *Transportation Reviews* 11: 131–141.

Maguire, D. J., M. Batty, and M. F. Goodchild, eds. 2005. *GIS, spatial analysis, and modeling.* Redlands, CA: ESRI Press.

Marchand, D. 1993. Expert system in urban planning: New tools or new toys? In *Systemes d'information geographique et systemes experts*, D. Pumain, ed., 88–91. Montpellier: GIP RECLUS.

Medsker, L. R. 1995. *Hybrid intelligent systems.* Norwell, MA: Kluwer Academic Publishers.

Mikkonen, J., M. Ristimaki, K. Oinonen, and H. S. Hansen. 2003. The planner's TOOLBOX: A web-based support. In *Planning support systems in practice*, S. Geertman and J. Stillwell, eds., 123–137. Berlin: Springer.

Miller, E. J., J. D. Hunt, J. E. Abraham, and P. A. Salvini. 2004. Microsimulating urban systems. *Computers, Environment and Urban Systems* 28: 9–44.

Miller, E. J., D. Kriger, and J. D. Hunt. 1998. Integrated urban models for simulation of transit and land-use policies. Final report. TCRP Web Document 9. Project H-12. Washington, DC: National Academy of Sciences.

Miller, E. J., and P. Salvini. 1998. The integrated land use, transportation, environment (ILUTE) modeling system: A framework. *Proceedings of the 77th Annual Meetings of the Transportation Research Board.* Washington, D.C.

Moeckel, R., C. Schurmann, and M. Wegener. 2002. Microsimulation of urban land use. Paper presented at the 42nd European Congress of the Regional Science Association, Dortmund, Germany, August 27–31.

Moore, T. 2007. The use of forecasts in creating and adopting visions for regional growth. In *Engaging the future: Forecasts, scenarios, plans, and projects*, L. D. Hopkins and M. A. Zapata, eds. Cambridge, MA: Lincoln Institute of Land Policy.

Myers, D. 2007. Promoting the community future in the contest with present individualism. In *Engaging the future: Forecasts, scenarios, plans, and projects*, L. Hopkins and M. Zapata, eds. Cambridge, MA: Lincoln Institute of Land Policy.

Myers, D., and A. Kitsuse. 2000. Constructing the future in planning: A survey of theories and tools. *Journal of Planning Education and Research* 19: 221–31.

Natural Resource Defense Council. 2000. *Environmental characteristics of smart growth neighborhoods: Sacramento case study.* Washington, DC: Natural Resource Defense Council.

———. 2003. *Environmental characteristics of smart growth neighborhoods: Nashville case study.* Washington, DC: Natural Resource Defense Council.

Nedovic-Budic, Z. 1998. The impact of GIS technology. *Environment and Planning B: Planning and Design* 25: 681–692.

———. 2000. Geographic information science implications for urban and regional planning. *URISA Journal* 12(2): 81–93.

Nijkamp, P., and H. Scholten. 1993. Spatial information systems: Design, modelling, and use in planning. *International Journal of GIS* 7(1): 85–96.

Nonaka, I., and H. Takeuchi. 1995. *The knowledge-creating company: How Japanese companies create the dynamics of innovation.* Oxford: Oxford University Press.

Onsted, J. A. 2002. SCOPE: A modification and application of the Forrester Model to the South Coast of Santa Barbara County. Master's thesis, University of California, Santa Barbara.

———. 2007. Effectiveness of the Williamson Act: A spatial analysis. PhD diss., University of California, Santa Barbara.

Openshaw, S. 1979. A methodology for using models for planning purposes. *Environment and Planning A* 879–896.

Ortolano, L., and C. D. Perman. 1990. Applications to urban planning: An overview. In *Expert systems: Applications to urban planning*, T. J. Kim, L. L. Wiggins, and J. R. Wright, eds., 3–13. New York: Springer-Verlag.

Ottens, H. 1990. The application of geographical information systems in urban and regional planning. In *Geographical information systems for urban and regional planning*, H. J. Scholten and J. Stillwell, eds., 15–22. Dordrecht: Kluwer.

Pallathucheril, V., and B. Deal. 2007. Coupled land use and transportation models: The LEAM/Trans-Eval experience in St. Louis, MO. *Proceedings of the 12th International Conference on Computers in Urban Planning and Urban Management*. Fas DeGuassu, Brazil, 11–15 May.

Pendyala, R., R. Kitamura, and A. Kikuchi. 2004. FAMOS: The Florida activity mobility simulator. *Proceedings of the Conference on Progress in Activity-based Analysis*. Maastricht, The Netherlands.

Pernici, B. 1990. Objects with roles. In *Proceedings of the Conference on Office Information System*, F. H. Lochovsky and R. B. Allen, eds., 205–215. 25–27 April, Cambridge, Massachusetts. Cambridge, MA: ACM Press.

Pettit, C. J. 2005. Use of a collaborative GIS-based planning support system to assist in formulating a sustainable-development scenario for Hervey Bay, Australia. *Environment and Planning, B: Planning and Design* 32(4): 523–546.

Pettit, C., A. Nelson, and W. Cartwright. 2004. Using on-line geographical visualization tools to improve land use decision-making with a bottom up community participatory approach. In *Developments in design and decision support system*, J. Van Leeuwen and H. J. P. Timmermans, eds., 263–274. Dordrecht: Springer.

Peuquet, D. J., and N. Duan. 1995. An event-based spatiotemporal data model (ESTDM) for temporal analysis of geographical data. *International Journal of Geographical Information Systems* 9(1): 7–24.

Plein, L. C., K. E. Green, and D. G. Williams. 1998. Organic planning: A new approach to public participation in local governance. *Social Science Journal* 34: 509–523.

Press, W. H., S. A. Teukolsky, W. T. Vetterling, and B. P. Flannery. 1992. *Numerical Recipes in C*. 2nd ed. Cambridge, Eng.: Cambridge University Press.

Putman, S. H. 1983. *Integrated urban models*. London: Pion.

———. 1991. *Integrated urban models 2*. London: Pion.

Putman, S. H., and S. Chan. 2001. The METROPILUS planning support system: Urban models and GIS. In *Planning support systems: Integrating geographic information systems, models, and visualization*, R. K. Brail and R. E. Klosterman, eds., 99–126. Redlands, CA: ESRI Press.

Quer, C., and A. Olive. 1993. Object interaction in object-oriented deductive conceptual models. In *Proceedings of 5th International Conference on Advanced Information Systems Engineering*, C. Rolland, F. Bodart, and C. Cauvet, eds., 374–396. 8–11 June, Paris, France. Heidelberg, Germany: Springer-Verlag.

Rittel, H. W., and M. M. Webber. 1973. Dilemmas in a general theory of planning. *Policy Sciences* 4: 155–169.

Rogers, E. 1995. *Diffusion of innovations*. New York: Free Press.

Rozwadowski, T. 2006. Dynamika przemian przestrzennych miasta I jej symulacja z wykorzystaniem modelu komorkowego na przykladzie rozwoju urbanistycznego aglomeracji gdanskiej. PhD diss., Polytechnika Gdanska Wydzial Architektury Zaklad Urbanistyki, Gdansk, Poland.

Saarloos, D., T. Arentze, A. Borgers, and H. Timmermans. 2005. A multiagent model for alternative plan generation. *Environment and Planning B: Planning and Design* 32: 505–522.

Sangawongse, S., C. H. Sun, and B. W. Tsai. 2005. Urban growth and land cover change in Chiang Mai and Taipei: Results from the SLEUTH model. In *MODSIM 2005 International Congress on Modelling and Simulation*, A. Zerger and R. M. Argent, eds., 170–176. Modelling and Simulation Society of Australia and New Zealand, December 2005.

Sarraf, S., V. G. Pallathucheril, K. Donaghy, and B. Deal. 2005. Modeling the regional economy to drive land-use change models. 46th Annual Conference of the Association of Collegiate Schools of Planning, Kansas City, MO. 27–30 October.

Schank, R., and R. Abelson, eds. 1977. *Scripts, plans, goals and understanding*. Hillsdale, NJ: Lawrence Erlbaum Associates.

Schank, R., and D. Leake. 1989. Creativity and learning in a case-based explainer. *Artificial Intelligence* 40(1–3): 353–385.

Scheer, A. W. 1992. *Architecture of integrated information systems*. New York: Springer-Verlag.

Scholten, H., and J. Stillwell, eds. 1990. *Geographical information systems for urban and regional planning*. Dordrecht: Kluwer.

Semboloni, F. 1997. An urban and regional model based on cellular automata. *Environment and Planning B: Planning and Design* 24: 589–612.

Senge, P. 1990. *The fifth discipline: The art and practice of the learning organization*. New York: Currency Doubleday.

Ševčíková, H., A. Raftery, and P. Waddell. 2007. Assessing uncertainty in urban simulations using Bayesian melding. *Transportation Research, Part B: Methodology* 41(6): 652–659.

Shen, Z., M. Kawakami, and P. Chen. 2006. A heuristic method for land-use plan generation in planning support systems. In *Progress in design and decision support systems*, J. Van Leeuwen and H. J. P. Timmermans, eds., 169–184. Eindhoven: Eindhoven University of Technology.

Shi, X., and A. G. O. Yeh. 1999. The integration of case-based systems and GIS in development control. *Environment and Planning B: Planning and Design* 26(3): 345–364.

Shiffer, M. J. 1995. Geographic integration in the city planning context: Beyond the multimedia prototype. In *Cognitive aspects of human-computer interaction for geographic information systems*, T. L. Nyerges, D. M. Mark, R. Laurini, and M. J. Egenhofer, eds., 295–310. New York: Kluwer.

———. 2001. Spatial multimedia for planning support. In *Planning support systems: Integrating geographic information systems, models, and visualization tools*, R. K. Brail and R. E. Klosterman, eds., 361–385. Redlands, CA: ESRI Press.

Shipley, R., and R. Newkirk. 1998. Visioning: Did anyone see it coming? *Journal of Planning Literature* 12: 407–416.

Siddiqui, M. Z., J. W. Everett, and B. E. Vieux. 1996. Landfill siting using geographic information systems: A demonstration. *Journal of Urban Planning and Development* 122: 515–523.

Sietchiping, R. 2004. Geographic information systems and cellular automata-based model of informal settlement growth. PhD diss., School of Anthropology, Geography and Environmental Studies, University of Melbourne.

Silva, E. A. 2004. The DNA of our Regions: Artificial intelligence in regional planning. *Futures* 36(10): 1077–1094.

———. 2006. Expert knowledge in land use planning: The role of information in workshops, scenario building, simulation modelling and decision making. SSRN Electronic Paper Collection, November 18, 2006. http://ssrn.com/abstract=945794.

Silva, E. A., and K. C. Clarke. 2002. Calibration of the SLEUTH urban growth model for Lisbon and Porto, Portugal. *Computers, Environment and Urban Systems* 26: 525–552.

———. 2005. Complexity, emergence and cellular urban models: Lessons learned from applying SLEUTH to two Portuguese cities. *European Planning Studies* 13(1): 93–115.

Skocpol, T., and M. P. Fiorina, eds. 1999. *Civic engagement in American democracy*. Washington, DC: Brookings Institution.

Smith, H. G., F. V. Burstein, R. Sharma, and A. Sowunmi. 2000. Organisational memory information systems: A case-based approach to decision. In *Decision support systems for sustainable development*, G. E. Kersten, Z. Mikolajuk, and A. G. O. Yeh, eds., 277–290. Boston: Kluwer.

Snoeck, M., and G. Dedene. 1998. Existence dependency: The key to semantic integrity between structural and behavioral aspects of object types. *IEEE Transactions on Software Engineering* 24(4): 233–251.

Solecki, W. D., and C. Oliveri. 2004. Downscaling climate change scenarios in an urban land use change model. *Journal of Environmental Management* 72: 105–115.

Stefik, M. 1995. *Introduction to knowledge systems*. San Francisco, CA: Morgan Kaufmann.

Stein, E. W. 1995. Organisational memory: Review of concepts and recommendations for management. *International Journal of Information Management* 15(1): 17–32.

Stillwell, J., S. Geertman, and S. Openshaw, eds. 1999. *Geographical Information and Planning: European Perspectives* (Advances in spatial science). Berlin: Springer, 454.

Sun, Z., and B. Deal. 2006. Managing the dynamics of geographic information systems: The case of urban land use transformation in St. Louis, MO. In *Geoinformatics 2006: The U.S. Geological Survey scientific investigators report*. S. R. Brady, A. K. Sinha, and L. C. Gunderson, eds. Washington, DC: U.S. Geological Survey.

Susskind, L., S. McKearnan, and J. Thomas-Larmer, eds. 1999. *The consensus building handbook: A comprehensive guide to reaching agreement*. Thousand Oaks, CA: Sage.

Syphard A. D., K. C. Clarke, and J. Franklin. 2007. Simulating fire frequency and urban growth in southern California coastal shrublands, USA. *Landscape Ecology* 22(3): 431–445.

Taleb, N. N. 2007. *The black swan: The impact of highly improbable events*. New York: Random House.

Teisseire, M., P. Poncelet, and R. Cicchetti. 1994. Towards event-driven modeling for database design. In *Proceedings of 20th International Conference on Very Large Databases*, J. B. Bocca, M. Jarke, and C. Zaniolo, eds., 285–296. 12–15 September, Santiago de Chile, Chile. San Francisco, CA: Morgan Kaufmann.

Theobald, D. 2001. Land-use dynamics beyond the urban fringe. *Geographical Review* 91: 544–564.

Tietz, M. B., C. Dietzel, and W. Fulton. 2005. Urban development futures in the San Joaquin Valley. Report, Public Policy Institute of California. http://www.ppic.org/main/publication.asp?i=341.

Timmermans, H. J. P. 1982. Consumer choice of shopping centre: An information integration approach. *Regional Studies* 16: 171–182.

———. 1997. *Decision support systems in urban planning*. London: E and FN Spon.

———. 2000. Decision support systems in urban planning. *Proceedings of the 5th conference*. Eindhoven: Eindhoven University of Technology.

———. 2002. Decision support systems in urban planning. *Proceedings of the 6th conference*. Eindhoven: Eindhoven University of Technology.

———. 2003. The saga of integrated land use–transportation modeling: How many more dreams before we wake up? Presented at the 10th International Conference on Travel Behavior Research.

———. 2006. The saga of integrated land use and transport modelling: How many more dreams before we wake up? In *Moving through nets: The physical and social dimensions of travel*, K. Axhausen, ed., 219–239. Oxford: Elsevier.

Tobler, W. 1979. Cellular geography. In *Philosophy in Geography*, S. Gale and G. Olsson, eds., 379–386. Dordrecht: Reidel.

Torrens, P. M., and D. O'Sullivan. 2001. Cellular automata and urban simulation: Where do we go from here? *Environment and Planning B: Planning and Design* 28: 163–168.

Tri-County Regional Planning Commission. 2001. *The Peoria-Pekin Future Landscape Project*. Spring-field, IL: State of Illinois Department of Natural Resources.

U.S. Census Bureau. 2002. *2002 census of governments*. Washington, DC.

U.S. Environmental Protection Agency. 2001. Our built and natural environments: A technical review of the interactions between land-use, transportation, and environmental quality. EPA 231–R–01–002. Washington, DC: U.S. Environmental Protection Agency.

Van Leeuwen, J., and H. J. P. Timmermans, eds. 2004. *Recent advances in design and decision support systems*. Eindhoven: Eindhoven University of Technology.

———, eds. 2006a. *Innovations in design and decision support systems*. Dordrecht: Springer.

———, eds. 2006b. *Progress in design and decision support systems*. Eindhoven: Eindhoven University of Technology.

Van Niel, K., and S. W. Laffan. 2003. Gambling with randomness: The use of pseudo-random number generators in GIS. *International Journal of Geographical Information Science* 17(1): 49–68.

Vancher, A., D. Andrey, P. Giordano, and S. Albeverio. 2005. Continuous valued cellular automata and decision processes of agents. *Proceedings of CUPUM 2005*, London.

Veldhuisen, K., H. J. P. Timmermans, and L. L. Kapoen. 2000a. Ramblas: A regional planning model based on the micro-simulation of daily activity travel patterns. *Environment and Planning A* 32: 427–443.

———. 2000b. Micro-simulation of activity-travel patterns and traffic flows: Validation tests and an investigation of Monte Carlo error. *Transportation Research Record* 1706: 126–135.

Vonk, G. 2006. Improving planning support: The use of planning support systems for spatial planning. Netherlands Geographical Studies 340. Utrecht: KNAG/Utrecht University.

Vonk, G., S. Geertman, and P. Schot. 2005. Bottlenecks blocking widespread usage of planning support systems. *Environment and Planning A* 37: 909–924.

———. 2006. Usage of planning support systems. In *Innovations in design and decision support systems*, J.Van Leeuwen and H. J. P. Timmermans, eds., 263–274. Dordrecht: Springer.

———. 2007a. A SWOT analysis of planning support systems. *Environment and Planning A* 39: 1699–1714.

———. 2007b. New technologies stuck in old hierarchies: An analysis of diffusion of geo-information technologies in Dutch public organizations. *Public Administration Review* 67: 745–756.

Voorhees, A. M. 1959. Land use and traffic models: A progress report. *Journal of the American Institute of Planners* 25: 55–105.

Voss, A., I. Denisovich, P. Gatalsky, K. Gavouchidis, A. Klotz, S. Roeder, and H. Voss. 2004. Evolution of a participatory GIS. *Computers, Environment and Urban Systems* 28: 635–651.

Waddell, P. 2000. A behavioral simulation model for metropolitan policy analysis and planning: residential location and housing market components of UrbanSim. *Environment and Planning B: Planning and Design* 27(2): 247–263.

———. 2002. UrbanSim: Modeling urban development for land use, transportation and environmental planning. *Journal of the American Planning Association* 68(3): 297–314.

———. 2005. *Integrated land-use and transport models: Building an integrated model—some guidance*. Washington, DC: Transportation Research Board, Workshop 162.

Waddell, P., C. Bhat, N. Eluru, L. Wang, and R. Pendyala. 2007. Modeling the interdependence in household residence and workplace choices. *Transportation Research Record: Journal of the Transportation Research Board* 2003: 84–92.

Waddell, P., A. Borning, M. Noth, N. Freier, M. Becke, and G. Ulfarsson. 2003. UrbanSim: A simulation system for land use and transportation. *Networks and Spatial Economics* 3: 43–67.

Waddell, P., G. F. Ulfarsson, J. Franklin, and J. Lobb. 2007. Incorporating land use in metropolitan transportation planning. *Transportation Research, Part A: Policy and Practice* 41: 382–410.

Waddell, P., L. Wang, and B. Charlton. 2008. Integration of parcel-level land use model and activity-based travel model. Transportation Research Board annual meeting 2007 Paper 08-2414. TRB 87th annual meeting compendium of papers DVD. Washington, DC: National Academy of Sciences.

Wang, Y., W. Choi, and B. Deal. 2005. Long-term impacts of land-use change on non-point source pollutant loads for the St. Louis metropolitan area. *Journal of Environmental Management* 35: 2.

Watson, I. D. 1995. An introduction to case-based reasoning. In *Proceedings of the first United Kingdom workshop on progress in case-based reasoning*, I. D. Watson, ed., 3–16. London: Springer-Verlag.

———. 1997. *Applying case-based reasoning: Techniques for enterprise systems*. San Francisco, CA: Morgan Kaufmann.

Webber, M. M. 1965. The roles of intelligence systems in urban-systems planning. *Journal of the American Institute of Planners* 31: 289–296.

———. 1969. Planning in an environment of change, Part II: Permissive planning. *Town Planning Review* 39: 277–295.

———. 1979. Personal communication, seminar given at the University of Reading, UK.

Wegener, M. 1982a. A multilevel economic-demographic model for the Dortmund region. *Sistemi Urbani* 3: 371–401.

———. 1982b. Modeling urban decline: a multilevel economic-demographic model of the Dortmund region. *International Regional Science Review* 7: 21–41.

———. 1983. Description of the Dortmund region model. Working Paper 8. Dortmund: Institut für Raumplanung.

———. 2005. Urban land-use transportation models. In *GIS, spatial analysis, and modeling*. D. J. Maguire, M. Batty, and M. F. Goodchild, eds., 203–220. Redlands, CA: ESRI Press.

Wegener, M., R. L. Mackett, and D. C. Simmonds. 1991. One city, three models: Comparison of land-use/transport policy simulation models for Dortmund. *Transportation Reviews* 11: 107–129.

Wen, C. H. 1998. Development of stop generation and tour formation models for the analysis of travel/activity behavior. Ph.D. diss., Northwestern University, Evanston, IL.

Wen, C. H., and F. S. Koppelman. 1999. An integrated system of stop generation and tour formation for the analysis of activity and travel patterns. *Transportation Research Record* 76: 136–144.

Wendt, D. 2002. Using CommunityViz™ for the Tacoma Dome Area Plan. Environmental Systems Research Institute User Conference, San Diego, CA, 10 July.

Wenger, E. 1998. *Communities of practice*. Cambridge, Eng.: Cambridge University Press.

West Churchman, C. 1968. *The systems approach*. New York: Delacorte Press.

White, R. W., and G. Engelen. 1993a. Cellular automata and fractal urban form: A cellular modeling approach to the evolution of urban land use patterns. *Environment and Planning A* 25: 1175–1193.

———. 1993b. Cellular dynamics and GIS: Modelling spatial complexity. *Geographical Systems* 1: 237–253.

———. 1997. Cellular automata as the basis of integrated dynamic regional modelling. *Environment and Planning B* 24: 235–246.

White, R., G. Engelen, and I. Uljee. 1997. The use of constrained cellular automata for high-resolution modelling of urban land use dynamics. *Environment and Planning* 24: 323–343.

Williams, I. N., and M. H. Echenique. 1978. A regional model for commodity and passenger flows. *Proceedings of the PTRC summer annual meeting*, 121–128. Warwick, Eng.: PTRC.

Worrall, L. 1994. The role of GIS-based spatial analysis in strategic management in local government. *Computers, Environment and Urban Systems* 185: 323–332.

Wu, F., and D. Martin. 2002. Urban expansion simulation of southeast England using population surface modeling and cellular automata. *Environment and Planning A* 34: 1855–1876.

Wu, F., and C. J. Webster. 1998. Simulation of land development through the integration of cellular automata and multicriteria evaluation. *Environment and Planning B: Planning and Design* 25: 103–126.

Xiang, W-N., and K. C. Clarke. 2003. The use of scenarios in land use planning. *Environment and Planning B* 30: 885–909.

Yaakup, A., Y. A. Bakar, M. N. A. Kadir, and S. Sulaiman. 2004. Computerised development control and approval system for City Hall of Kuala Lumpur. *Geo-Spatial Information Science* 7(1): 39–49.

Yang, X., and C. P. Lo. 2003. Modelling urban growth and landscape change in the Atlanta metropolitan area. *International Journal of Geographical Information Science* 17: 463–488.

Yeh, A. G. O. 1999. Urban planning and GIS. In *Geographical information systems: Principles, techniques, applications, and management*, P. A. Longley, M. Goodchild, D. Maguire, and D. Rhind, eds., 877–888. 2nd ed. New York: John Wiley.

Yeh, A. G. O., and X. Li. 2001. A constrained CA model for the simulation and planning of sustainable urban forms by using GIS. *Environment and Planning B: Planning and Design* 28: 733–753.

Yeh, A. G. O., and X. Shi. 1999. Applying case-based reasoning (CBR) to urban planning: A new PSS tool. *Environment and Planning B: Planning and Design* 26(1): 101–116.

———. 2003. The application of case-based reasoning in development control. In *Planning support systems in practice*, S. Geertman and J. Stillwell, eds., 223–248. Berlin: Springer-Verlag.

Index

About the Authors

Back row, left to right: Nikhil Kaza, George Janes, Lew Hopkins, Harry Timmermans, Paul Waddell, John Landis, Stan Geertman, Joe Ferreira, Richard Brail, Richard Klosterman, Brian Deal, Terry Moore, Eliot Allen, Michael Flaxman
Front row, left to right: Keith Clarke, Lyna Wiggins, Michael Batty, Richard Bolan, Armando Carbonell, Judith Grant Long

Eliot Allen, AICP
Principal, Criterion Planners Inc., Portland, Oregon

Eliot Allen is an urban and regional planner whose career has focused on the use of information technology and collaborative decision making to help planners and citizens create places that are measurably more sustainable. He is a former chair of the City of Portland's Sustainability Commission, a member of the Remaking Cities Institute advisory board at Carnegie Mellon University, and the primary certification consultant for the U.S. Green Building Council LEED for Neighborhood Development program.

Michael Batty
Bartlett Professor of Planning, University College London

Michael Batty directs the Centre for Advanced Spatial Analysis (CASA) at University College London. From 1990 to 1995, he was director of the NSF National Center for Geographic Information and Analysis (NCGIA) at the State University of New York at Buffalo. His research work involves the development of computer models of cities and regions, and he has published many books and articles in this area. He is editor of the journal *Environment and Planning B: Planning and Design*.

Richard K. Brail
Professor Emeritus, Edward J. Bloustein School of Planning and Public Policy, Rutgers University, New Brunswick, New Jersey

Richard Brail's interests include the applications of information technology in urban planning, geographic information and planning support systems, and urban transportation. Brail wrote *Microcomputers in Urban Planning and Management* (1987) and was coeditor of *Spreadsheet Models for Urban and Regional Analysis* (1994) and *Planning Support Systems: Integrating Geographic Information Systems, Models and Visualization Tools* (2001). He is former chair and program director of the urban planning program and founding director of the National Transit Institute at Rutgers.

Keith C. Clarke
Professor, University of California, Santa Barbara

Keith C. Clarke works in the areas of GIS, cartography, remote sensing, and computational simulation modeling. Clarke was the primary developer of the SLEUTH regional simulation model. He is chair of the National Research Council's Mapping Sciences Committee, is a member of National Geographic Society's Committee on Research and Exploration, and was a 2005 recipient of the U.S. Geological Survey's John Wesley Powell Award.

Brian Deal
Assistant Professor of Urban and Regional Planning, University of Illinois at Urbana-Champaign

Brian Deal is director of the LEAM Modeling Systems Laboratory, director of the Smart Energy Design Assistance Center, and director of research at the University of Illinois's Robert Allerton Park. His current research includes the study of sustainability and urban land use transformation. Central to this research is the Land-use Evolution and impact Assessment Model (LEAM) Laboratory, an interdisciplinary laboratory dedicated to the study of the spatio-temporal dynamics of land use change and their social, economic, and environmental consequences.

Stan Geertman
Associate Professor of Geographical Information Science, Utrecht University

Stan Geertman has specialized in topics like planning support systems and methodological issues concerning GI applications. He is a regular author and reviewer for about fifteen international journals and associate editor of the international journal, *Applied Spatial Analysis and Policy*. He is coeditor of several books, including *Geographical Information and Planning* (1999) and *Planning Support Systems in Practice* (2003). He is an appointed member of the National Board of

Land Use Modelling (LUMOS), and of the Scientific Advisory Committee of the Dutch Research Programme for Geo-Information Sciences (RGI).

George M. Janes, AICP
Executive Director, Environmental Simulation Center, Ltd. (ESC), New York

George Janes has led several of the ESC's simulation modeling efforts including the land development model used by the City of Houston to evaluate the results of forecasts produced by their metropolitan planning organization. Prior to joining ESC, Janes managed the development of several of IBM's (formerly PricewaterhouseCoopers Consulting) simulation modeling programs including CommunityViz's Policy Simulator component and TRANSIMS, the traffic simulation model developed by Los Alamos National Laboratory.

Richard E. Klosterman
President and CEO, What if? Inc., Hudson, Ohio

Richard Klosterman is professor emeritus of planning, geography, and urban studies at the University of Akron. He has published widely in the areas of information technology, planning analysis, and planning theory, and is the author of *Community Analysis and Planning Techniques* (1990) and coeditor of *Spreadsheet Models for Urban and Regional Analysis* (1994) and *Planning Support Systems* (2001).

Michael Kwartler, FAIA
President, Environmental Simulation Center, Ltd. (ESC), New York

Michael Kwartler is founding director of ESC, a non-profit research laboratory created to develop innovative applications of digital technology. He is an architect, planner, urban designer, and educator, and principal of Michael Kwartler and Associates. His 30 years of professional practice and teaching have focused on urban design and the theory and practice of legislating aesthetics and good city form. He has served as deputy director of the Mayor's Urban Design Council and associate director of the Division of Land Planning and Environmental Management.

Xuan Liu
Manager of Data Center, Southeast Michigan Council of Governments (SEMCOG), Detroit

Xuan Liu leads SEMCOG's land use modeling work and focuses on the interaction between land use and transportation models. He oversees demographic, economic, and land use data development, analysis, and forecasting at SEMCOG. He is a Ph.D. candidate at University of Michigan, where his research focuses on the relationships between land use and transportation systems in metropolitan regions.

Terry Moore, FAICP
Vice President and Planner, ECONorthwest, Portland, Oregon
Terry Moore has has managed over 500 projects in land-use and transportation planning, policy analysis, and market analysis for private and public clients. Recent projects focused on growth management, the interaction between land use and transportation policies, and integrated regional planning at the metropolitan scale. He was a visiting researcher and professor at the National Center for Smart Growth Research and Education at the University of Maryland in 2007. His recent publications include *An Economic Development Toolbox* (2006) and *The Transportation/Land Use Connection* (2007).

Varkki Pallathucheril
Associate Professor, School of Architecture and Design, American University of Sharjah, United Arab Emirates
Varkki Pallathucheril is a coprincipal investigator in the LEAM Modeling Laboratory at the University of Illinois at Urbana-Champaign. His research interests include planning support systems, specifically the use and representation of planning information. This work has led to an interest in innovative planning processes using PSS and information technology.

Harry Timmermans
Professor of Urban Planning, Eindhoven University of Technology, The Netherlands
Harry Timmermans is director of the Design and Decision Support Systems in Architecture and Urban Planning Research Programme, which models various types of behaviors and embeds these models into various kinds of support systems, ranging from GIS to spatial decision support, expert and virtual reality systems. Research projects focus on retailing, housing, leisure and tourism, and transportation in addition to general process models in architecture and urban planning.

Paul A. Waddell
Professor of Public Affairs, Urban Design, and Planning, University of Washington, Seattle
Paul Waddell is director of the Center for Urban Simulation and Policy Analysis. His research focuses on the analysis and modeling of urban development, and the effects of major transportation investments and land policies on these processes and on outcomes related to efficiency, equity, and the environment. Over the past several years he and several collaborators developed the UrbanSim model system for integrating land use and transportation modeling and planning, and applied it in several metropolitan areas.

Liming Wang
Ph.D. Student, University of Washington, Seattle
Liming Wang is a Ph.D. candidate of the Interdisciplinary Ph.D. Program in Urban Design and Planning. His main research interests include land use and transportation modeling and planning support systems.

Anthony G. O. Yeh, FRTPI, FPAI, FHKIP, FCILT, FBCS
Chair Professor in Urban Planning and GIS, University of Hong Kong
Anthony Yeh is a member of the Chinese Academy of Sciences. He initiated the International Conference on Computers in Urban Planning and Urban Management in 1989 in Hong Kong. He is the founding secretary general of the Asian Planning Schools Association and Asia GIS Association. He is on the editorial board of *Environment and Planning B*; *Computers, Environment and Urban Systems*; and *Transactions in GIS*. He has published widely in international journals and has published two books in Chinese on GIS and planning support systems. He has been the chairman of the Geographic Information Science Commission of the International Geographical Union (IGU).

About the Lincoln Institute of Land Policy

The Lincoln Institute of Land Policy is a private operating foundation whose mission is to improve the quality of public debate and decisions in the areas of land policy and land-related taxation in the United States and around the world. The Institute's goals are to integrate theory and practice to better shape land policy and to provide a nonpartisan forum for discussion of the multidisciplinary forces that influence public policy. This focus on land derives from the Institute's founding objective—to address the links between land policy and social and economic progress—that was identified and analyzed by political economist and author Henry George.

The work of the Institute is organized in four departments: Valuation and Taxation, Planning and Urban Form, Economic and Community Development, and International Studies. We seek to inform decision making through education, research, demonstration projects, and the dissemination of information through publications, our Web site, and other media. Our programs bring together scholars, practitioners, public officials, policy advisers, and involved citizens in a collegial learning environment. The Institute does not take a particular point of view, but rather serves as a catalyst to facilitate analysis and discussion of land use and taxation issues—to make a difference today and to help policy makers plan for tomorrow. The Lincoln Institute of Land Policy is an equal opportunity institution.

LINCOLN INSTITUTE
OF LAND POLICY

113 Brattle Street
Cambridge, MA 02138-3400 USA

Phone: 1-617-661-3016 x127 or 1-800-LAND-USE (800-526-3873)
Fax: 1-617-661-7235 or 1-800-LAND-944 (800-526-3944)
E-mail: help@lincolninst.edu
Web: www.lincolninst.edu